Getting into
the Mail-Order
Business

Getting into the Mail-Order Business

Julian L. Simon

University of Maryland
Julian Simon Associates

with a chapter by John Caples

An abridged version of Julian Simon's famed bible on mail-order success,
How to Start and Operate a Mail-Order Business, Third Edition

McGraw-Hill Book Company
New York   St. Louis   San Francisco   Auckland
Bogotá   Hamburg   London   Madrid
Mexico   Montreal   New Delhi   Panama   Paris
São Paulo   Singapore   Sydney   Tokyo   Toronto

Library of Congress Cataloging in Publication Data

Simon, Julian Lincoln, 1932–
  Getting into the mail-order business.

  Abridged version of: How to start and operate a mail-
order business. 3rd ed. c1981.
  Bibliography: p.
  Includes index.
  1. Mail-order business. I. Caples, John. II. Title.
HF5466.S54 1984   658.8'72   83-16281
ISBN 0-07-057474-X (pbk.)

    5 6 7 8 9 0   DOC/DOC   8 9

ISBN 0-07-057474-X

The editors for this book were William Sabin and Christine Ulwick,
the designer was Richard Kluga, and the production
supervisor was Sally Fliess. It was set in Melior
by Waldman Graphics.
Printed and bound by R. R. Donnelley & Sons Company.

This paperback edition, first published in 1984, is an abridged version
of *How to Start and Operate a Mail-Order Business.*

For Rita and for
David, Judith and Daniel

Contents

Preface

Do you want to make money in mail order? If so, this book can help you. If you have the capabilities to make it in mail order, either with a new business or by buiding up another non-mail-order business you are now in, this book can help you be successful. (There are people who began by reading this book who now make a million dollars a year. That's right, income of $1,000,000 each year.) And if you do not have the capabilities, this book can save you from wasting your capital in a losing venture or from being ripped off by fraudulent start-in-mail-order deals.

This paperback is an abridged version of the hard-cover book *How to Start and Operate a Mail-Order Business, Third Edition*. The primary purpose of this book, like its parent book, is to teach newcomers to the mail-order business what they need to know to make money in mail order. By "newcomers" I mean those of you who want to start a business from scratch. I also mean businesspeople who now sell retail or through sales representatives, and who want to utilize the mail-order selling method to increase their profits or to expand their operations.

The step-by-step organization of this book is tailored to newcomers to mail order. It tells you what to do first, second and third. It teaches you exactly how to proceed from one stage to the next, until you are reaping the profits you want.

This book teaches the *business* of mail order and the *business decisions* a mail-order operator must make. This is unlike most previous books about mail order, which have concentrated on how to write advertising copy.

Choosing a product is the first and crucial decision you must make; hence we tackle that problem first. I show you the real "professional method" that is the secret of the big operators who find one profitable product after another.

The book collects in one place the important facts and data that will be of interest and help to experienced mail-order operators. I've tried very hard to separate *proven facts* from mere opinions and old wives' tales, not always an easy task.

How to Use This Book

Begin by flipping through the book. Study the table of contents. Browse around to find out just what is in the book, and where. Read Chapter 2, "What Is the Mail-Order Business?" to give you some background on the industry you want to enter.

Then *study* Chapter 3, "The Professional Method of Finding Products," and Chapters 4 and 5. If you are already in another line of business, those chapters will help you evaluate your product for mail-order selling. If you are starting from scratch, Chapters 3–5 will make it relatively simple to solve the problem of what to sell *profitably*. And you don't even need to have a bright idea!

Make no mistake about it—Chapters 3, 4 and 5 are the key to the mail-order business. They teach newcomers to select products in the same way the biggest operators do. Read these chapters again and again, and then begin to follow the instructions. If you *really* want a mail-order business, you must follow through the steps in those chapters.

Once you are satisfied that you have selected one or more salable products, read Chapter 6 to make sure that your products may be sold by mail. Then Chapter 7 on mail-order strategies will help you prepare a road map for the sale of your products. Chapter 7 will also direct you to the other chapters in the book that will be most helpful in solving your particular problems. Your further study will depend upon your choice of type of business, product and general strategy.

Anyone who has completed eighth grade and has a knowledge of arithmetic has enough education to understand the ideas in this book. Nevertheless, it may seem hard going sometimes. And I say, let it be a little difficult. If a reader is not smart enough or hardworking enough to plow through this book, he or she is probably not smart or diligent enough to make money in mail order.

(It is sad but true that a dullard or a lazybones will not make money in mail order any more than he or she will in farming or selling insurance or running a flower shop. The sooner some of the dreamy fortune seekers quit kidding themselves, the better for all.)

Mail order requires specialized knowledge, which this book will help you gain. The ignorant beginners who *intend* to stay ignorant are surely wasting their time and money. Even those who tackle the business with plenty of intelligence and energy may get hurt until they learn what mail order is all about.

There are two important sources of knowledge about mail order. You must learn from *both* these sources. The first source is your observation of other mail-order businesses. Chapter 3 tells you how and what to observe. A unique advantage for the beginner is that it is easier to learn the inner workings of a mail-order firm than those of any other type of firm. You don't need to work there or spy on them. All you need to do is to watch their advertisements. Much that is important about the operation of any mail-order business is revealed in its advertising.

Books and articles about mail order are the second source of mail-order knowledge. This book rounds up for you most of the important general mail-order knowledge. But you must also read other books. Buy or borrow as many of the books I mention as you have time to read. It will be the best investment you can make in your mail-order future.

There are two important reasons for reading what other writers have written about mail order: (1) some books cover specialized aspects of mail order that I cannot cover here; and (2) you must constantly refresh your knowledge. Even the old-time professionals never stop their mail-order education.

Here's a piece of general advice. Get to know people who are already in the mail-order business. You will soon learn which mail-order businesses are in your area. Call the owners, and ask if they will talk with you. Don't be shy; tell them what you want. Probably they will be hospitable. The mail-order business can be a lonely one, and mail-order people, like everyone else, like to give advice. If you seem intelligent and willing to listen, they'll be glad to spend some time with you, to your great advantage.

The Relationship between the Abridged and Unabridged Versions

This book contains most of the general advice about starting and operating a mail-order business found in the parent unabridged version. Left out is most of the material on how to write advertising copy and how to use particular media such as classified ads and match books, and detailed business information on such matters as filling orders, printing, and calculating costs. If you will actually start a business, I suggest that you go beyond this introduction and read the full version.

And with Gratitude to Many Others . . .

I am grateful to the many persons who graciously gave their help to the three editions of *How to Start and Operate a Mail-Order Business* and who are mentioned by name there. It has given me great satisfaction that many people have read the unabridged editions of this book. And a fair number of those readers have written me about their progress, mentioning that the book helped them start successful businesses and avoid costly mistakes. That is the kind of reaction that makes any writer feel good. I've also met many nice people through this correspondence. And it is very gratifying that the book continues to help enough so that this edition is needed.

The preface to the unabridged edition begins with the hope that the book will help you make money in mail order. I'll end this preface with the same hope for your success—and with the additional wish that you will also enjoy your adventure and success in the mail-order business.

June 1983   **Julian L. Simon**
                                   Chevy Chase, Maryland

Getting into
the Mail-Order
Business

The Possibilities of Mail Order

Who Can Make Money in Mail Order? • *Can You Start Part-Time?* • *Can You Still Make a Fortune in Mail Order?* • *Can You Make a Nice Living without Much Capital to Invest?*

WHO CAN MAKE MONEY IN MAIL ORDER?

An official U.S. government booklet on establishing a mail-order business says:[1]

> With a little determination and sagacity, the average person can easily master the principles of selling by mail. A principal requirement is good common sense and a mind made up to build a business. . . . As well suited for women as for men. . . . Age only a secondary consideration. . . . Advanced schooling helpful, but not essential.

And in this book you will be reading some astonishing success stories of men and women who started businesses at their kitchen tables with a few hundred dollars, and from that start built businesses grossing millions.

All true! But let me add, loud and clear and repeatedly, so no one can miss it: *Mail-order success is only a dream to many people who get interested in it.* Fast-money mail-order "deals" fan the delusion of quick, easy fortunes. But few people who come to mail order have the necessary characteristics to make a go of it.

1

Robert Baker checked eighty-seven advertisers and found that only ten were advertising five years later.[2] He also found that only 27 percent of 500 advertisers had run ads the previous year.

Baker's figures are interesting, though not very scientific. Still, what he says is helpful in pulling you down from the clouds. And of course you should remember that even the *biggest* firms in the mail-order business and in the economy as a whole expect not to succeed with a big majority of the ventures—perhaps three out of four—that they try out.

And why should the mail-order business be easy? It is probably the most desirable business in the world to be in. As with all good things, the fight to get a piece of it will not be easy.

The government booklet is right in saying that you don't need to be brilliant or well-educated to succeed in mail order. Many remarkably successful operators had little formal schooling. And some of the smartest professors at the world's major universities have made suggestions to me at parties ("I have a great idea for mail order") that would make them go broke in no time at all. The successful mail-order operators have studied mail order and know it inside out. That's about all the education they need.

CAN YOU START PART-TIME?

One of the great advantages in starting up a mail-order business is that you *can* start part-time. There is no store to open in the morning, no interference with your present job.

Furthermore, it is usually *wise* to start part-time. Mail order is a rough, tough business, and you can't learn it overnight. Learning will be much less painful if your livelihood, and that of your family, doesn't depend on immediate success.

And you have an *advantage* if you start part-time. As you will learn later, one of the important skills in mail order is to be able to move fast on the basis of skimpy evidence. The part-time operator doesn't need to move so fast, and therefore he can move more surely. His slower pace helps keep him from making wrong and expensive guesses.

Here are a few examples of businesses that were started part-time but grew to be sizable enterprises: Lee Wildeman started Holiday Gifts, Inc., in 1964 while running a laundry, and didn't go into mail order full-time until 1967.[4] He began with one ad in *House & Garden* for the Melody phone, which plays a tune while you ask someone to wait on the telephone. Because that ad succeeded, he continued in business, losing a few hundred dollars the first year. He didn't make a profit until 1967. By 1974 he was spending $450,000 a year in magazine advertising alone, which indicates that the size of the business has grown to a good many millions of dollars by now—from a part-time start.

Another example: Ex-GI Sam Lauderdale and his wife Mary Lauderdale were in college. Mary's mother sent her a pecan fruitcake which someone suggested to them was good enough to sell. Their first advertising was 500 letters to prominent people in nearby Texas towns. Now after 25 years in business they have a very profitable list of 27,000 people, 12,000 of whom buy regularly and about 1,100 of whom buy amounts ranging from $50 to $4,000 yearly for gifts.[5]

One last example: Larry Newhouse and his wife Madeleine started selling costume-jewelry rings in 1969 from their kitchen table with a $1,500 investment.[6] During the day Larry was a salesman selling jewelry. In the evening he made up orders in his basement. Five years later the sales of their firm, House of Camelot, were over $3 million yearly.

Some mail-order ventures can continue to be profitable part-time hobbies. A special skill that you can sell by mail—bookbinding, for example—can be a perfect mail-order product.

Or, you can run a small mail-order business part-time if you spend some time developing an item for which there is a limited appeal. (Successful items with wide appeal cannot remain small. Big competitors will find you out, horn into the field with their versions of the product, and steal your market.)

An example of a limited-market ad: "CIGARETTES—Make 20 plain or filter-tip for 9¢. Facts free. . . ." That ad has appeared almost word for word for years—an unquestioned profit-maker. But because of the small size of the operation (the ad runs in only a few magazines) and small profits, it can continue relatively safe from competition.

Another example of a limited-market business is that of Lee Mountain, who from his base in the little town of Pisgah, Alabama, has been buying and selling used correspondence school courses and educational books since 1919. You can find his little classified advertisements in the classified columns of many such magazines as Popular Science and Sports Afield.

Limited-market mail-order businesses need not be small in size. L. L. Bean has been selling hunting, camping and fishing equipment by mail for 60 years. Now the firm has 640,000 customers, and it grossed $12.5 million in 1971 (the most recent date for which I could obtain figures).

CAN YOU STILL MAKE A FORTUNE
IN MAIL ORDER?

Sears, Roebuck and Montgomery Ward are not the only great success stories in mail order. Fortunes have also been made in recent years. Examples include Hudson Vitamin, Spencer Gifts, Sunset House and many more.

It *is* possible to pyramid your winnings and get rich fast in mail order because you can increase your market tremendously in a great hurry. A retail store can increase its patronage only slowly. It takes time for its reputation to become known and for customers to become steady patrons. In mail order, however, if you find a very profitable item, you can spread into a great many media practically overnight. You can quickly increase the amount of space bought and profit made.

In case you worry about there being too much competition, read this squib written over *eighty years ago* in 1900: "Of course it is not so easy to succeed in the mail-order business now [1900], as it was a few years ago, when there was much less competition. This is especially true in case the business is started and conducted along the same lines as followed by scores of other mail dealers."[3]

Many, many fortunes have been made since then, and even more will be made in the future. In fact, the prospects in mail order now are probably better than ever.

An example is Arthur S. De Moss and National Liberty Insurance Company. In 1959 insurance agent De Moss got interested in selling health insurance by mail. He offered low rates to people who do not drink alcoholic beverages. In his first year he made a profit of $55,000— and in 1972 the company earned *$20 million.*

Furthermore, the high profit margin above the product cost for most mail-order products means that you can earn a huge return on your investment if your advertising is successful. As an example, read this letter from a Los Angeles advertising agency specializing in mail-order advertising to *Golf World:*

> Enclosed is our check in the amount of $195.89 to cover the full page ad for the XXXXX Book Co., less agency discount and 2% discount. This was the ad on the book, XXXXX, by XXXX. We thought you would be interested in knowing that as of this date the ad has pulled exactly 1187 orders.
>
> Sincerely,

If XXXXX's figures are correct—this letter was sent out by *Golf World* to help boost space sales, and you should therefore give credence to it only with caution—these are my guesses as to the profit results of the ad:

```
1,187 orders in 3 weeks
1,187 orders estimated after first 3 weeks
2,374 × $2.98 = gross revenue                                    $7,074.52
    Less: Advertising                           $  195.89
        Estimated cost of books, shipping, etc.    1,600.00
            Total cost                                             1,795.89
            Gross profit                                          $5,278.63
```

Needless to say, this ad probably will not pull as well in other media. Successes like this one are all too rare.

Two other examples: (1) An ad for the book *How to Collect from Social Security at Any Age* was recently run in *Parade*. The cost of the ad was $33,214, and the sales generated were $228,492. The costs of printing and mailing the book probably were about $25,000 to $40,000—which leaves a tidy profit. Of course this offer will not do this well very often, if ever again, but even with a much lesser response there is a nice profit.[7] (2) In 1963 Martin Faber started Film Corporation of America, a mail-order photo finisher and film seller, with a cash investment of $1,000. In 1973 sales were $44 million, and pretax earnings were somewhere between $4 and $5 million (of which taxes took about half). The firm operates in several foreign countries, and sells to 18 million families in the U.S., about one family in four.[8]

On the other hand, it is no snap to make a fortune in mail order. Competition is keen. If you show signs of doing well, competition finds it easy to imitate you and cut into your market. And once you are really in business, you face all the problems of any other business: personnel, stock, housing, taxes and the rest. Bankruptcies and reorganizations of several large mail-order firms should convince you that mail order is no easy-magic way to make money.

R. H. Macy went into the mail-order business in a big way for a while. But eventually Macy's got out.

Furthermore, you can't make a huge fortune unless you have capital to use as leverage. Even if you *know* you have a tremendous winner, you must have cash or credit to purchase stock, advertising and printing. Even if your winner is terrific, you can't make a fortune in a hurry just by plowing back earnings. By the time you have a respectable stake your competition will have swamped the market.

A Few Other Examples of Successful Mail-Order Businesses

Here are a few more examples of mail-order businesses, to give you some idea of what mail-order businesses are. In this section, and elsewhere where actual businesses are named, I stick to facts that are in print, rather than give examples of businesses I have worked with, because that way there is no danger of giving away trade secrets.

This section is based on the facts about mail-order businesses given in the lists of mail-order buyers that are offered for rent in *Direct Mail Lists, Rates and Data* (DMLRD).[9]

1. LeeWards has a list of 850,000 people who bought hobby materials from them in 1977 with an average sale price of $17 and two to three purchases per year. That suggests a gross of about $20-25 million per year.

2. American Handicrafts rents out their list of 2.77 million persons who bought in the years 1977 and 1978.

3. Harry and David is the name of a firm in Bedford, Oregon, that sells fine foods including fruits, and that has a fruit-of-the-month club. They offer for rent a list of 813,000 people who were buyers of their products in 1975 through 1978. The average unit of sale is $30. If you figure that perhaps 200,000 of those buyers buy each year, a calculation comes to almost $10 million a year gross. And the size of their advertising schedule suggests that their gross is considerably larger than that.

4. One of the most active, respected and biggest mail-order businesses in the country is the Fingerhut Corporation. They sell all kinds of merchandise, but especially merchandise related to automobiles. Their list of paid buyers who purchased on the installment plan in 1978 contains 1.44 million names. The average unit of sale is $45. Revenues for fiscal 1977 were $190 million.

But these selected examples of big mail-order firms don't truly represent what the business is about. Let's take a random sample of mail-order firms by taking the first firm listed alphabetically in the first category of merchandise in the alphabetical listing of merchandise categories in DMLRD—until we get tired. For example:

1. The first alphabetical category is "Almanacs and Directories," and the first listing is Bobley Publishing. In 1977 the total list was 130,000, and the average unit of sale was $40.00. These are owners of encyclopedia for active buyers of supplementary books. No information is given about how many years are covered by the list, so we have no basis to estimate the size of the business.

2. The first B category is "Babies," and the first firm listed is the American Bronzing Company, which metalplates baby shoes and other keepsake items. In 1977, there were 150,000 buyers, and in 1976, 123,000 buyers. The average unit of sale was $12.00.

3. The first C category is "Children," and the first firm listed is Americana Portraits. This is a firm that does business mostly by personal solicitation, so let's move on to "Children's Record Buyers." These are children between the ages of 6 and 14 who purchase records by mail. The list of 1975 buyers included 18,000, the average unit of sale was $5.00 for records, $8.00 for tapes.

4. The first D category is "Dancing," and Booksellers to the Dance World offers to rent a list of 40,000 people who in 1975 bought books on dance by mail. Average unit of sale was $12.00.

5. The first E category is "Education and Self-Improvement," and the first listing is American Consumer, Inc., which offers lists of 310,000 1978 diet-product buyers, 300,000 buyers of pills, 10,000 1978 buyers of exercisers. Average unit of sale was $6.00 to $20.00.

6. The first F category is "Fashions." Aldens offers to rent their list of 2,500,000 1978 buyers, whose average unit of sale runs between $5 and $600. These are people who bought from general merchandise catalogs.

The firms mentioned give you only a clue to the size of the mail-order business. One cannot reason from the examples to the total size of the mail-order business in any easy way, because a very few firms represent a disproportionate amount of business—Sears, Roebuck, Montgomery Ward, Spiegel, Aldens, Penney's and so on. But you can deduce from the DMLRD listings that there are far more than the 3,000 mail-order firms whose lists are big enough to advertise for rental, plus a lot more mail-order firms in the United States whose lists are too small for such rental. How many such there are, no one has any idea. (The fact that there are approximately 350,000 active mailing permits does give some indication, though of course this figure includes many firms that do not sell by mail order but only advertise by direct mail.)

A good many other examples of mail-order firms are found in Appendix B, some with bits of their histories.

An example of success in marketing industrial rather than consumer products by mail is that of Revere Chemical.[10] Until 1954, Revere sold building and grounds maintenance materials through salespeople. Then about a decade ago they went into mail order seriously with ads in business magazines and direct mail, using ice-melting material as the main offer. In 10 years they developed 100,000 customers, and became much bigger in volume than the business had become in the previous 53 years.

CAN YOU MAKE A NICE LIVING WITHOUT MUCH CAPITAL TO INVEST?

There are also many small mail-order businesses, netting their owners a nice living, that started from scratch with practically no capital (a few hundred dollars, maybe). Many of these businesses originally depended upon some special skill or knowledge of the owner: hat restoring, playing cards for collectors, bee supplies. Many of these businesses were built slowly, as customers were gained and kept. There is a cosmetics firm in California from which all my aunts have bought by mail ever since one of them visited the store in 1927. And in the last few pages you read the examples of Lee Wildeman, the Lauderdales, the Newhouses and Martin Faber, all of whom started their businesses with roughly $1,000 or less.

Another example: Arizona lawyer James E. Grant began part-time, selling Arizona legal forms to other lawyers and office-supply firms. In his first year of part-time work he grossed $50,000, and when last heard from he was about to go into the business full-time.

These small mail-order businesses that make nice livings yet neither grow big nor die off usually are too small to attract much competition. But "small" could mean an income of $25,000 per year.

Some of these successful small firms are tied to retail or manufacturing operations. The people who successfully sell wrought-iron furniture by mail probably could not survive if they had built solely as a mail-order business.

Other small mail-order businesses scratch out a specialized corner in a profitable market—perhaps by straight price appeal. There are several successful operators who operate this way in the photographic supplies market. But take my word for it: This is a rough way to make money. The competition is extremely tight, and woe to the inefficient!

In mail order, more than in any other business, you must be able to go it alone. You must be able to do without people with whom to talk things over. There is no boss, of course. But there is also no competitor nearby, nor are there any face-to-face customers, or salespeople coming by to sell you. And unlike a doctor or lawyer or plumber who goes into business for himself, you can't just sit in your office until something happens. Nothing will happen until you make it happen.

So—you need real gumption and self-reliance. This is one reason why a part-time start may be wise. While you have an outside job, you have financial and social support to keep you going.

Still, the mail-order business has a wonderful advantage for one who wants to go into business for oneself; it is relatively cheap to get into business long enough to find out whether your plan is profitable. To open up and test out a restaurant may require $20,000 and 2 years. You can test most mail-order products for $50 or $500, though $5,000 may be necessary to test a large, repeat-order business.

This is the long and short of it: Mail order is a terrifically desirable business, and it has many advantages. Because it is so desirable it is also very competitive and tough. And trying to find "one great item" is not the way to solve the problem, as we shall explain later.

What Is the Mail-Order Business?

Introduction ● *Why Do People Buy by Mail?*

INTRODUCTION

"Mail-and-phone-order" or "telemail-order" should be the name of this branch of business, rather than just "mail-order business." But historically it has been "mail-order business" and so it will probably remain, despite industry attempts to relabel it "direct marketing," which would include house-to-house selling.

When we talk about "the mail-order business," we mean all businesses that deal with customers at a distance, without face-to-face selling. We also include the appropriate departments of firms that do some business at a distance, e.g., the mail-selling and telephone-selling activities of stores.

Firms that sell over the telephone resemble mail-order businesses, too. The selling techniques they use are like mail-order techniques, those of direct mail in particular.

Department stores have for many decades sold much of their newspaper-advertised goods by telephone orders. And now Sears, Roebuck and Montgomery Ward find that much of the business generated by their catalogs comes by telephone instead of mail.

Until recently, the high cost of long-distance telephone calls, direct or collect, discouraged both buyers and sellers. But now the cost of long-distance telephone calls has fallen, compared with other costs.

And there are convenient methods of having buyers call direct with an 800 number. And now that it is possible to obtain wide-area WATS service for part or all of the United States at a flat monthly rate, there will surely be more business done by telephone order.

Businesses that sell through agents recruited by mail are in the mail-order business, too. Fuller Brush started that way. In 1913 Fuller used tiny classified ads in *Popular Mechanics* magazine.

When you think of mail order, you probably think first of Sears, Roebuck and Montgomery Ward, the correspondence schools, and book and record clubs. But don't forget the magazines, from *Reader's Digest* and *Time* to the *Journal of Marketing*, all of which sell subscriptions by mail. For example, the magazine *Bon Appétit* formerly distributed 150,000 of its 450,000 copies through liquor stores, but in 1976 the new publisher decided to cut out that practice. He went to direct-mail sales, and was able to profitably raise circulation back to 400,000 within a year, with further increases to come, and at a very satisfactory cost.[2] Magazine subscription sales are perhaps the biggest mail-order operation of all. They account for 9.6 percent of all the direct mail that is sent out each year in the United States. (Next come general mail-order houses with 4.5 percent, book publishers with 3.4 percent, and newspaper publishers with 3.4 percent. But don't forget that direct mail only takes in a *part* of the mail-order business.)[3]

And keep in mind the fancy foods, prescription eyeglasses, artists' supplies, auto accessories, motors and generators, chemicals and the hundreds of other categories of goods sold effectively by mail (see Appendix B).

It is important that when you think about possibilities for your mail-order business, you should *not* restrict yourself to those products narrowly thought of as "mail-order products." Remember that there is *some* truth in the old saying that "if it can be sold, it can be sold by mail." And if you already have a business of your own of almost any kind, you should consider doing some of your business by mail—even if you only hang up a sign that says "Packages Mailed Anywhere in the World," as the candy and novelty shops do, or "Meals To Go" if you run a restaurant. (Later, we shall discuss your choice of product at length.)

WHY DO PEOPLE BUY BY MAIL?

Some people genuinely like to buy by mail. Many get a thrill from waiting for the mail carrier to bring their packages of goodies. But most people buy through mail order because a mail-order merchant makes them an offer of merchandise or price that no store nearby can match, or because no salespeople call on them in person to sell the product. Mail-sold novelty goods are seldom available in nearby stores. Sex books are available in book stores but can be bought by mail without embarrassment.

Very little mail-order merchandise competes on a price basis with merchandise sold through nearby stores. Actually, selling by mail is often an *inefficient* and *expensive* sales technique. Staple merchandise usually can be sold cheaper over the counter in a retail store than it can be sold by mail. The retail merchant can operate on a gross margin of 60 percent down to 20 percent, while mail order usually operates on a margin of 60 percent and up.

But mail order can usually compete very well on products for which a salesperson makes *outside* calls for the firms selling the item. The cost of an outside sales call may be anywhere from $5 to $500; sales calls to businesses now average an astonishing $95 to $100, according to a McGraw-Hill survey (though remember that McGraw-Hill is a publisher and has a stake in having advertising look good by comparison). Sales can often be made by mail at considerably cheaper cost than that.

The Small Business Administration classifies mail-buyers this way.[4]

1. Those interested in novelties. They want something different from their neighbors. These people look over magazines for items that appeal to them. Frequently they find products, relatively inexpensive, of novel appearance and design.

2. Those pursuing a hobby or some particular line of interest. Included here are such groups as home gardeners, stamp collectors, how-to-do-it enthusiasts and many others.

3. Those who buy by mail as a matter of convenience. They find it easier to buy by mail, and especially so if they live in a location removed from adequate shopping facilities. Often they send away for merchandise to benefit from a wider selection. They fill much of their staple goods needs in this way.

4. Those who buy by mail purely for what they consider a price advantage. They look over mail-order catalogs and also the advertisements of stores in their area or farther away to make comparisons and selections in the same manner that women shop for bargains in the local stores.

Many people in the mail-order business have suggested that the increase in the number of women who have 9–5 jobs, and who therefore have less time to go shopping, accounts for the recent boom in the mail-order business. Maybe so, but I think that this is only one small factor among many that are responsible for the increase in Americans' (and Europeans') desire to buy by mail and telephone. Better mail-order selling has helped and so have credit cards, but people's good experiences with buying by mail could be most important of all.

The Professional
Method of
Finding Products

*Types of Mail-Order Marketing • Correspondence
Courses and Other High-Priced Inquiry-and-Follow-Up
Propositions • "The Method": Take Off Your Thinking
Cap • Theory behind "The Method" • Why This
Unlikely Business Principle Holds True • Step by
Step—How to Find and Evaluate Successful Products •
Developing Markets: How to Make a Slow Horse Run
Fast*

Chapters 3 to 5 are certainly the most crucial in the book. Read them through several times. Be sure you are familiar with everything that is within them.

Everyone who has ever dreamed the American dream even a little bit wants a nice, cozy mail-order business for his own. Preferably he'd like a mail-order business he can run with his left hand, from his hammock, and between fishing trips.

The sad truth is that if you ever do find a dream product that sells like hotcakes, at a fantastic profit, the dream won't last much longer than it takes you to quit your steady job and get used to easy living. Competition will pour in so fast, squeezing your profit margins, that you'll be half drowned before you know it.

But that sad truth can also be your key to success in mail order. That's what this chapter is all about.

HOW TO GET RICH THE LAZY MAN'S WAY

I used to work hard. The 18-hour days. The 7-day weeks.

But I didn't start making big money until I did less—a lot less.

For example, this ad took about 2 hours to write. With a little luck, it should earn me 50, maybe a hundred thousand dollars.

What's more, I'm going to ask you to send me 10 dollars for something that'll cost me no more than 50 cents. And I'll try to make it so irresistible that you'd be a darned fool not to do it.

After all, why should you care if I make $9.50 profit if I can show you how to make a lot more?

What if I'm so sure that you will make money my Lazy Man's Way that I'll make you a most unusual guarantee?

And here it is: I won't even cash your check or money order for 31 days after I've sent you my material.

That'll give you plenty of time to get it, look it over, try it out.

If you don't agree that it's worth at least a hundred times what you invested, send it back. Your uncashed check or money order will be put in the return mail.

The only reason I won't send it to you and bill you or send it C.O.D. is because both these methods involve more time and money.

And I'm already going to give you the biggest bargain of your life.

Because I'm going to tell you what it took me 11 years to perfect: How to make money the Lazy Man's Way.

O.K.—now I have to brag a little. I don't mind it. And it's necessary—to prove that sending me the 10 dollars . . . which I'll keep "in escrow" until you're satisfied . . . is the smartest thing you ever did.

I live in a home that's worth $250,000. I know it is, because I turned down an offer for that much. My mortgage is less than half that, and the only reason I haven't paid it off is because my Tax Accountant says I'd be an idiot.

My "office," about a mile and a half from my home, is right on the beach. My view is so breathtaking that most people comment that they don't see how I get any work done. But I do enough. About 6 hours a day, 8 or 9 months a year.

The rest of the time we spend at our mountain "cabin." I paid $30,000 for it—cash.

I have 2 boats and a Cadillac. All paid for.

We have stocks, bonds, investments, cash in the bank. But the most important thing I have is priceless: time with my family.

And I'll show you just how I did it—the Lazy Man's Way—a secret that I've shared with just a few friends 'til now.

It doesn't require "education." I'm a high school graduate.

It doesn't require "capital." When I started out, I was so deep in debt that a lawyer friend advised bankruptcy as the only way out. He was wrong. We paid off our debts and, outside of the mortgage, don't owe a cent to any man.

It doesn't require "luck." I've had more than my share, but I'm not promising you that you'll make as much money as I have. And you may do better; I personally know one man who used these principles, worked hard, and made 11 million dollars in 8 years. But money isn't everything.

It doesn't require "talent." Just enough brains to know what to look for. And I'll tell you that.

It doesn't require "youth." One woman I worked with is over 70. She's travelled the world over, making all the money she needs, doing only what I taught her.

It doesn't require "experience." A widow in Chicago has been averaging $25,000 a year for the past 5 years, using my methods.

What does it require? Belief. Enough to take a chance. Enough to absorb what I'll send you. Enough to put the principles into action. If you do just that—nothing more, nothing less—the results will be hard to believe. Remember—I guarantee it.

You don't have to give up your job. But you may soon be making so much money that you'll be able to. Once again—I guarantee it.

The wisest man I ever knew told me something I never forgot: "Most people are too busy earning a living to make any money."

Don't take as long as I did to find out he was right.

Here are some comments from other people. I'm sure that, like you, they didn't believe me either. Guess they figured that, since I wasn't going to deposit their check for 31 days, they had nothing to lose.

They were right. And here's what they gained:

$260,000 in eleven months
"Two years ago, I mailed you ten dollars in sheer desperation for a better life . . . One year ago, just out of the blue sky, a man called and offered me a partnership . . . I grossed over $260,000 cash business in eleven months. You are a God sent miracle to me."
B. F., Pascagoula, Miss.

Made $16,901.92 first time out
"The third day I applied myself totally to what you had shown me. I made $16,901.92. That's great results for my first time out."
J. J. M., Watertown, N.Y.

'I'm a half-millionaire'
"Thanks to your method, I'm a half-millionaire . . . would you believe last year at this time I was a slave working for peanuts?"
G. C., Toronto, Canada

$7,000 in five days
"Last Monday I used what I learned on page 83 to make $7,000. It took me all week to do it, but that's not bad for five day's work."
M. D., Topeka, Kansas

Can't believe success
"I can't believe how successful I have become . . . Three months ago, I was a telephone order taker for a fastener company in Chicago, Illinois. I was driving a beat-up 1959 Rambler and had about

". . . I didn't have a job and I was worse than broke. I owed more than $50,000 and my only assets were my wife and 8 children. We were renting an old house in a decaying neighborhood, driving a 5-year old car that was falling apart, and had maybe a couple of hundred dollars in the bank.

Within one month, after using the principles of the Lazy Man's Way to Riches, things started to change — to put it mildly.

• We worked out a plan we could afford to pay off our debts — and stopped our creditors from hounding us.
• We were driving a brand-new Thunderbird that a car dealer had given to us!
• Our bank account had multiplied tenfold!
• All within the first 30 days!

And today . . .
• I live in a home that's worth over $250,000.
• I own my "office". It's about a mile and a half from my home and is right on the beach.
• I own a lakefront "cabin" in Washington. (That's where we spend the whole summer — loafing, fishing, swimming and sailing.)
• I own two oceanfront condominiums. One is on a sunny beach in Mexico and one is snuggled right on the best beach of the best island in Hawaii.
• I have two boats and a Cadillac. All paid for.
• I have a net worth of over a Million Dollars. But I still don't have a job . . ."

$600 in my savings account. Today, I am the outside salesman for the same fastener company. I'm sitting in my own office and have about $3,000 in my savings account."
G. M., Des Plaines, Ill.

I know you're skeptical. After all, what I'm saying is probably contrary to what you've heard from your friends, your family, your teachers and maybe everyone else you know. I can only ask you one question.

How many of them are millionaires?

So it's up to you:

A month from today, you can be nothing more than 30 days older — or you can be on your way to getting rich. You decide.

Sworn Statement:
"On the basis of my professional relationship as his accountant, I certify that Mr. Karbo's net worth is more than one million dollars."
Stuart A. Cogan

Bank Reference:
Home Bank
17010 Magnolia Avenue
Fountain Valley, California 92708

Joe Karbo

Joe, you may be full of beans, but what have I got to lose? Send me the Lazy Man's Way to Riches. But don't deposit my check or money order for 31 days after it's in the mail.

If I return your material — for any reason — within that time, return my uncashed check or money order to me. On that basis, here's my ten dollars.

Name _____

Address _____

City _____

State _____ Zip _____

© 1978 Joe Karbo

Figure 3-1 Rare example of successful one-shot products—don't try it.

TYPES OF MAIL-ORDER MARKETING

Before you go looking for a mail-order product, you had better decide which general type of operation you are interested in. These are the important types.

One-Shot Items

This is everyone's idea of the mail-order business. You advertise in magazines or by direct mail, and you either sell enough of the advertised product right from the ad to make a profit, or you lose money.

The advantage of a one-shot product is, first, that you know *immediately* whether you succeed or fail. You don't pour money into a business for a year before finding out it won't work. The one-shot product also gives you back your investment in the shortest possible time. This means that one-shot items have the greatest get-rich-quick potential.

But one-shot items are also the toughest, most competitive business in all the world. It is easy for *you* to get into business, and it is just as easy for your imitators, who will jump in just as soon as they detect you are making a pile—a fact that is hard to conceal in mail order.

As Paul Bringe says:[1]

> If you are in a business where every new customer brings an immediate profit *you are in a dangerous business*. The fast buck boys will be swarming in on you soon. There are few who have the courage to invest in future customers—and that's just what makes such an investment a wide open opportunity for the man who looks ahead.

Not only do successful one-shot items draw direct competition, but they also get indirect competition. The catalog houses like Spencer Gifts, Sunset House and Walter Drake leap on any inexpensive novelty sold through mail-order advertising, and they insert the item into their catalogs. The cost of selling through a catalog is considerably less than one-shot selling costs, and therefore you can't stand catalog competition for long. Furthermore, catalog merchants can saturate a market.

You never really build a *business* when you sell one-shot items. You do not have a loyal clientele who come back and back just as long as you are in business. The one-shot merchant's business is dead 3 months after the last ad is run. The entire business is in one's head.

There are two types of one-shot items: (1) the explosive fads that sell furiously in full-page ads till the market is saturated, and (2) the one-shot staples. The staples never have a big enough market to make big ads pay off, but some of them go on and on, year after year, in 1-inch, 2-inch and 3-inch ads.

What is generally true of one-shot items is especially true of the explosive fads. If you really are looking for a quick million, that's where to cast your eye. But beware the fantastic odds even if you are a thoroughly experienced mail-order dealer. Note also that even if you hold a patent on an item, there isn't one product in 10 years that will support a whole mail-order business. It takes many items to do that. The one-shot dealer is constantly discarding old products.

And yet—there are one-shot success stories. Ed Stern got interested in prescription drugs when a member of his family suffered from some side effects of a drug. He tried to find a book for consumers on the subject, and when he couldn't, he wrote one himself: *Prescription Drugs and Their Side Effects*. He sold more than 70,000 through mail-order ads in *TV Guide* (his first test medium), *Redbook*, *Parade* and other magazines and newspapers. He also sold about that many in stores.[2] But, Stern is director of mail-order sales with major publishers Grosset and Dunlap, who published the book for him. And the book is not strictly a one-shot deal, because Grosset includes package inserts with Stern's book that sell another medical book, which increases the total intake.

CORRESPONDENCE COURSES AND OTHER HIGH-PRICED INQUIRY-AND-FOLLOW-UP PROPOSITIONS

Correspondence courses are like one-shot items in this respect: You expect to make only a single sale to the customer. But correspondence courses are different from inexpensive one-shot products in most other respects.

Correspondence courses and other high-priced merchandise are never sold directly from display advertisements, and they seldom are sold from a cold-canvass direct-mail piece. Instead, they are sold by a series of letters sent to people who have been made to inquire for information by display ads.

Furthermore, correspondence courses cannot usually be bought wholesale by you. They require careful and expensive preparation by the firm that sells them by mail. Other high-priced merchandise also usually requires more work to obtain supplies than does low-priced merchandise.

For these reasons, it is not quite so easy to put this type of merchandise on the market. And therefore the successful operator won't be

Figure 3-2   Examples of successful repeat-order businesses.

swamped so quickly with imitating competitors, and profits are sheltered for a while.

Repeat Lines

Most mail-order businesses that are successful for a long time sell a product that the customer buys again and again: cigars, uniforms, office supplies, etc. Invariably, they "lose money" on the first order from the ad, but they make their profit on the second or tenth sale to the customer.

The strength and the weakness of a repeat-line mail-order business is that it requires more capital and more courage to get started. It takes more time and money before you can tell whether or not you're going to make a success. You can't cut your losses as quickly in a repeat-line business as you can with one-shot items.

But because you must risk more to get into business, you have greater protection from competition once you're established. It is just as tough for *them* to get in. Furthermore, your customers are an ever-growing asset that your competition can't reach. The customer list *is* your business, and no one can ever take that away from you.

Repeat-line businesses are also more profitable, I believe. A rule of thumb is that the harder and more costly it is to break into a line of business in which some firms are operating profitably, the higher the profits will be once you have broken in.

A catalog is almost always part of a repeat-purchase business. But the catalog need not be large or elaborate at first; it can start small and plain and go from there.

Repeat-purchase businesses often obtain their first orders from a customer at a "loss"—that is, the sale by itself does not cover the expense of advertising and goods. But you make up the "loss" on subsequent sales. It takes patience to wait for the later sales to make up for the initial loss, but you must think of this as a necessary process of investment.

Best of all is what Joffe calls a "self-liquidator," an item that will continue to bring in new customers and yet pay for itself immediately. Joffe tells us that Mack the Knife, has been a successful self-liquidator for his firm (Henniker's), which he follows up with his specialty-and-gift catalog.[3] And I'd guess that the "Tidi-File" in Figure 3-4 is a self-liquidator for Frank Eastern Company, which sells a full line of office supplies.

Figure 3-3

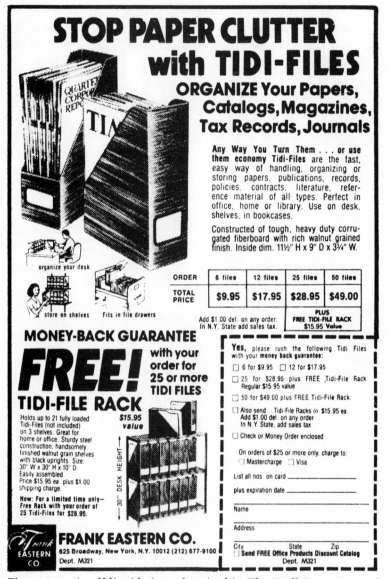

Figure 3-4 A self-liquidation advertised in *The Wall Street Journal.*

The General Catalog Business

This section is about Sears, Roebuck, of course, and also the novelty catalog people like Spencer Gifts, Sunset House, Walter Drake and several others.

Forget this type of business. At least for now. That's my best advice for all newcomers to mail order.

Mail Order through Agents

Many firms that employ house-to-house canvassers as their sales force recruit their agents exclusively through mail-order ads in magazines and newspapers. Firms selling Christmas cards, cosmetics, fire extinguishers and shoes are good examples. The agents and the firm never meet in person. All business between them is done by mail.

You are not likely to tackle this aspect of mail order unless—through other outlets—you already sell a product that is adaptable for this type of mail-order operation. And that's another long story that we won't tell here.

Commercial and Industrial Products

Some commercial products are sold by firms that sell only by mail. Office supplies are an example. But a good deal of mail-order sales of commercial and industrial products is handled by manufacturers or wholesalers who sell through a sales force, also.

One-Shot Items Will Be Our Examples

Throughout the book we shall talk mostly about one-shot items, but *only* because they make the clearest examples and demonstrations of mail-order techniques. *Everything* that applies to finding a good one-shot item applies to repeat lines and other aspects of mail order. And I *strongly advise* that you try not to build a business that is based on one-shot, sold-from-the-ad products.

"THE METHOD": TAKE OFF
YOUR THINKING CAP

Proof First. Before telling you what "The Method" is, I'll try to prove it to you with real examples. And I'll try to ram the lesson home by making you work through the experience.

Below and on the following pages you will find display advertisements D and E and classified ads A, B, C and F. Each advertisement is for a different product. Your problem is to decide (1) whether D or E brought in more dollars, and (2) which two of the four classified ads did best.

All the ads were written by the same copywriter, so you need not concern yourself with the *quality* of the ads. D and E appeared in the same issue of the *National Enquirer,* and the ad that did better had by far the worse position on the page. A, B, C and F all appeared in *Popular Science* classified. The classifications they ran under were not the crucial factor.

Advertisement A

"MAKE YOUR OWN WILL." Forms, Instruction Booklet $1. (Guaranteed!)

Advertisement B

HARMONICAS. Excellent imported chromatic harmonica now only $3.95. Satisfaction guaranteed. Catalog free.

Advertisement C

"HOMEBREWING .. Beers .. Wines!" Instruction Manual $1. (Guaranteed!)

Advertisement D

**$2.98 CONTRAPTION
SQUELCHES SOUND
OF TV COMMERCIALS**

Mad at loud, nasty TV commercials? Now with AD-SQUELCH you can shut up those advertisers that annoy you.

AD-SQUELCH is a brand-new contraption that allows you to shut off, & turn on, TV sound right from your chair. The picture stays on. Works with any TV set made in U.S. Hangs out of sight when not in use.

To install AD-SQUELCH on your set, first open the back with All-model screwdriver included in kit. Then make two connections that a 7-year-old child can do in 3 minutes. That's all!

Complete AD-SQUELCH contains everything necessary to equip your set, plus simple, step-by-step, illustrated directions.

Lean back & enjoy your TV without extra-loud, unpleasant commercials. Send $2.98 to-day to XXXXXXX....................AD-SQUELCH mailed postpaid same day order received. Complete Satisfaction Guaranteed or Money Refunded.

Tear Out and Mail To-day

Advertisement E

Advertisement F

Made your decisions? These are the answers:

E outpulled D by a ratio of 15 to 1. D was one of the most complete fiascos of all time, while E was a success. (Actually, the paper's typographer set up E in a terrible format. The ad did well *despite* the bad typography.)

A and C were profitable ads. B and F would have to have pulled three to four times as much as they did to become really profitable.

Unless you know the mail-order business, it is unlikely that you picked the winners. But any experienced mail-order operator would probably have got them all right—*without thinking hard, and without guessing*. He would *know* for sure.

The mail-order operator's secret in this: he would recognize that E, A and C offer products that have been, and are now, sold successfully by mail. He knows that they are sold successfully because he has seen ads for them repeated again and again over long periods of time. But the D, B and F products are not now being offered repeatedly by anyone.

The principle of the theory is: *Do what is being done successfully.*

The first corollary of that principle is: *Never innovate, never offer really new products.* It's as simple as that.

The second corollary is: *Offer your product in a similar manner and in exactly the same media as the innovator,* at least until you know the situation intimately. At that time you may test new copy against the old, and you can use additional media to *add* to your schedule.

The words of authority never *prove* anything. But the words of a man who has demonstrated success can be very persuasive. So I quote John D. Rockefeller: "When you hear of a good thing—something already working for the other fellow—don't delay but get in while you can."

THEORY BEHIND "THE METHOD"

The artist in you that thrills to novelty, boldness of thought and "creativity" will point to the good new ideas that have made people rich. The examples you will give are true and well known. But the number of people who have sunk big chunks of their lives into schemes that failed badly is not known. And the failures vastly outnumber the successes. Few of us can afford the time that it takes before rare success turns up for us. (Don't forget that each person who backs a losing scheme is always quite sure he has a winner. But, of course, the losers are not as smart as you are!)

It may be true that the total *amount* made by winners exceeds the *amount* lost by losing schemes. This would explain why large corporations can afford to try many new schemes. But only large corporations have the time and money resources to wait till a great many tries bring in the inevitable profit.

My personal experience should help prove what I have said. This is the story of how I learned this secret.

Before I went into mail order, I had a fine college education, service in the Navy as an officer, plus experience working in one of New York's top advertising agencies selling by direct mail and in the advertising promotion department of a huge Madison Avenue publishing house. I had received the degree of Doctor of Philosophy in Business Economics. Furthermore, I had been an advertising consultant to, among other firms, one of the biggest department store chains in the United States.

Then I decided to go into the mail-order business for myself. I read every available book, but found little to help me. I talked with everyone I could find, some of the smartest and most successful people in the country. I asked each one of them what I should sell.

Finally, I had a list of four major product lines to try. And I went full steam ahead!

Sounds as if I was perfectly prepared, doesn't it? Maybe you can guess what happened—a complete *bust!*

One after the other, the products proved unsuitable for mail order. I hadn't lost much money. (I didn't have much to start with.) But I was bewildered and discouraged. Where should I go from here?

But I knew that *some* operators had the knack of finding successful products. So I went back and studied the operations of the most successful mail-order dealers. I studied them, and studied them, and studied them until . . . *finally I knew.* I had found out what the top money-making mail-order dealers—many of whom *had never finished high school*—knew all along.

And it was so easy! How I regretted the time I had wasted. All my education and experience did me no good in learning the secret of "The Professional Method." In fact, even now I have trouble convincing professor friends of mine that the secret is real—that is, until I show them the *results.*

WHY THIS UNLIKELY BUSINESS PRINCIPLE HOLDS TRUE

The principle says that brilliant and artistic thinking is of little use in this aspect of business. Sad but true. Psychologists tell us that the best administrators do not have "creative" minds. The best businesspeople do not generate new ideas. They choose between the ideas suggested by others.

But note that the standards and goals of business are very different from those of art and scholarship. Innovation for its own sake has value in art and science. If a painting or a story fails in every other way, mere innovation gives us some pleasure and wins some praise for the artist. The same goes for a wonderfully imaginative but wrong-headed theory in the sciences. But the yardstick in business is simply how well the idea works and how much it makes.

So if you're looking for an outlet for your creativity, stay away from the mail-order business. You'll save yourself money and frustration.

The *first reason* why the copycat principle works so well is that both the mail-order industry and business as a whole do a great deal of trial-and-error experimentation. Much of this experimentation is carried on by people highly qualified to do it. All this trial-and-error investigation makes it highly unlikely that a single innovation by a nonprofessional will find a wide and profitable market.

Your chances are better when the innovation requires specialized knowledge, such as that of a chemical engineer or of an airplane pilot or of a biologist. But anyone can dream up a new kind of can opener.

The chances against your making a fortune with a new kitchen gadget are astronomical.

The *second reason* why copycat works is the outsider's lack of information. Newcomers to mail order don't know what has been tried and found to fail. They don't know what the market needs. And the newcomer doesn't have information with which to project the profit potential of a totally new product.

The *third reason* why copycat works is *especially* true in the mail-order business. The first person to sell a product has very little advantage over those who follow. The pioneer has less advantage than in almost any other line of business because it is so easy and cheap for mail-order competition to duplicate the product and its advertising. The "barriers to entry" against competitors are low indeed. So the time advantage of the leader is only a matter of months. That's why the one-shot mail-order business is such a toughly competitive field.

The *fourth reason* why the copycat principle works is also peculiar to mail order. A mail-order campaign is remarkably open to inspection by all who care to look. Reading all the likely magazines, and checking the mail sent to major mailing lists, will tell you much of what you need to know about a competitor's campaign. There is little in the way of trade secrets that the leader can keep hidden. What was learned by the sweat of the brow and costly experimentation, all others learn free and at ease.

And *fifth*, the copycat even has an *advantage* over the leader. The leader had to bear the cost of testing until he found the most effective copy and the media that would pay out. The copycat then follows as closely as consistent with business ethics. He can explode into a great many media just as soon as he has tested his copy, and this means that he will reach peak volume much faster than the innovator did.

It may be that the market is too small for both of you, though this is true much less often than you would imagine. Perhaps you have developed better copy or a better offer than the leader, and are able to force him out. But if your test ads are well done and your results are still borderline, you'd better seek another product.

The only advantages the leader has over imitators are: (1) The leader has already developed tested copy, and has information about the relative performance of the various media; and (2) the leader's development costs are "sunk," so that, in a true economic sense, cost for future operations will be less than that of the followers. Like any other lower-cost producer, the leader can last longer in a struggle than can the higher-cost producers.

Those are the reasons why the best mail-order product for you to market is a presently successful product. The same reasons also show that the media you should expect to use are exactly the media used by the leader. You will first use the media that the competition uses most heavily—in terms of space or frequency—because those are the media in which his (and your) payout will be greatest.

In this chapter I have tried to be as blunt as I can be in saying: If you try to sell any *new* mail-order product or service—that is, a product or service that you don't know is now being sold successfully in mail-order—the odds are very strongly against you. At the very same time, I can safely tell you that if you operate intelligently and efficiently you have an excellent chance of making good in selling whatever products and services successful mail-order firms are now selling. Even though I have tried to make this message as crystal-clear as can be in previous editions, I still get phone calls and letters from readers who say: "But you still haven't told us how to find a successful product." So maybe I better look for another way of explaining what's going on here.

Let's say that a friend of yours is thinking about opening a retail business. What kind of a store would you advise your friend to open? Or better, how would you advise your friend to go about finding out what kind of store to open? I think that you might look around your city, or in other towns, to see which kinds of retail stores seem to be doing well. You might look especially closely at those which have been growing particularly fast recently. You might then reason that since they are doing well, your friend might also do well in the same line. If your friend instead began to think up ideas for a new sort of retail store that is not now operating successfully—a rope store, say, or a store to sell old beer cans—I think that you might look skeptically on the venture, and think that the odds of success are low. Of course, some new ventures that have never been seen before come to do well in each decade—yogurt stores, and ice cream stores, and sneaker stores, in the last decade, for example. But for each such new success like those, there must be many, many attempts that failed. The odds simply are much greater against such a totally new venture than in starting a store of the same sort that others now are operating successfully.

You might say, however, that in the retail business one has to have a lot of capital to get started, and that keeps out every Tom, Dick and Harry who might want to do the same thing that others have done successfully, a barrier to entry which allows opportunity to be there. And you might say that the small capital requirement is the reason that you want to go into the mail-order business. The fact of the matter, however, is that there is a barrier to getting started in the mail-order business too, though it perhaps is not as visible as the need for capital in opening a store and stocking it with inventory. As I have emphasized throughout the book, almost all successful mail-order businesses sell a line of *repeat* goods. Therefore you must invest in getting customers who will buy from you again and again, and that needs capital, just as for retail stores. Perhaps more important in the mail-order business, however, is the investment of time and thought that is needed to begin small, and gradually learn and build on your mistakes. This may mean starting with a classified ad or two, or a small display ad somewhere, working part-time, and gradually building your personal skills and your tested advertising sales methods for the business. It is this requirement of go-slow patience and trial-and-error learning which keeps most people out of the mail-order business—or, at least, keeps them from operating successfully in the mail-order business. It is also this factor which keeps it from being so competitive that no one can make any money at all.

I hope that this explanation, by analogy to retail stores, makes clearer why I recommend to you that you look for opportunities among products and services where there is already evidence of successful mail-order activity.

A Big Difficulty of "The Method"

When you try to copy a successful operation, you must be sure that you learn *all* the essential facts about the operation you are copying—or you may find yourself in big trouble. Stone tells the story of how one copycat drowned.[4]

> Years ago, when I was a principal of National Research Bureau, we had a division which sold collection stickers to business men by mail. We sold millions and millions of collection stickers. I bragged about this to a Texan once, and it wasn't six months later that he started a company to sell collection stickers by mail. He copied us "right off the page." In less than a year this Texan was hopelessly bankrupt.
>
> There was just one thing I neglected to divulge when I was bragging to this Texan. I neglected to tell him *we lost money on every collection sticker order.* He didn't know we "bought" new customers in volume with our collection sticker offer so we could sell Christmas greeting letters to those same customers at a substantial profit.

Here are two examples:[5]

> The World of Beauty, for example, passed through several hands before the idea was perfected, simplified and made profitable by GRI.
>
> My friends Steve Brown and Vic Schiff of Cheeselovers International took their financial lumps for years until they got their system to work. Then they were able to go to Jay Norris for support, and now everyone concerned seems on the way to riches. You may be able to invest in a loser at a bargain—if you know how to turn it into a winner. Even if it should remain a loser, somebody else's loser will usually cost you a lot less than your own.

As an individual you want to reap the profits yourself, and now. So follow The Method, and leave the new concepts for others, or until later.

STEP BY STEP—HOW TO FIND AND EVALUATE SUCCESSFUL PRODUCTS

The first step to finding successful products is to get hold of a copy of *Standard Rate & Data,* Consumer Magazine and Farm Publication section, and write to every magazine listed in it with circulation over perhaps 100,000 in these classifications: Men's, Romance, Women's, Sports, Almanacs, Mechanics and Science, Motion Picture, Fraternal, Religious and Denominational, Exposure, Fishing and Hunting, Gardening, Newspaper-distributed Magazines, Health, Home Service and Home, TV and Radio, Veterans, Business and Finance, plus every single farm magazine. There are other mail-order media, but these will do for a start. Give yourself a company name, and write to each magazine for a sample copy and a "rate card." A postcard will do the job except for *Esquire* and two or three other standoffish magazines.

Look through each magazine you receive, and for each one make notes on an index card of the types of products sold in it. You should be learning that there are hundreds of magazines you have never seen in all your well-bred, high-thinking life. And those magazines of which you are not aware are probably the best mail-order media of all. They carry a tremendous proportion of the one-shot products we are using as our examples here. For goodness sake, do not limit yourself to the Home Service magazines. Much of the advertising they carry is amateurish and unsuccessful, and much more is of products and lines that are tough for a newcomer to mail order.

Keep your eye on the classified sections, too. There is much to be learned from classified.

Next, go to a back-date magazine shop, and buy 100 back copies of *Popular Science, Workbasket,* farm magazines, *House Beautiful* and low-life men's and women's magazines—especially the latter. Not only are the "gray matter" low-life magazines important, but you can't find them in any library.

Now you should begin reading ads in earnest. Don't try to form conclusions. Just look and look and look at all kinds of mail-order ads. At first you will think there are 100,000 products on the market. But soon the various ads will become familiar. Then you will recognize the addresses of some companies offering several different products.

You are making progress when you recognize *most* of the ads you see. And you have learned almost enough when you can recognize the layout styles of the important mail-order firms. By that time you will know that there are relatively few products and advertisers on the market, and even fewer big and successful companies that have been around for several years.

Of course, the successful products are the ones that you recognize as appearing again and again over a period of years and in a great many magazines. The most successful among the successful are those that even run ads in the slow summer months.

(Why do once-successful products disappear? Some go off the market because the Federal Trade Commission or the Post Office Department finds them fraudulent or deceptive. Others, some full-page-ad products, may exhaust their fads after a while. Many do not really disappear, but reappear intermittently.)

Next, get acquainted with the direct-mail mail-order offers. Get a few friends to save all the direct mail they get. Write to every single free offer, or offer of information, that you come across in the magazines, especially in one full issue of *House Beautiful*. This means writing for *hundreds* of catalogs and offers. And try to find some products you want to buy or try by mail. Buy some things by mail (not from Sears) that you wanted anyway. Don't be afraid to accept offers of a free trial or offers to refund your money if you're not satisfied. You'll get your money back, just as you'll give it back once you're in the mail-order business.

Important: Use a different set of first initials in the name you sign for each firm you write to, and keep a record of which initials went where and on which date. Then record which offers you receive addressed to which initials, and the date. Your initial code will then teach you which lists are rented to whom, very important information later on. The card below is an edited example from our files.

G. H. Smith

Sent to
  Miles Kimball Company, Sep 1, 19— HOUSE BEAUTIFUL

Rented by:
  Publishers Clearing House. Jan 21
  American Home Magazine, Feb 12
  Saturday Evening Post, Mar 31
  Publishers Clearing House, July 18
  etc.

Study the direct-mail offers the same way you studied the magazines.

Then, one way or another, get your hands on a copy of Standard Rate and Data Service, Inc.'s *Direct Mail List Rates and Data* (DMLRD). This wonderful publication is a gold mine of information for the person who wants to learn about the mail-order business, and it is indispensable for the mail-order operator who gets new orders from list solicitations. DMLRD is a compilation of data on most of the important lists. The lists that interest the person who wants to learn about mail order are the lists of mail-order *customers* of various firms. You can tell how many customers a firm has had and the average unit of sale in dollars, which tells you a great deal about the firm. More about this publication later.

Getting your hands on a copy—even a back copy, which will be sufficient for the beginner's needs—can be tough unless you're prepared to fork out the $59.50 (1979) subscription price for the two semi-annual editions. Some big libraries have a copy. Or you can try to look at a copy belonging to a mail-order business or an advertising agency in your area. Maybe you can persuade your local library to buy it. So you'll have to scrounge. But try *somehow* to get your hands on a copy of DMLRD.

Study the lists being offered for rent, and the size of the lists. This will give you further information on the number of firms in any line (even though the firm names are not given) and the amount of business they do in the various products. These data will also be important later on when you try to estimate the profit potential for various product lines.

All this time you should be watching the mail-order section of your Sunday newspaper, examining the magazines that come into your hands, and keeping a sharp ear for mail-order offers on the radio.

Appendix B in the back of the book contains a long sample list of successful mail-order lines.

Two Storied Exceptions

If you are not convinced by what I said about the humdrum, copycat routine method being the best way to find successful products, here are the stories of a couple of exceptions that you can use to prove that I'm all wet. (But don't say I didn't warn you of disaster if you try to follow their examples.)

Al Sloan[6] is the fellow behind the famous Bell & Howell camera promotions. Way back in the 1930s, he began by developing an arrangement with jewelry stores by which he sold them circulars that had the store's merchandise on one side, and Sloan's merchandise—boudoir chairs, comforters and the like—on the other. And Sloan's merchandise was also offered as a premium—as a gift, or for $1—if the customer bought any of the jewelry store's merchandise from the circular. Sloan "syndicated" the offer across the country, and hence Sloan is known as the pioneer of this sort of deal. And he also worked up a deal that sold hundreds of thousands of sets of Wearever aluminum as premiums, using the same store-circular strategy.

The deal that made Sloan famous in the mail-order business was an extension of his syndication method—the sale of a $150 movie camera for Bell & Howell in coordination with gasoline companies and others who had large lists of customers with solid credit. Traditional mail-order operators doubted that the deal would work because, until then, big-ticket consumer items had never been sold this way. But Sloan's deal pulled fantastically—selling $50 million worth in 24 years—and enriched everyone connected with the deal.

Now Sloan has a new deal in the works, a centrifugal paint sprayer, which he is selling in conjunction with such major firms as Fingerhut's, World Book and an oil company; it is reported to be doing well.

But—here's the other side of the coin. Disaster overtook even as experienced and talented an operator as Sloan. This was the report in the trade press in 1972:[7]

"The syndicators of merchandise programs have sustained impossible losses for mysterious reasons." Al Sloan of Whitney-Forbes, Inc. told this reporter last week in Chicago, during a visit with Sloan in Michael Reese Hospital. Syndication pioneer said he has mounted 14 promotions in the last four years. Each tested carefully to oil company active and inactive charges. Based on tests, continuation to full lists indicate substantial profits. Instead says Sloan, sustained lost of almost $2 million. Test projections considered timing (seasons), recession factors. Showed this reporter detailed results, by product promotion, by accounts. Continuation often halved test results. Most often because inactive portion of lists failed. Problem many sided. Sloan's system was to supply all up-front promotion money with commission to oil company. Not uncommon to risk million dollars based on the successful test.

Continuation brought losses due to insistence of clients to run inactive accounts, the major client interest and ahead of hefty commissions earned on a percentage of sales, whether effort was profitable or not. According to Sloan reactivated customers, secured through merchandise mailings, worth better than $400 per year in gas, oil and tires to oil companies. Thus no risk mailing syndicator's offer even to bad list. Other side of problem: unused merchandise committed and made based on test and unexpected continuation results. Mistakes in box car figures, tens of thousands of unsold units."

Joe Sugarman is another such story and—relax—Sugarman's story has strictly an upbeat ending as of this date. Here are excerpts from a front-page *Wall Street Journal*[8] article on Sugarman:

Back in 1971, when electronic pocket calculators were still primitive and costly, an advertising man named Joseph Sugarman figured he could make a pile of money by selling the little gadgets through the mails.

Mr. Sugarman raised $12,000 with the help of friends, persuaded Craig Corp. to let him market its calculator, and mailed out 50,000 fliers extolling the new product. "I lost my shirt," he recalls. But then the manufacturer dropped the price to $180 from $240. Mr Sugarman wrote a new ad, mailed it to a million people and hit the jackpot.

"I made $20,000 in 10 days," he says, and by the end of 1972, he had done "a half-million dollars in volume, grossed $100,000 and netted $50,000." As sales took off, giant retailers such as Sears Roebuck and Montgomery Ward took an interest in the Craig calculator, and they, too, began selling it.

In the seven years since then, the 40-year-old Mr. Sugarman has done his mail-order number on dozens of other electronic gadgets, ranging from burglar alarms and home pinball machines to remote-control model speedboats. In every case, his methods have remained the same: pick an emerging product, plug it with ads in general magazines and special brochures, and distribute it through the mail. His company, JS&A National Sales Group, once occupied his basement but now employs 50 people in modern offices. The company's annual sales are approaching $50 million, and its profits provide Mr. Sugarman with an enormous mansion and a matching ego. . . .

"I like gadgets," Mr. Sugarman says. He is a connoisseur of gadgets who carefully selects for his largely upper-income, male clientele an array of toys that look nifty and do nifty things. "Maybe you're just looking at a guy who has good taste," he says in explanation of his knack for picking winners.

Mr. Sugarman scrutinizes a product's styling, which can make or break it on the marketplace. One reason he agreed to sell a $150 Japanese-made "jogging computer" this year was its "space-age styling" and "digital read-out," he says. The machine consists of a platform on which the jogger runs in place and a sleek console that measures the pace and "distance" of the jog and prints the results on a lighted screen.

But Mr. Sugarman has more than an eye for styling. One of his merchandising tricks is to infuse a product with a timely marketing angle. "Someone offered me a small walkie-talkie in the middle of the CB craze," he recalls. "Instead of using the walkie-talkie idea, I focused on the mini-CB angle" and called the product the "Pocket Com." In the three years since he introduced it, Mr. Sugarman has sold 250,000 Pocket Coms. . . .

Not all of Mr. Sugarman's efforts succeed, however. He got caught with a $1,500 laser-beam mousetrap, brought to market in April 1977. The gadget detected the presence of a mouse with a laser beam, which activated a spring-loaded wire trap. The device was mounted on a polished walnut base that could be "handsomely displayed in any office, boardroom, or rodent-infested area," Mr. Sugarman said in his ad. Unfortunately, he didn't sell a single one. Mr. Sugarman said he was trying to test the adage that "if you build a better mousetrap, the world will beat' a path to your door." Not always, apparently.

Financially speaking, Mr. Sugarman's biggest flop was a $250,000 loss he sustained in 1975 on a "checkbook with a brain," a $40 electronic device that recorded savings deposits, checking balances and the like. Mr. Sugarman has concluded that people would rather write such information in their checkbooks by hand.

Another noteworthy flop was "Mickey Math," a Mickey Mouse calculator. "I thought I had the next 'pet rock,' " Mr. Sugarman says. He now believes that the product flopped because a calculator "is a pretty serious product. People don't buy it for a joke."

DEVELOPING MARKETS: HOW TO MAKE A SLOW HORSE RUN FAST

You *may* be able to increase the size of the market and force the volume of a product much higher than your competitors have managed to do. In this section we shall discuss ways of developing proven products. But heed this warning: Do *not* count on expansion potential when you estimate the size of a product's market unless you are already a highly skilled mail-order dealer.

These are some ways you can develop or increase the size of a market:

1. *Advertise classified products in display advertising.* Some firms that advertise in classified have insufficient skill, initiative or capital to push out into display, and an enterprising firm can take advantage of this. For example, coin catalogs have been successfully sold in classified for years. Then a big operator began to sell coin catalogs in full-page ads in dozens of magazines, spending hundreds of thousands of dollars in advertising.

   But—many of the firms that use classifieds are wise birds that *also* use display, or that have found out from hard experience that display advertising won't work for their purposes.

2. *Another way to increase a market is by personalizing items with the customer's monogram or initials.* This is actually a special

case of increasing a market by improving the desirability of the product offer. But be careful—personalizing can be costly.

3. *Search through old magazines (10 to 40 years old) for products that were once sold successfully but that outlived their fads.* Sometimes you can bring these products back to life. But sometimes their market has died with them because times have changed and Americans no longer are interested in the product.

4. *Find successful mail-order products in English magazines and transplant the ideas to this country.* Again, be careful: the British and Americans are very different in many ways.

5. *Sell a product similar to existing products.* If one outfit successfully sells a franchised business to clean rugs, for example, you might consider selling a franchised business to clean walls.

6. *Upgrade a successful book or short correspondence course.* The "Little Blue Books" of Emanuel Haldeman-Julius represent a gold mine of tested mail-order material. The subject matter of many of the books he originally sold for 5 cents can be amplified and upgraded into full-scale mail-order successes. (But be sure not to copy his material!) Read Haldeman-Julius's book *The First Hundred Million*,[9] the best book ever written on the technique of choosing and selling books by mail order, if you can lay your hands on a copy (it is out of print).

More about Finding Products to Sell

Follow Your Hobbies Into Mail Order • From Stores to Mail Order • If You Are Already in the Mail-Order Business

Chapter 3 discussed how to find products if you are starting from scratch. In this chapter we'll talk about how to exploit some special advantages you may have—hobbies, a retail business, connections with others who have products to sell and so on.

FOLLOW YOUR HOBBIES INTO MAIL-ORDER

A path to mail-order success that many successful operators have used— even starting with nothing but the legendary kitchen table—is to capitalize on your knowledge of, and interest in, one of your hobbies. Let's consider some examples:

1. Pat Baird started Ships Wheel Inc.[1] because she always loved the sea and boating. She had had a heart attack and needed an activity to keep her busy. Her first step was a single ad for four items in *Yachting*. At that time she did her paperwork on the kitchen table, and stored her inventory in the garage. Now her items fill an 80-page catalog, of which Ship Wheel sends out hundreds of thousands, or millions, of copies each year. Many of the items—drinking glasses for example—are personalized. A big success any way you look at it, out of Pat Baird's hobby interest.

39

2. Jean Shramm had an aunt who ran a "doll hospital," and Mrs. Shramm got fond of the dolls. She and her husband had a real-estate office in Vermont, so she borrowed some dolls from the aunt and put them on display shelves in the office, withdrawing $500 from her savings account to finance the early stock. People bought the dolls. So she next decided to sell by mail order, and borrowed $2,000 from the bank. Eventually the business grew so much that she sold it to a major corporation.[2]

3. Ewing Hunter had been a Ferrari auto buff for years. In 1973 he found it difficult to obtain the owner's manuals and parts manuals for a Ferrari he bought. So he decided to reproduce and sell manuals himself. He invested only enough for some brochures and $250 in postage. In six months he was grossing $1,000 per month. Five years later the firm was grossing perhaps $1 million annually, largely on parts sales. (An interesting feature of the business is that people pay $2 for the catalog.)

FROM STORES TO MAIL ORDER

Few people who start in mail order from scratch would decide to sell airplanes or farms. But if you are already in one of those businesses, you may decide that you can increase your volume by mail-order selling.

Remember: We are *not* talking about ordinary direct mail that so many firms use to *help* them close deals. We're talking about mail-order deals in which the customer is first contacted with printed material, and in which the whole transaction takes place without face-to-face meeting.

Businesses that may not be practical to *begin* purely for a mail trade may be very profitable to expand by mail. The art-supplies business is a good example. You would require a stock of perhaps $100,000 to back up a mail-order business—expensive indeed. But if you are already a large retail dealer in art supplies, you already bear the cost of the stock, and you do not need to charge any of that cost to the mail-order operation as you would if you sold by mail only.

Lamps, rugs and advertising specialties are other examples of the same principle.

There is still another good reason why an established retailer or manufacturer may find it profitable to develop a mail-order operation. Mail-order advertising can stimulate the sale of goods through regular outlets, too. Book publishers often find that a mail-order campaign will increase sales of books in stores by between 100 percent and 400 percent. This means that the mail-order sales campaign can bring back *mail-order* sales far less than its cost and still be very profitable.

In some cases retailers have shifted over completely from retail to mail order, as seen in this report.[3]

SHOES FOR HARD TO FIT WOMEN

Starting with retail stores in Greater Boston area, [Hill's] branched out into direct mail six years ago. The operation has been so successful there is a possibility that only one retail store will remain and all efforts will be concentrated on mail. With 120,000 mail customers now, the market can become much larger, since all sizes of shoes are carried, including regular sizes. Lawson Hill Jr., president, says he can carry 118 different sizes vs about 19 for a regular retail store. He stocks over 15,000 different pairs of shoes. Two major mailings are made each year to 1.5 million names each time. . . . Hill is an advocate of "scientific marketing" and describes the formulation of his catalog in these terms, using "eye flow" pages. His average sale is $22 and the average order is for 1½ pairs of shoes.

And traditional department stores are getting ready to participate in what many think is a "new marketing revolution," as these examples suggest.[4]

Neiman-Marcus, a Texas-based department store, has developed a mail-order operation that is highly personalized; that offers an intensely edited selection of merchandise, frequently exclusive and of high quality. . . . Saks Fifth Avenue published a Christmas catalog for the first time in 1972, and Bloomingdale's in New York City mailed a catalog recently for the first time in over 20 years. Harrod's of London has long published catalogs.

The most impressive case is that of J. C. Penney. This was the story as of 1973.[5]

The J. C. Penney Company is the second largest merchandise retailer in the United States. Our total sales in our 1973 fiscal year will be over $6-billion. We are second to Sears Roebuck. But unlike Sears and Montgomery Ward who started in the catalog business and later added stores, we began with our stores. Mr. Penney opened his first store in 1903. He called his early stores the Golden Rule Stores. Each store manager was a partner in the Company. *Today* we have 1,700 Penney Stores.

We did not enter the catalog business until 1963, when we purchased a small regional catalog company to get us started.

Today we do about $500-million with our catalog in 40 states and are well on our way to becoming national. Sears Roebuck today does well over $2-billion in catalog sales. So you can see we have a little way to go.

We operated our catalog business at a loss for eight years until we earned our first profit in 1971. The obvious question we were asked during those difficult years was: "why?" Why did we believe it was so necessary to bring in a catalog operation in which we were willing to invest for so long a period?

There are several answers, which provide good testimony to the importance of the catalog as an example of direct marketing. First we saw it as a way to increase our share of the market. We were unwilling to concede that important segment of the market to Sears, Wards, and others.

Second, our best judgment, backed by some hard research facts, told us that just as our store business would help us get a catalog business started, a catalog would help build volume in our stores.

Finally, there were good indications that direct marketing by means of a catalog was a rapidly growing business, fitting more and more into the changing lifestyles of Americans. If catalogs were to become increasingly important in the future of retailing, we certainly didn't want to stand by and watch.

A nice example of how mail-order selling can be used to take advantage of an existing product you control is the success of selling Bob Dylan's comeback tour in 1974:[6]

The times, Bob Dylan is telling us, they are a'changin'.

And he's also telling us something about advertising. In his first concert tour in eight years, the young poet-songwriter-performer is demonstrating the power of advertising. It seems that his 21-city tour had a sellout capacity of 650,000 seats (at between $9.50 and $10.50 a ticket).

To fill those seats with denim and corduroy-clad bottoms, the tour promoters ran a newspaper ad once in each tour city last December. According to the latest estimates, these one-time-only ads pulled between 2,000,000 and 3,000,000 mail orders.

And here is an example of how a clothing retailer branched out into mail-order selling.[7]

HOW CASEY JONES RAILROADED US INTO MAIL ORDER BUSINESS

If you look in the New York Times or National Observer lately, you might see our ad for a "Casey Jones 5-Piece Outfit." It looks like a railroad engineer's outfit in little boy's sizes. It is made of sturdy denim ticking. And each ad pulls around 60 orders. At an average of $19 each. Or a total of $1,140. . . .

Those of you with a good memory had read of many examples of retail stores growing many times their size through mail order. Why not us? Why not our retail store? . . .

We leafed through our newspaper ads for the previous year. One item pulled so well we repeated it often. Each time we appealed to the same audience . . . and each time it drew mail, phone and in-person orders. The item: the above-mentioned dungaree set by Oshkosh B'Gosh, manufacturers of men's sturdy work clothing. Would this item pull as well in a national ad as in a local ad? Why not? People are people. . . .

You must have exclusivity in your presentation that cannot be knocked off by someone else. But Oshkosh is available to other stores. It is not sought out by many specialty shops since they make only this one item in a huge and diversified men's line. But it *could* be bought by other stores. And promoted.

What would make it ours alone? Something added. What do you associate with a train conductor? A lamp. A train. A whistle. We leafed through a wholesale toy catalogue and found a marvelous four-inch hardwood whistle. Great. We added the bandana made by Oshkosh and we now had an "exclusive 5-piece set." We named it "The Casey Jones Set."

As an added fillip, we offered to monogram the name on the jacket for an extra $2. . . . We knew our customer sought out gift items. Something different . . . and for children. We geared our advertising a month or two before Christmas. We selected our first media buy, the National Observer whose reader profile closely matches our existing customer. The Observer can be bought by regions. (We recommend you test with the region nearest you first. Cost is about half the national $4.10 per line rate.) We bought the Eastern edition first. It pulled well enough to try for the national circulation (half-a-million).

The two ads sold a total of 153 sets.

Here's what that figure means in terms of money made:

Eastern edition	$109.80
National edition	246.00
Cost of set ($8. × 153)	1,224.00
Cost of set and ads:	$1,579.80
Total sales (153 × 18) =	$2,754.00
Less expenses	1,579.80
Net profit	1,174.20

Each order included an extra $1.00 for postage which took care of mailing charges. More than half included the monogramming $2.00 fee which means an *extra* $100. profit.

In 1967, bar owner Eddie DiNicolantonio got interested in message-printed T-shirts. In eight years he built up Printed Sportswear, selling to stores in the Atlantic City area. Then he thought to sell to businesses by mail rather than in person, and within a few months he had the makings of a successful operation.[8]

Lou Burnett has owned a golf course near Interstate 76 in Georgia for 19 years. A few years ago the golf pro at a local military installation began to eat into Burnett's pro-shop sales of clubs and other equipment with what Burnett considered unfair price competition. So Burnett began to advertise even lower prices in local newspapers, then in regional media, and finally in national magazine classified ads. Soon he had done so well that he was ready to sell the golf course and concentrate on the mail sales alone.[9]

Small manufacturers also can develop successful mail-order businesses with products they have formerly sold through other channels. For example, Burton Bank had manufactured men's slacks for 25 years, starting in 1948. After selling his slacks business in 1975, he tried selling just a single item—the "bush jean" or "bush short"—by mail-order. He ran one ad in the *National Observer*, made a good profit, and within a year he had a twelve-page catalog of men's and women's wear, and did half a million dollars in business the first year.[10]

"But I haven't got a store or a product," you may wail. OK, but maybe you can hook up with someone who *does* have a store or a product, to your mutual benefit. How about making a deal with the fellow who sells tires for foreign cars in your town? Sell those tires by mail out of his inventory. Or the aggressive camera dealer in town who has lots of interesting specials? Or the "war surplus" dealer down the road? Or golf clubs? And so on. Look around, use your imagination and be willing to walk in and suggest the idea. Almost anyone will hear you out when you have a deal like this to propose.

IF YOU ARE ALREADY IN THE MAIL-ORDER BUSINESS

If you are already in a mail-order business, you almost surely are actively looking around for new products to sell, in order to keep growing and to increase your profit. Of course you have an enormous advantage over your situation when you were first starting out in business. But the odds still are strongly against any single new idea panning out. Luckily for you, in the mail-order business you can try out new ideas cheaply until you find ones that work.

The guiding principle, if you are already in the mail-order business, is to develop new ventures that take advantage of some existing features of your present business. The most important possibilities are: (1) your customer list, (2) your shipping and warehousing capacities, and (3) any special skills of your staff that may be underutilized during some periods of the year.

Selling new—though related—products to your old customers is the basic tried-and-true method of mail-order growth. Haband started out selling neckties; now their main business is pants and shoes. Richard Sears started with watches, and by now Sears, Roebuck has branched out into almost everything. You can expand your offerings by increasing the size of your catalog, or by increasing the number of mailings to customers. Either way, however, remember that the new merchandise must appeal to similar sorts of people as your existing merchandise does, or else you are not taking advantage of your customer list (except for their trust in you, which is a help), in which case you are little better off than starting from scratch.

Taking advantage of the firm's knowledge of a market, its skills and its facilities is a bit less obvious than taking advantage of the customer list, so let's consider an example:[11]

The company is Chap Stick in Lynchburg, Virginia. For many years we have handled Chap Stick's mail order companies, the principal one being Blair Quality Products. Blair is an Avon-like business. Its dealers sell toiletries and cosmetics to their friends and neighbors. There are no field managers; however, the Blair dealers are, in fact, simply mail order customers of the company. Blair recruits its dealers through advertising in TV Guide, and in the big circulation movie and fan magazines. But Blair dealers cannot be recruited profitably in Glamour, Cosmopolitan, Mademoiselle or Seventeen.

But those magazines comprise a huge market. How could Chap Stick develop a new business for this market? Well, let's add two other factors to the equation. Chap Stick Company has an excellent and flexible consumer-oriented computer operation. Secondly, the Chap Stick Company has a superb capability for manufacturing cosmetics, packaging them, and mailing them to individual customers. Analyze these strengths—and the media market—and you might well come up with Chap Stick's new business—the Kenneth Beauty Program.

Chap Stick was brought together with Kenneth, the famous hairdresser and beauty expert. Drawing on Kenneth's strong ideas about beauty, Chap Stick put together a highly individualized 40-page beauty-guidance report, printed by computer at relatively low cost. This report is uniquely the customer's own. She answers about 50 questions which are fed into the computer, and gets a highly personal one-of-a-kind analysis.

We sell the Kenneth Beauty Program for cash—using a very editorial-looking ad which incorporates a full page questionnaire. Buyers get a periodic newsletter, which is—of course—a vehicle for selling the Kenneth line of cosmetics.

If you already sell a product, these are some of the factors to consider when you decide whether to market your product through mail order:

1. Do any of your competitors sell by mail? If they do, your problem is almost solved. If they don't, don't let their example stop you.

2. How many customers do you have who *now* buy from you only by mail? If you already have a good many people or firms on your books who have moved to other parts of the country or whom you never see, and who still buy from you, then you probably have a product that lends itself to mail order.

3. These rules of thumb may be helpful:

● Is the product light in weight per dollar of sales price? Mailability is very important if you are to obtain a profitable return. Books are ideal because of the cheap postage rate they enjoy.

● Can you get a high markup on the cost to you? Three-to-one is a familiar formula, but there are too many situations to which it does not apply. Don't be hamstrung by the formula.

● Is it a product that is not readily obtainable in stores near most consumers?

● Can the sales appeal be communicated on paper? Perfume is hard to sell by mail because prospects want to smell before they buy.

● Will you have to offer credit? It is generally true that you must offer credit if the sales price is over $10 or $20. Do you have the capital and the organization to offer terms?

● Do outside salespeople sell your product? Examples: insurance, industrial equipment, commercial supplies. All are sold both by outside salesmen and through mail order.

● Is your product a regular seller year after year? The effort and money necessary for a mail-order campaign are often too great for a novelty item that will soon have no market.

Finally, you must determine whether or not your product will sell by mail by actually *testing* it. But since you already sell the product, you have the great advantage of knowing your product and what aspects of it appeal to customers. Furthermore, you also have stock to fill test orders with. The next chapter and Chapter 18 tell you how to make the necessary tests.

Which Products Are Best for You to Sell?

Profit-Potential Estimates ● *How Much Investment Will It Require?* ● *Is the Product Strictly Legal?* ● *How Long Does It Take to Make Money?* ● *Specialty and Novelty Products* ● *Why Is a Profitable Mail-Order Product Profitable?* ● *Testing the Potential of the Product Line You Choose*

By now you should have started making a list of products that you know are being sold successfully and that might be possibilities for you. Our job in this chapter is to narrow that list down to the five, one or no product(s) that are right for your interests, your capital, your background and your energies.

PROFIT-POTENTIAL ESTIMATES

One of the most important factors that you must consider when choosing a product is its profit potential. It is not enough that you can make a high *percentage* of profit on your advertising investment. You must also be able to invest enough money in advertising so that the *total profit* return is great enough for your desires, and great enough to repay your investment of energy and time in organizing the project.

For example, this ad has run for over 30 years, month after month, practically without change: "Earn money evenings, copying and duplicating comic cartoons for advertisers." Ordinarily, any ad running for many months will draw competitors like flies to honey. But the cartoon-duplicating ad runs in only a few classified sections, and hence, no matter how profitable each ad might be, the total profit each month will not amount to much. This may explain why there is no competition.

Of course, if there is no competition, it may also mean that there is only room for one firm. It may be that the market cannot be widened with new kinds of product offers, by finding new media or by using display ads.

Cardmaster ads for hand postcard duplicators are another example of a long-running ad that has probably drawn little competition because of a too-restricted market. Cardmaster does use display ads, however, which puts it in a much bigger profit class than cartoon duplicating. Or it may have the market to itself because it can obtain the merchandise more cheaply than anyone else can. But that would be unusual.

Many more of these limited-profit product situations occur in specialized and trade markets.

What you seek, then, is a product that can generate enough *volume* so that it can also generate considerable profit. You can estimate a product's market and its volume and profit potential by searching out the media where the product's ads presently appear. Add up the dollars spent for space in a given month and you will have an underestimate, because you will never manage to find all the insertions.

Estimating the volume of a product sold by direct mail is much harder, because you have no easy way of determining how many and which mailing lists are being used. This is one more good reason why the beginner should stick to magazine advertising until he has some experience.

HOW MUCH INVESTMENT WILL IT REQUIRE?

You must make an estimate of the expenditure of time, energy and money required for developing the product and the campaign to sell it by mail. Then compare the time-and-energy expenditure to the estimated profit to see if the profit is worth the investment of your time.

For example, selling a law-study course may be profitable and interesting to you. But unless you can think of a shortcut, the development of the course and the backup texts will require vast resources of time and money.

To sell wallet-size photo duplicates, you need either photographic equipment or a connection with a firm that will do your processing. A photographic plant may well cost more than you want to invest, and lining up a reliable connection may be difficult to arrange.

Remember, though, that the greater the costs in time and money for you to get into a particular line, the harder it is for future competitors to get in, too. So a hard-to-begin product line may offer you some protection and security.

IS THE PRODUCT STRICTLY LEGAL?

A large proportion of one-shot mail-order items advertised at any one time are close to the line of legality, some on one side of the line, some on the other. Sooner or later many will be forced out of business by the Federal Trade Commission or the Postal Service, while others will be assaulted by the Better Business Bureau.

What is legal and what is illegal are discussed in the next chapter. In brief, you will remain on safe ground if:

1. The buyers get from you exactly what even the most gullible of them expect to get.

2. The customers don't feel gypped.

3. Every word and picture you put in your ad are true in spirit as well as in letter.

4. Your product is neither pornographic nor obscene.

5. The product is not a lottery or gambling scheme of any kind.

6. It is not a "chain" scheme in which your customers make money by doing the same thing you do.

Be especially careful of drug products and of plans and equipment designed to make money for the purchaser.

There are two good reasons why you should not imitate others in venturing to the edge of what is legal:

1. The experienced shady mail-order operators, together with their legal advisors, have spent a long time learning what they can get away with. Even then, the biggest of them have been caught and thrown in jail. As an inexperienced newcomer, you're the guy who is sure to get hurt.

2. Perhaps more important, you may be surprised to find that you have a powerful conscience when you least expect it. Before carrying out a sharp scheme, you may feel, like P. T. Barnum, that

it's a game to fleece the suckers that are born every minute. But after the deal is done, you may feel a terrible remorse and guilt that you never anticipated. This has wrecked many a person.

Don't laugh at what I say as being naive. I warn you: Don't take a chance. Sell a product you can respect, in a manner you will not be ashamed of.

HOW LONG DOES IT TAKE
TO MAKE MONEY?

If you settle on a repeat-business item—as I hope you will—you must also think about how *long* it will take for your customers to return you a profit, and what else can be sold to them. The longer it takes to get into the black ink and the greater the capital you need to start, the greater the risk you are taking *and* the more valuable and secure your business if all goes well.

SPECIALTY AND NOVELTY PRODUCTS

Despite everything I have said up until now, you are going to be interested in novelty and specialty products. Since that's the way it is, I'll tell you a success story. But remember that there are few success stories like this one.

In 1951 Leonard Carlson started Sunset House with one mail-order item: a $1 name-and-address rubber stamp. Then he developed a catalog of novelty items such as a nose-hair remover and an electric toilet-seat warmer, getting new customers mostly from ads in a wide variety of magazines. In a little more than a decade, Sunset House sales hit $10 million, and now are far more than that.[1]

Sounds easy, doesn't it. Sure, Sunset House makes money. But for every Sunset House that has made it big in the mail-order specialty business, there must be a hundred people who have failed because they do not have a good nose for specialty mail-order items, or because they could not handle the advertising and business end.

WHY IS A PROFITABLE MAIL-ORDER
PRODUCT PROFITABLE?

I have already argued that at first you should never ask or answer this question. All you should need to know is that an item *is* already a good seller for someone else. Forget about *why* it is, or is not, a good mail-order item.

Nevertheless, if you stay in the mail-order business for a while, or even if you don't, you will probably get involved in considering whether an untried mail-order product will be a winner.

This idea should help you to understand mail-order products: except for novelty, repeat and catalog items, most items that can profitably be sold by mail can also be sold profitably by an *outside* salesperson. Those items that are sold *within* stores will *not* make a mail-order profit.

This is the reasoning behind the idea: Outside selling and mail-order selling are both expensive methods to sell goods, figured as a proportion of sales. Only those items that continue to support a high markup are good for mail order.

Repeat-order and catalog mail-order businesses have a much lower cost of selling, because the largest expense is making a *new* customer.

Here are some questions you can ask yourself about a product, if there is no competition to guide you:

1. How many media (or, for direct mail, how many lists) do I expect to be able to use profitably?

2. Are these media large?

3. How much will it cost to stock the product and prepare the advertising?

4. Will I be able to use only tiny ads, or bigger ads also?

If the product falls into one of the following classes, it has a very *poor* mail-order prospect:

1. Standardized and branded goods, unless you can offer a substantial price advantage.

2. Goods whose characteristics are hard to communicate in ads, e.g., perfume and high-style women's dresses.

3. Goods sold on a small profit margin, e.g., coffee and food (except gourmet food).

4. Goods that don't lead to profitable repeat sales.

If you are considering a product to be sold through sales agents, consider John Moran's checkoff list of the requirements of an agent-sold item.[2]

1. Must appeal to agent

2. Must appeal to agent's customers

3. Little investment for agent

4. Not seasonal

5. No choice of size or color (but shoes do well, and dresses)

6. Light weight

7. Easy for agent to carry samples

8. Not obtainable in stores

9. No breakage or spoilage

10. 100% or more commission

TESTING THE POTENTIAL OF THE PRODUCT LINE YOU CHOOSE

Never think that you have "found a product line" until you have successfully tested the product, the offer and the copy. Until then, all you have is an idea, and it is exceedingly unwise to invest much time or energy in a product line that is only at the idea stage.

The actual mechanics of testing are fully described in Chapter 18. But these points are relevant here:

1. *It is customary to run test advertisements before you have the merchandise.* This allows you to beat a cheap and hasty retreat if your ad doesn't pull. Return the money and letters as "Out of Stock." When the late Bennett Cerf was still president of Random House, one of the largest U.S. publishers, Cerf's practice was to make small test mailings "to determine whether or not a given book is worth publishing at all or possibly to determine how to price a book or how to package it or how many copies to print."[3] This may not be the nicest practice in the world and you must conduct yourself in accordance with both general fairness and with the new FTC regulations on this subject.

   One of the great virtues of mail order is that you *can* put your toe into the business and test it fully without getting in up to your neck. This is not the case with any other kind of business I know of.

2. *Mediocrity of results is the most likely test outcome.* Chances are you'll get neither a runaway winner nor a dud. The professional

is the fellow who can tinker with a so-so proposition and make a winner of it.

3. *Failure of an ad can mean that the product* or *the offer* or *the copy is at fault.* But a clear failure is *most likely* to be the fault of the product.

A Closing Note

Now I'm going to sound like a fortune-teller. The best way to find a good mail-order product is to *have another* good mail-order product already. This isn't just double talk. It's my guess that any successful mail-order dealer has a file of a dozen good products that he doesn't have time or capacity to develop at the moment, or that are too big or too small for him to tackle.

What this should mean to you, however, is the importance of getting into business with *some* product. Even if your first product is not tremendously profitable, it will at least lead you to evaluate other products, and that is the way you will find better products.

So—think of your first venture as an investment in getting into business. And if you're willing to work on a thin margin, almost *any* already proved product will do for you. You can then compete successfully because you won't be charging for salary or overhead, or demanding a profit margin, as your established competition will be. You can't go on that way for very long, of course, but it's a way to break in.

What You May, and May Not, Do in Mail Order

Why Is the Law So Important in Mail Order? • *What*
They Used to Get Away With • *What Is a Racket?* •
Special Products You May Not Sell by Mail • *How to*
Check on Legality

Don't, DON'T, *DON'T* skip this chapter. Don't make the mistake of
thinking that it doesn't apply to you. Sooner or later—probably sooner—
you will have reason to understand why I make this appeal so strong.

A quick example to make you see how important this chapter is: I
might have advertised this book by saying, "*You, too, can earn money
in mail order*" or "*Make $10,000 yearly in mail order.*" I would not
have used those headlines for two reasons:

First I know they might get me in trouble with the law; and second,
I would feel bad about misleading some people about how easy it is
to make money in mail order.

But if I *had* used those headlines, there is a good chance that some
legal agency (probably the Federal Trade Commission) would have
jumped on me sooner or later. No matter what the legal outcome, I
would be caused trouble, and aggravation, and a big money loss.

Here is a recent news story to dramatize some of the rackets and
some of the trouble that one can get into:[1]

Bill Manning, 62, a retired electrician in Lyford, Texas, was looking for a
way to cushion his savings against inflation. Last summer, he got a brochure

from an Arizona-based firm named DeBeers Diamond Investment Ltd. Thinking he was dealing with the South African diamond giant, Manning mailed off a check for $5,000. He was still waiting for his diamonds in November when DeBeers—which has no connection with De Beers Consolidated Mines of South Africa—filed for bankruptcy, with the FBI at its heels. Now, Manning is queued up with other disgruntled investors, hoping someday to recover his savings.

DeBeers is one of dozens of mail-order diamond firms under investigation in three states for allegedly defrauding investors of hundreds of millions of dollars. Buoyed by soaring prices for fine gems, diamonds have emerged as the latest investment scam. . . .

In New York, the state attorney general's diamond task force has focused on Diamond Resources Corp., a now-defunct Manhattan firm that allegedly passed off zirconium chips as real gems. Three company officials are convicted felons, and sources say Donald Nixon, nephew of the former President, made several $50,000 telephone sales for the firm. Nixon's attorney denies his client was connected with the firm, but concedes that "he may have called some of his friends to see if they would be interested in purchasing diamonds. . . .

I am *not* a lawyer, and I have *not* studied the law of mail order carefully. Therefore, what I say here is not legally precise or perfectly accurate. It does not deal with the subtleties that are the very essence of legal practice. I shall try to tell you in *businessperson's* terms how I think the law affects you as a mail-order businessperson.

If you have *any* doubts whatsoever about the legality of a plan of action, refer *immediately* to *The Law for Advertising and Marketing* by Morton J. Simon.[2] (No relative, we have never even met.) If you can't find a *definite* answer there, you might—if you are a good researcher—look at *The Law of Advertising* by George and Peter Rosden,[3] or consult the sources mentioned in those books; better yet, see a lawyer. Don't make a move until you are sure the move is within the law.

WHY IS THE LAW SO IMPORTANT IN MAIL ORDER?

An unscrupulous or overzealous operator can cheat the public more successfully (until the law puts a stop to it) in the mail-order business than in almost any other line of trade, for several reasons.

Unlike a retail store owner, the seller of one-shot items does not depend upon the goodwill of satisfied customers. You have the money whether or not the customer grumbles. A satisfied customer does you no more good than an unsatisfied customer.

Even unconditional guarantees do not remedy the situation. Many dissatisfied customers will not trouble themselves to wrap and ship a piece of shoddy merchandise to get back $1, $2 or $3.

A dissatisfied customer of a local store will tell his or her neighbors about being cheated. Not only will the store's business suffer, but the store owner will have to face the loss of personal reputation among the neighbors. Someone may even punch the proprietor in the nose.

But the dissatisfied mail-order customer has no way of getting back at the unscrupulous mail-order operator—except by reporting him to the authorities. And the mail-order person's neighbors seldom know the exact nature of the business. So this important community control of a businessperson's actions does not exist in mail order.

The mail-order seller has great control over what the buyer knows about the product. The buyer cannot ask sharp questions of the seller or examine the merchandise carefully. The advertisement tells the buyer exactly what the *seller* wants him to know, and nothing more. This increases the possibility of a cheated customer.

That's why you *must* know about what you can and can't do in mail order.

And it's not just dishonest people who get into legal trouble in mail order. Anyone can get carried away with the desire to make a sale.

WHAT THEY USED TO GET AWAY WITH

The majority of mail-order operations are, and always have been, respectable. They are respectable because many of them sell repeat items that demand a satisfied customer, because of the law, and because of the conscience and ethics of most mail-order operators.

But 70 and more years ago when mail order was a brand-new way of doing business, the law did not have sufficient remedies against hanky-panky. The laws that worked to regulate face-to-face business dealings were inadequate to deal with business at a distance by mail. And so, sharp operators ran wild.

Verneur E. Pratt told the following stories.[4]

One ad, for example, offered a "Steel Engraving of George Washington" for 50 cents. The copy beneath the headline described the excellence of the engraving, the beautiful, deep, rich color used, and the fact that the paper was deckled on all four edges. In return for his 50 cents, the buyer received a two-cent stamp.

Another well-known example was that of the "Patented Cigarette Roller" that rolled with equal ease either round or oval cigarettes. It was made entirely of metal, heavily nickel-plated, with only one moving part. It fitted the vest pocket and was so simple that it could not get out of order. In return for $1.00 the buyer received a three-inch nickel-plated spike. The instructions read: "Lay either a round or oval cigarette upon the table, pushing the spike directly behind it, upon doing which you will find the cigarette to roll easily and with almost no effort."

Every statement in the copy was true. The individual merely placed his own interpretation upon it, and his curiosity as to how the device would roll the cigarettes led him to part with his dollar bill.

In the advertisement for the "Patent Potato Bug Killer" stress was laid on the fact that "$1 equips you to kill all the potato bugs in a ten-acre field." In return for the dollar, two little slabs of wood were sent, accompanied by ironically elaborate instructions as to how to pick the bugs off the vines with fingers, laying them down on one slab, pressing the other firmly down upon the bug, and thus quickly and efficiently extinguishing its life.

Another mail-order ad was headed "$3.95 for this 5 piece Wicker Set." The illustration showed a handsome, sturdy wicker table, a settee, two straight-backed wicker chairs, and a rocker. The copy, after extolling the virtues of the materials used, guaranteed the set to be "exactly like the illustration." When the set arrived, the discomfited buyer found it to be in truth exactly the same size as the illustration.

And some 80 years ago, Samuel Sawyer related this yarn.[5]

A manufacturing concern, in Connecticut, produced an interesting little novelty in the form of a sun-dial enclosed in a watch-case. It was the same size as a gentleman's watch and when the case was opened, revealed the dial by which time could be determined from the sun, in the good old-fashioned way of our forefathers. This article was produced and supplied at wholesale for a few cents to any concern that wanted to buy.

One New Yorker conceived a bright idea. He had an illustration made of the article in such a manner that anyone who glanced at it could naturally say it represented a nice watch. Then he prepared an advertisement describing "the new timekeeper; warranted for twenty years, not to get out of order," and called it a timekeeper, which was true enough, and by the general language of his announcement led the reader to believe that a watch could be obtained with a subscription to a cheap periodical. . . .

People showered their complaints upon the police and postal authorities, but as there was really nothing in the advertisement which described the article as a watch, the authorities were afraid to undertake legal action. . . . No misstatement in language could be found by the district attorney and no prosecution ever went very far, but the promoter of this scheme was compelled to submit to columns of unpleasant newspaper exposures. . . .

WHAT IS A RACKET?

By now the situation has changed drastically. As always, the law may be slow, but it eventually finds ways to deal with injustice. Today, practically any shady mail-order proposition is within the long reach of one or another branch of the law.

The law covers a lot of ground. For example, telling the literal, technical truth is *not* enough. You may be in the wrong for what you *don't* say; for example, you must reveal that imported goods are made abroad, in most cases.

You may fall into the clutches of the law because your ad *suggests* an untruth, even if it doesn't say it. And you can err by hiding the truth away in small print or big words, or in many other ways.

Fraud, false advertising and deceptive advertising constitute the likeliest problem you must avoid. Here are some general guides:

- "Fraud" means "taking money under false pretenses," but almost anything that a jury thinks is a "racket" will qualify to get you into jail.

- Your advertisement must not fool even "gullible" people, or "ordinarily trusting people." The test is not what a *university graduate* would find in an ad, or even a "reasonable man." If you fool any substantial portion of *your public*, you are in the wrong. And what counts is not your actual words, but what people believe after they have read your ad.
  Some kinds of exaggeration may be permissible, however. You could probably get away with saying that a cheap dress is "the most beautiful dress in the world." But that probably would not be successful advertising practice.

- Good intentions on your part *may* save you from going to jail— if you can prove your good intentions—but they will *not* prevent the Postal Service or the Federal Trade Commission from shutting down your operation. That is sufficiently painful, and sufficiently costly, so that you should make every effort to prevent its happening.

- Your advertisement *can* be illegal even though the customer is not obviously injured. For example, if you get the customer to write for full further information by misleading him or her, you are outside the law even though the information you send is perfectly truthful in describing the product. An example is advertising a correspondence course in a "Help Wanted" column.

- Whether or not your ad is legitimate is *not* obvious from the content of the advertisement itself. Other evidence may be necessary. For example, perhaps you advertise that your correspondence course on bicycle repairing will teach people how to earn $10 an hour. Whether the ad is legitimate depends upon how many bicycle repairers make $10 per hour and how many graduates of your course actually do so.

Here are some specific examples of mail-order operations that the law gets after. These examples are all taken from just one of the Postal Service's press releases, stating that it had upheld complaints for false advertising through the mails.[6]

Jay Norris Corp., Freeport, N.Y., charged with marketing a "Lincoln-Kennedy" coin—a Lincoln penny upon which a profile of President Kennedy had been stamped—under the pretense that the Treasury Department had minted the coin.

National Opportunity Research Service, Princeton, N.J.; charged with selling $10 memberships in an organization which promised members an opportunity to earn up to $10,000 in return for each one dollar investment, and to buy merchandise at 35 percent below wholesale.

James Allen, of Atlanta, Ga., for advertising a $6.95 "scientifically evolved" plan guaranteed to help persons lose as much as 22 pounds within a week by means other than caloric dieting.

Hartford Publishing Corp., Denville, N.J., for promoting a weight reduction program called the "Digital Diet Method" which consisted only of a diet booklet.

Greenland Studios, Miami, Fla., for the sale of a massage band guaranteed to firm up muscles and significantly reduce sagging skin.

And here's another one:[7]

American Consumer (Philadelphia, PA) has been charged with 1,000 counts of mail fraud in Federal District Court in Philadelphia, by U.S. Attorney Peter F. Vaira. The charges could cost the company $1,000 per count or $1 million if the government's case prevails. The firm which is reported to have sales of $32 million annually was indicted for its "Cross of Lourdes" promotion. The company's promotion said that the $15.95 item had been dipped in holy waters at Lourdes, the site of 58 miracles and had been blessed by Pope Paul VI in the Vatican. In another action before the Pennsylvania Bureau of Consumer Protection, the company signed a consent decree and paid a fine of $45,000 for marketing a tomato plant which promised to produce tomatoes by the ton. Consumer was also hit for a walnut tree promotion that offered a $3.95 tree which would produce 3,000 walnuts.

Please notice in the above examples that, in addition to some firms that I never heard of and that may be new small ventures, there are two huge mail-order outfits being attacked by the U.S. Postal Service— Greenland Studios and Jay Norris—each of which sells many millions of dollars worth each year. This should teach you that you may not feel legally safe even if you do the same thing that the big firms do. Both you *and* the big firm may get clipped by the law—although I think it is fair to say that if a large firm and a small firm do the same thing, the small operator is in more danger from the law. The reason is that the legal agencies expect that the small operator will be more likely to give in because he can less well afford to pay for a lawyer. Large firms, in contrast, often count on their lawyers' being able to stall the government until they reap most of the profit—and then go out of business (in which case the court is asked to drop the case as no longer being material).

An example of how the law sometimes discriminates against the little guy is the sale of *will forms*. Despite the fact that there is nothing illegal about selling or advertising them in a proper fashion, the Federal Trade Commission has had a standing rule that sellers of will forms are told to cease their selling. If you begin to sell them, you will sooner or later get a letter from the Federal Trade Commission that will frighten you out of your wits. The FTC knows that the threat will probably work even if they cannot back up the threat. But at the same time the largest novelty firms go on advertising and selling will forms year after year. How about that for justice? But then, it is not yet a perfect world.

Correspondence schools that promise students good jobs, and insurance plans that misrepresent the insurance, are two major classes of mail-order activities that are presently under attack by the law. Work-at-home schemes are always in trouble. The owner of one of the largest, whose ad read "Part time, work home, mailing our catalog" went to jail for 5 years a few months before I wrote this.

Read what the Chief Postal Inspector has written about one of the most common mail-order-business frauds, work-at-home schemes:[8]

WORK AT HOME SCHEMES

"Send just $1—Find out how you too can earn $25 a week addressing envelopes at home during your spare time," promised an ad running in dozens of newspapers across the country. Fortunately, postal inspectors moved quickly against this bogus scheme. Within a few weeks 13,000 letters, all containing dollar bills, were returned to the senders stamped: "Fraudulent— Return to Sender." The scheme was phony because today large mailers rarely "job-out" envelopes for manual addressing. The promoters were sentenced to long prison terms for mail fraud.

In many advertised schemes the victim receives something for his money, but it may be useless. One promoter advertised a booklet on how to make more money for one dollar. The pamphlet merely explained that honesty and leadership are among the necessary traits for success. It also invited the reader to take a course in self-improvement, at additional cost. A $2 booklet promising to show one how to attain wealth, revealed that hard work is the secret. For a dollar another company promised information on job opportunities. All it furnished were a few classified ads clipped from a newspaper.

Many work-at-home mail-addressing jobs are actually chain-letter schemes. In answering the ad promising such work the victim may receive a letter saying that a dollar will bring additional information and material for making money addressing mail. After sending a dollar a person may receive identical copies of the same letter he answered.

One "work-at-home" promoter started a small operation which rapidly grew into the largest and most complained-about promotion of this type in the United States. Beginning with a sure-fire method for applying a velvet-like finish to any material, he soon branched out into enterprises involving silk-screen printing, miniature trees, moulding machines for making plastic novelties, tropical fish, and other activities which might appeal to those seeking work in their home. He and his office manager were convicted of mail fraud and sentenced to prison.

A fraud artist preyed on invalids, shut-ins, and others in need of extra income by charging $3 for "instructions" which guaranteed large incomes from addressing envelopes and clipping newspapers. His victims lost an estimated $300,000 to this promoter before complaints developed and postal inspectors investigated. He was sent to prison.

Do not make the mistake of assuming that because you see ads for an offer that it is legal. Often ads will run for quite a while until the authorities get around to chasing them down. Here is a list of offers which postal authorities say they often investigate:

Classified directory solicitations to simulate billings for listings in established directories

Distributorships

Endless chains
Chain letters
Referral plan (selling, etc.)
Pyramid selling

Estates (missing heirs)

Franchises

Gambling

Lottery dealer (includes distributors or agents of sweepstakes, etc.)

Turf tipsters

Home improvement (includes aluminum siding, remodeling, fall out shelters, etc.)

Insurance

Investments
Oil and gas leases
Stocks

Job opportunities (sale of information purporting to lead to employment—domestic and foreign)

Loans
  Debt consolidation
  Mortgage

Literary
  Manuscript
  Song promotion

Matrimonial (lonely hearts)

Medical
  Body ailments (includes devices, vitamins, drugs)
  Cosmetics
  Hypnotism
  Reducing (including chin straps, vibrating gadgets, drugs)
  Sexual (devices and stimulants)

Merchandise
  Coins

Nursery (trees, plants, evergreens, etc.)

Real estate
  Improved
  Unimproved (sale of submarginal land for homesites, vacation resorts, etc.)

Schools
  Correspondence courses
  Diploma mills

Solicitations
  Begging letters
  Charity
  Religious cults

Vending machines

Work at home
  Addressing envelopes
  Clipping newspapers
  Sewing baby shoes

Without comment I reproduce in the following pages a couple of direct-mail offers—"$100,000.00 Club" and "The Letter"—that may fit into one or more of the above categories (Figures 6-1 and 6-2).

Here are some specific things to watch out for:

- Medical and drug products usually need valid *scientific* proof that they will work. Testimonials from satisfied users are not enough to prove that your product relieves a disease. Many diseases go away by themselves and your product may get false credit in the user's mind. You need *clinical* evidence, scientific *experimentation* or *chemical* evidence, furnished by qualified people.

  Recently the Federal Trade Commission suppressed a business that sold a plan to increase height, though the seller claimed to have scientific evidence of the *possibility* of its doing so.

- Be triply careful of such words as "cure," "banish" and "remedy" when selling drugs. See the literature mentioned at the end of the chapter for further information.

- You can't use a company name that includes such words as "Laboratory," "Manufacturer," "Refiner," etc., unless you really

Dear Friend,

    I am inviting a limited number of people to become members of a very unusual club. I can promise you adventure, excitement and out of the ordinary benefits beyond your wildest dreams. One of the numerous benefits will be the opportunity to profit by $100,000 during your first year of membership. You buy nothing, you sell nothing you just have fun. Impossible?

    Your receiving this letter was not a matter of chance. You were among a select group of people throughout the world that I chose to receive this letter. Why? Because, unless I am wrong you possess certain qualities not found in the majority of people. These qualities are a necessity to this club to provide a secret strength. Once you learn this strength, I can assure you that you will never reveal it to anyone.

    Let's say I have misjudged you, that you live a dull everyday existence. That adventure is not part of your makeup. That the "unusual" is for the other guy. That the thrill of making a lot of money doesn't give you a "kick."

    If this is true and I have misjudged you, there is no point in wasting your time reading any further. For those who are mildly curious please read on, for as I wrote this letter I could remember a short time ago when I fit the unadventuresome category myself. I lived each day in a high pressure business, seeing little of my family and friends and seeing nothing of the world except on occasional TV. How has this changed?

    Let me tell you an incredible, but true story.

    As you may remember some time ago in history a man from Cuba, named Fidel Castro, formed a new government and purged his country of all businesses, night clubs, gambling casinos, and persons that did not suit his needs for a new peoples Cuba.

    One of the thousands of persons caught in Castro's purge escaped to this country but was somehow separated from his family during the escape. Arriving here he was penniless and left with little hope of ever seeing his family again.

    Perhaps it was fate that brought this man to me. I gave him a job with my company. He was promoted rapidly as he seemed to have a talent for business and a winning way with other employees. During the next two years we became good friends and he began telling me of his past life and all he had accomplished as a successful business leader in Cuba. He was the principal owner of seven night clubs and casinos. He vaguely told me how he and a small group of men had almost overnight acquired their first casino; then how this same group multiplied their efforts to practically monopolize the casino industry in Cuba.

Figure 6-1

URGENT!

The LETTER...

This is the most important letter you will ever read! Please spare me five minutes right now. It is in your interest!

You can

earn up to $813,800 in the next 50 days*

*Based on 5% return as described in detail on other side

...and reach up to seven million people in direct mail for a very low investment!

Dear Reader,

This is no joke and in the next five minutes I will prove it to you. You can make this much, and perhaps even more, since the only limit is your own initiative . . .and it's all perfectly *legal!*

At various times through the years, you have probably received a few "chain letters," all of them asking you to send $2 to someone, for nothing of value in return. It probably occurred to you that if you continued the letter by mailing out duplicate copies to other people, these people would likewise not really want to send you money for nothing of value in return.

But, you *do* know how appealing the *multiplying power* of a "chain letter" can be. I am now going to tell you about a most fantastic *"Co-op Advertising Program"* that has all the multiplying power of a "chain letter" but *is perfectly legal!*

This *"Co-op Advertising Program"* offers the people you send *this* letter to a *double incentive* to send you their two dollars! The first incentive is the valuable report that they will be buying. The second incentive is that the *same report they buy from you can be resold by them* to people they send this letter to. As a result, *your offer is legal!*

Please read the four "advertisements" on the back of this letter. Each one of them offers a unique and valuable *one-page* report of useful money-making information that took years of time and money to obtain. These reports are exclusive and *not available anywhere else!* No matter how knowledgeable and experienced you may be, you will find a wealth of information and new ideas in each report that you can't afford to ignore! You owe it to yourself to purchase these reports *for the valuable knowledge they contain*, which is well worth the two dollars . . .but remember, by buying the four reports advertised on the reverse side, you will also be buying *the right to reproduce and sell them* to other people, by your participation in this novel *"Co-operative Advertising Program."*

The one-page reports that you will be buying *can be easily duplicated* at a cost of as little as 5¢ each, by Xeroxing (photocopying) or inexpensive offset printing (remember, you will be reselling them for $2 each). And there is no need to duplicate a large supply initially until you begin to receive orders for your reports. Even if you have never been in the mail-order business, this is an easy, legitimate way for you to get started and possibly make up to $10,000 to $1,000,000 in a very short amount of time with a very small investment of time and money!

HERE'S HOW THE ENTIRE DEAL WORKS!

❶ Order the four reports from the advertisers printed on the reverse side of this letter by sending *each* of them $2 plus a self-addressed stamped return envelope (to get a faster reply). When you receive the four reports, you may then duplicate them *and offer them for sale to others* (I will show you how in a moment). Be sure to *ask for each report by title when ordering* since each advertiser sells all four reports, *as you will shortly be doing too.*

❷ Using your home or office typewriter, type *your* name and address and the names and addresses of the *first three* advertisers printed in the "Co-op Advertisers Ad Section" on the reverse side of this letter (those selling Reports #1, #2 and #3). With scissors or a razor blade, cut out your name and address and the other three names and addresses that you typed and neatly paste *your* name and address *under ad #1* (you'll be selling Report #1). Paste each name and address down one position. The original name and address now printed in the number four position will no longer be used. *Example:* Let's say the four advertisers on the reverse side are (1) Smith (2) Jones (3) Edwards (4) Blake. You will type your name and address in where "Smith's" name and address now appears. "Smith" will move down to #2. "Jones" will move down to #3 and "Edwards" will move down to #4. "Blake's" name will be eliminated. *Don't worry about "Blake."* He was once in the number one position *and has possibly received several hundreds of thousands of dollars by now.* So don't worry about "Blake." It's your turn now!

❸ After neatly pasting in *your* name and address in the #1 position and the names and addresses of the other three advertisers into positions 2, 3 and 4, take the letter to an offset printer (listed in the Yellow Pages of your telephone book) and tell him to run off 500 copies (or more if you wish). Do not make any other alterations of this letter as you may harm its "pulling power."

[Reprint this letter]

Figure 6-2a

Page 2

❹ You then mail out 500 (or more) copies of this letter (with your name and address in the number one position) to friends, relatives, smart business people in your local telephone directory, or to names of mail-order buyers or opportunity seekers that you can rent cheaply from mailing list brokers (listed in your Yellow Pages under mailing lists).Use your business skills to choose the most productive lists since this is the key to making a profit! You can be in the mail with 500 pieces for about $165, including postage. You can mail less than 500 if you are low on funds just to get started, or until the money starts to roll in, which should take only a week or ten days.

*HERE'S HOW YOU CAN MAKE THOUSANDS OF DOLLARS

[Reprint this letter]

After carefully following the instructions above, you mail out your 500 letters (with your name and address in ad position #1). With a 5% response, 25 of the five hundred people to whom you mailed this letter will send you two dollars each (that's $50) for Report #1 and they should also continue mailing this letter by mailing out five hundred letters each (25 x 500 each). Remember, each of *those 12,500* letters will have your name and address in the number 2 position selling Report Number Two for $2. Now those 12,500 letters may pull in a 5% response, or 625 new people, each sending you two dollars for Report #2 (that's $1,250 total) and if each of *those people continue the letter by mailing five hundred each, this will increase the circulation of your ad* to 312,500 (625 x 500 letters each). Your name will now be in the number 3 position, selling Report Number Three at $2. Now a 5% return would produce *15,625* new people, each sending you $2 for Report Number Three (that's *$31,250.00* for you) and if each one of those people continues the letter by mailing five hundred letters each, the circulation will be over seven million (*7,812,500* to be exact). And finally, with your name and address in the number four position, selling Report Number Four for $2, a 5% return would produce *390,625* new people, each sending you two dollars for Report Number Four (that's *$781,250.00* cold cash for you). This would bring the total money you would receive to a whopping $813,800. Not bad for an initial investment of *$165!* What percentage of new people your mailing will pull will depend on the mailing list that you use. Many lists will pull less than 5%. Some "hot" mailing lists can pull *more* than 5%, which will mean more money for you! Even only a *1%* return would bring you *$1,560.00*, nearly 10 times your investment on only 500 pieces mailed (or *$15,600.00* if you mail 5,000 letters). As you can see, *it's hard not to make money!*

So *get started now!* Time is wasting. If *you* do not want to seize this opportunity *which knocks this once*, give it to someone else who will (maybe you can get them to share it with you for telling them about it after they start rolling in the dough). *Don't do what you've too often done and let this chance for real big money go by. If there is something you do not understand, please Read This Letter Again.*

[Reprint this letter]

————— CO-OP ADVERTISERS AD SECTION —————

Send $2 to each of the four advertisers whose names and addresses appear below. Order each report by its title, and enclose a stamped self-addressed envelope for each report. You have the unconditional right to copy and resell these reports.

1 **REPORT #1   HOW TO MAKE BIG MONEY IN YOUR SPARE TIME** $2.00
    One-page report on making big money working out of your home.
EQUAL OPPORTUNITY
▲ (Your name and address will go here when you reproduce this letter.) ▲

2 **REPORT #2   HOW TO RAISE $10,000 OVERNIGHT** $2.00
    One-page report on raising $10,000 in 24 hours or less.
PROFITS UNLIMITED

3 **REPORT #3   HOW TO GET RICH ENJOYING YOURSELF** $2.00
    One-page report—how to make big money while letting other people do the work.
MR. LES BENNETT

4 **REPORT #4   GETTING LOANS, LEASES, MORTGAGES & CREDIT FAST** $2.00
    One-page report teaches you how to borrow without co-signers, red-tape, collateral, etc.
MR. Z. FOLI

Each Report carries a 7-day money-back guarantee, if returned with self-addressed stamped envelope.

Remember, you now have a chance to get in on this early. As this spreads in the weeks ahead, others can beat you to the punch. You'll never forgive yourself if someone you know makes a fortune right under your nose. Don't let that happen. *Join us now* and *"get in on the ground floor." Opportunity seldom knocks twice!*

Legal Notice & Disclaimer: We cannot and do not represent or guarantee how much profit you will make, or indeed that you will make any profit, by participating in this plan. There is no condition that you purchase anything from us. You may freely reproduce our reports or use this sales technique to sell your own merchandise if you choose to.

Figure 6-2b

perform those activities. And names that suggest nonprofit organizations, such as "Institute" and "Bureau," are highly suspect.

- Guaranteeing a refund to dissatisfied customers probably does not keep you safe from the charge of defrauding your customers. (I say "probably" because the law does not seem to be clear on this point.)

- Phony prices are illegal. For example, you can't say "formerly sold at $10.98" unless a *substantial number* were really sold at that price. However, there is no restriction on your charging as high a price as you like for anything you sell.

- Testimonials must be true. You are as responsible for the correctness of a statement you quote from a customer as if you made the statement yourself.

Here goes an unlawyerlike statement of how you can test whether your advertisement or offer is free of fraud or deceptive advertising. You are safe if:

1. Your customers get from you exactly what the most gullible of them expect to get.

2. The customers don't feel "gypped."

3. Every word and picture in your ad is true in spirit as well as in letter.

A customer can be dissatisfied without feeling "gypped." For example, a month after buying from you his taste may change, and he may no longer like the style or design of your product. He won't be happy, but he won't feel cheated.

A customer may also be dissatisfied at some later time because he comes across an opportunity to buy for less. He will then be dissatisfied, but our society generally recognizes that it is not theft to charge as much as the traffic will bear as long as you stick to the truth.

It may help you evaluate the honesty of your offer if you consider the information that the potential consumer *needs* to evaluate your offer. The less information about the product the customer has to start with, the more responsibility you have to inform the customer completely.

As examples, compare selling fabric by the yard to women sewers with selling a patent medicine. As long as you don't lie about the quality, width, pattern or type of yarn in the fabric, women sewers have plenty of knowledge to decide whether your offer is what they want. Furthermore, as soon as they receive and examine the goods, they can tell whether you really told them the truth. So you can take some liberties in puffing the beauty and quality of your merchandise.

But the potential consumer of a patent medicine is neither a scientist nor a doctor. A person has no way of testing whether your medicine will help him, or even whether it is any good for anyone. The customer does not understand the difficult and subtle scientific tests of a drug's efficacy, and he can easily be swayed by misleading evidence. The customer may believe testimonials of people who *thought* the medicine helped them, without considering that many patients get well even if they only take sugar pills.

Furthermore, the consumer may not have sufficient information to evaluate your product until long *after* his purchase. Correspondence courses and money-making plans are good examples: The purchaser must often try them out for quite awhile before finding out whether they are helpful or worthless.

Sawyer long ago wrote accurately about what is and is not legitimate:[9]

> To explain what I mean, let me give you a few brief examples. First I write this lying statement:
>
> *"Our stogies are made of pure Havana tobacco."*
>
> That's a lie because the stogies are made of Virginia tobacco.
>
> Here is a sample of evasion that might be used if deemed necessary:
>
> *"Smoke some of our stogies, then smoke the best 15 cent Havana cigar you can buy and we believe you will like our stogies better."*
>
> That's an ingenious evasion. You've probably become so used to Virginia tobacco that it suits you better than Havana and you assume that everyone else will think likewise.
>
> Some persons might criticize your opinion, but nobody can successfully accuse you of deceiving if you train yourself to believe what you suggest. The first statement may bring you to jail, the second never can. In fact, this very expression would tend, by psychological operation, to lead a person to think the same as yourself (after he had smoked a box of stogies at one cent each) that they tasted better than Havanas.
>
> I repeat, tell the exact truth whenever and wherever you can. If you feel that it is necessary to your success to make a strong statement, use ingenuity and don't put yourself in a position where you can be proved a downright liar under cross-examination.

To cover the principal argument of your ad, and yet tell the strict truth without the slightest bother from your conscience as to black or white lying, you can say:

Our stogies are made of Virginia tobacco and after smoking a box of them, we believe you will continue their use, even though you have been accustomed to smoking 15 cent Havanas.

. . . . The same idea will apply to any commodity. I have simply undertaken to show the difference between a deliberate lie, a unique and legal evasion, and an ingeniously told actual truth. Even the statement I have given as truthful is as a salted and buttered baked potato compared to a raw potato, but the advertiser who cannot at least write up his goods with some enterprise, better try another line of trade.

Times are different now, though, and much of what got by when Sawyer wrote would not pass muster now. Standards are higher now, I'm glad to say. Bringe describes the standard which we are now aiming for (but don't always reach)—that the advertising should simply not deceive.[10]

THE USES OF DOUBLE SPEAK

What is it? It's the statement that appears to say one thing but gets through to our mind with quite another message. "Nine out of ten doctors use aspirin," when sandwiched in a block of copy for Bayer Aspirin, seems to say that the aforesaid doctors are using the advertised product. Here is a headline on an investment service ad:

WHEN THESE 22 STOCKS SPLIT
The Number of Shares Held Could Double or Triple

Seems like a big promise, doesn't it? Seems to point to a speculative killing. Yet it is a simple statement of fact that promises nothing.

"Clients in nine states depend on our ability to create advertising which gets measurable results at the lowest possible cost."

The sleeper word in that statement is "measurable." It could mean one order or one thousand. The reader, looking for the big promise and wanting it, interprets the word as pie in the sky and will impatiently brush aside the truth *even when he knows it.*

You would not use such deceptive statements in your mail? Any statement you permit your reader to twist to fit his emotional needs can be a deceptive statement for him.

SPECIAL PRODUCTS YOU MAY NOT SELL BY MAIL

Lotteries. Straightforward gambling schemes are forbidden, of course. But also be careful of any "contest" idea, because many of them are found to be forms of lotteries.

Pornographic and Obscene Literature, Films, Etc.

"Chain" Schemes. These are many money-making plans in which your customer is taught to make money in the same way you do. Example: you sell him a plan to sell the same plan to other people. These schemes are illegal.

"New Drugs." This includes all drugs that are not standard, well-accepted medical remedies. You may not sell "new drugs" without special permission from the Food and Drug Administration.

Pay attention to this: Even if a doubtful scheme does not land you in jail, the effects can be disastrous. Here are the things you can lose:

1. You can lose the lawyer's fees to fight your case. Even in the unlikely event that you come out clean, it will take you a long time to make up what you have to pay your counsel.

2. You can lose the heavy investment of time, energy and money required to set up a going business. Nothing could be more discouraging than to slave and spend until finally you see a neat profit coming in, only to have to close up shop by order of the law. This is a losing proposition no matter how you look at it.

3. You can lose your self-respect and your pleasure in the mail-order business. Don't shrug your shoulders at this. Many a good person has found out with terrible regret that what seemed like a prank wound up as a terrible burden on the conscience. Don't think you can play footsie with the public without coming to feel guilty and losing your esteem for yourself. Few happenings can cause more misery and unhappiness.

HOW TO CHECK ON LEGALITY

Here are some ways to find out if your offer is legal.

Don't Assume That What Others Do Is Legal. Some of the advertisements you see will eventually be squelched by the authorities. Others are prepared by very slick operators who know the law well, employ smart lawyers and are not frightened of going to jail. If you try to imitate them, you will either play too safe and make no money, or go too far and land in trouble.

Use Your Common Sense about Whether Your Offer and Advertisement Are Honest. Show the ad to friends and ask them what they think it means. If they are misled by the ad, rewrite it.

If you are ashamed to show the ad to friends because of your good name, then the offer is probably shady and illegal.

Get Information. Write to the Federal Trade Commission and ask for the Trade Regulation Rule on Mail Order Merchandise and for their weekly "News Summary." Write to the Information Service of the Post Office and ask for their monthly bulletin "Enforcement Action—Fraud and Mailability." Do this today, and by the time you are ready to go into business, you will have learned a great deal about what is legal and what is not.

Call or write the Council of Better Business Bureaus, 1150 17th St. N.W., Washington, D.C. 20036 or 845 3d Ave., New York, N.Y. 10022. Ask if they have had any complaints about the concerns that will be your competitors.

You may request opinions about the legitimacy of your product, your offer or your advertisement from the Federal Trade Commission, the Food and Drug Administration or the Attorney General of the United States, all in Washington. Make sure that your request is routed to the appropriate addressee. Do *not* ask your local post office head for an opinion. He or she is prevented by regulation from doing anything more than refer you to the appropriate section of the regulations.

Check with a Lawyer. Try to find a lawyer who has experience with advertising and marketing problems. If you select a general practitioner, he or she may appreciate your referring him to the sources below.

Read and Research. Refer to *The Law for Advertising and Marketing* by Morton J. Simon and the *Advertising Truth Book*, which Simon wrote for the Advertising Federation of America.[11] If you are a good researcher and know your way around a law library, you may also want to consult these references:

Honesty and Competition, George J. Alexander, Syracuse University Press, 1967.

Trade Regulation Reporter, a Commerce Clearing House publication.

Do's and Don'ts in Advertising Copy, National Better Business Bureau.

"The Regulations of Advertising," *Columbia Law Review*, vol. 56, p. 1018, November 1956.

Postal Frauds and Crimes, Mack Taylor (1931).

The Law of Advertising, George and Peter Rosden, New York: Mathew Bender, 1974.

Strategies of
Mail-Order
Selling

Which Media to Use for Your Test? ● *Direct Mail
versus Display Advertising* ● *The Advantages and
Disadvantages of Classified Advertising* ● *Selling
through Agents versus Other Mail-Order Methods*

By this time I assume you have selected a product. Either it is a product that you already sell at retail, or a product you decided upon after following the procedure in Chapters 3 to 5. If you have not yet decided on a product, you should go back and follow the instructions in Chapters 3 to 5.

But you're not in business yet! You won't *really* be in business until you have tested a particular ad for your product in one or more media—and obtained successful results!

The greatest thing about the mail-order business is that you can reserve final judgment until you have the best possible evidence for your decision to go full steam ahead. Generally you can't know whether a retail store or other kinds of business will succeed until you have invested $5,000, $15,000, or $50,000. But in mail order you hold back all but $50 or $500 of your stake till you almost *know* your business will succeed.

You can't get off so cheaply if you choose to sell a line of repeat-order goods or a line of catalog items. In that case, you must test not only the pull of your original ads, but also the subsequent reorders from your customers. Chapter 17 tells you how to calculate. In any case, your original ad or mailing will not break even on repeat-order goods. The amount you "lose" on that first ad is your investment in the customer list which will form the backbone of your business.

Selling by inquiry–and–follow-up requires somewhat more investment than a one-shot item. One of the biggest correspondence-course operators budgets $20,000 to test a new correspondence course; $10,000 of that is for the writing of the course, and $10,000 is for testing ads. But if you have time and the knowledge to do your own work, you can get by with far, far less. The *out-of-pocket* expense to me in setting up a correspondence course of mine was much less than $500.

Selling through agents also requires more testing investment than one-shot sales, but less than a catalog business.

Our problem now is to spend your $50 to $500 wisely so that you can get a positive test. We must draw up a blueprint for your mail-order selling effort. We want to make the blueprint as successful as we can, right from the start.

The three most important decisions you must make are decisions about:

1. The *type* of media to use, and the *specific* media in which you will place your test ads.

2. The proposition you will offer.

3. The copy and layout of your ad.

At the test stage, the order of importance of the decisions is the same as in the list above.

WHICH MEDIA TO USE FOR YOUR TEST?

If you choose a product that is already being sold by several competitors, your choice of media in which to test is obvious. Advertise in exactly the same magazines the competitors advertise in *most frequently* and with the *biggest ads*. That's where the best chance of success is.

Some mail-order people advise against testing in the most promising media. They say that you are likely to get inflated expectations of how your product will sell. They have a point in their argument.

But I believe in trying the very best media first, because even if you have only a mild success there, and can never improve your technique, you have found a *small* profit anyway, a profit you can tap again and again.

Besides, it is much less painful to test various offers and copy if you make a couple of bucks at the same time, instead of having to shell out of your pocket for the test.

If your product is *not* being sold by mail by competitors, then choose media in which *similar* products are advertised. If you intend to sell garden furniture, go where other furniture or garden advertisers are— maybe to magazines like *House Beautiful,* or the Garden Section of *The New York Times.*

If you have a new correspondence course to teach a skilled trade, go where other trade correspondence courses are advertised—maybe to magazines like *Popular Science,* or the *Premium Men's Group* magazines, or *Specialty Salesman.*

If you have a new type of low-cost insurance offer, try the mailing lists used by advertisers of auto insurance, casualty insurance and life insurance. A good list broker can steer you to those lists.

Still in the dark? If your product is so different from anything else on the market (and it should *not* be), you may not even know whether to use direct mail, display advertising or classified advertising. The following sections will teach you the advantages and disadvantages of the three basic mail-order media.

You may use television, radio, matchbook covers and other exotic media—but only *after* you are successful in the basic types of selling channels.

If you sell a line of goods by catalog, there are two ways you can test whether an item should become a permanent part of your catalog—as permanent as anything can be in the mail-order business.

1. Throw a 2-inch or 3-inch ad into mail-order media with which you are well acquainted—perhaps a regional edition of *The Wall Street Journal,* or a Sunday newspaper supplement, or *The New York Times Magazine*—for a quick test. After several such tests of different items, you will learn what a set of results in that medium indicates about the probable pull of the items in your own catalog.

2. Or, run the product in one edition of your catalog. This is the fairest test of all, of course. Its only disadvantage is the time it takes to obtain results.

DIRECT MAIL VERSUS DISPLAY ADVERTISING

When should you use direct mail? The answer is *not* "always," as some beginners in mail order think. In fact, direct mail is not the first medium you should think of for products. I think you should first consider whether your offer will sell profitably in display ads. If it seems to be a toss-up between display and direct mail, try display first. Here are reasons for trying display first:

1. Testing is cheaper in display. For $200 to $300 total cost for space *and* preparation, you can often get an accurate idea of whether a product will succeed. But preparation costs alone, for the simplest direct-mail piece, will be many times as expensive.

2. Testing is also more *informative* in display. Some magazines are very general in appeal, partly because of their huge circulation—Sunday supplements and the "shelter" magazines, for example. Unless your offer is very specialized, you can rest assured that poor results in a very general medium are not due to an idiosyncrasy of the medium, as might often be the case with lists.

Use direct mail if your competitors use it. Their success promises your success. That is the basic logic of this entire book.

Use direct mail if you can shoot at prospects with a rifle instead of a shotgun. (That is the favorite metaphor of the direct-mail enthusiasts.) If your product has much greater appeal for some groups of people than it does for others, and if your potential customers can be identified by any external characteristics and a list of them is available, then you should use direct mail.

For example, if you want to sell a course on raising children, any general magazine *may* be satisfactory. If you sell a book on Catholic religious instruction, Catholic magazines deliver the audience you want. But if you sell a teaching device of special interest to priests who head Catholic schools, you will use direct mail (unless Catholic educators also have their own magazine).

Compiled lists are the most specialized of all. Lists of mail-order buyers are not so specialized except with reference to the product they bought originally. A list of customers who buy cheese by mail is tremendously specialized for another cheese company (which isn't likely to be able to rent the list). It is much less specialized for gift sellers, though it may nevertheless be a very profitable list for them.

Industrial and commercial lists are very specialized, of course. Businesses that sell to a particular industry will generally use both direct mail and the trade magazines. But direct mail is far more essential to them. Trade-magazine space costs are very high compared with space costs in consumer magazines, and that narrows the gap between display and direct-mail costs.

Direct mail is also more flexible for the form of the copy message, the timing of the message, the addressee of the message and the length of the message. It is also much more satisfactory for repeat-order businesses.

Office supplies are a favorite product sold by direct mail to many industries and trades. Economic information services are another very successful direct-mail product to businesses.

Any *particular* nonfiction book is an extremely specialized item. Few books on special topics in anthropology or mathematics are likely to have a wide general audience. There is seldom a magazine circulation that corresponds perfectly with the focus of the book—even an anthropology or mathematics journal, though they may be good media anyway. Furthermore, the publisher can do the necessary *complete* selling job only in direct mail. That's why publishers of specialized nonfiction use direct mail so much.

Use direct mail only if you expect to get at least $25 out of the average customer, including all future purchases. This estimate is based on:

1. The minimum costs to get a mailing into the mail (perhaps $150 to $250 per thousand, in 1980); and

2. The highest rates of response you can possibly expect in any large-scale mailing.

An example: Correspondence-course sellers seldom are willing to pay more than $1, $2, or $3 at most, for inquiries from display ads. But to get inquiries that cheaply from direct-mail solicitation, they would need to obtain a response of around 10 percent—very unlikely, indeed.

But if you can afford a much higher inquiry cost and if the specialized prospects cannot be obtained through magazines, direct mail might be a good bet.

You are more likely to use direct mail to develop new customers if you sell a "repeat item." Repeat items obviously produce more revenue in the long run than items that the customer never buys again, and therefore a new customer is worth more to you. In fact, if you sell a repeat item, you usually expect to "lose money" on the first order (if you count in the cost of developing the customer, as you should).

Repeat-item catalog houses use direct mail to solicit for all orders subsequent to the first, of course.

Use direct mail when you have a story to tell that is too long and complicated for a display ad. Use direct mail when your product requires illustration, especially in color. There are virtually no limits to the methods you can use to tell your story in direct mail.

Catalogs are an example of a form of *material* that can be carried by direct mail but not by magazines.

Sometimes you don't want the whole world to know about a special proposition you are offering to some part of your market. Magazine publishers, for instance, sell some subscriptions at full price and others at a cut rate. If they offered cut-rate deals in display ads, no one would ever renew a subscription at the full rate. That is one reason magazine publishers use so much direct mail.

The relative privacy of direct mail provides *some* screen from the prying eyes of your competitors. The display advertiser does business in a fishbowl and is often eaten by predatory cats.

Direct mail can search a limited geographical area for customers, and a periodical cannot. A manufacturer of fire alarms developed a lovely small-area technique. First he saturates a town to develop leads for his "sales engineers." Then he circularizes the immediate neighbors of each family that buys, telling the neighbors to ask the person who purchased what he or she thinks of the fire-alarm system. This follow-the-leader method helps instill confidence in the product.

After saturating each town, the sales force moves on like an infantry company following an artillery barrage. This is a great way to use direct mail.

Some advertisers use both direct mail *and* display advertising to develop new contacts. Firms that sell through agents use plenty of direct mail because only a few magazines reach a heavy proportion of potential agents.

Novelty and gift-catalog firms often use both display ads and direct mail.

The moral to the story is that you should use *every* medium that will pay you any profit on your money. Only in that way can you maximize your earnings.

In two important ways, direct mail is *easier* to use than display advertising:

1. The time lag between mailing and getting enough returns for accurate predictions is much less than the lag between placing your ad in a magazine and getting predictable returns from it. This means you can make more money *quicker* in direct mail than in display advertising. And you recover your investment quicker.

2. Some direct-mail advertisers will scream to high heaven that I'm wrong about this, but—direct-mail *testing* is much more accurate than display-ad testing (except for split-run copy testing). From

any set of results the direct-mail advertiser can get a much better idea than the display advertiser about what will happen when the original advertising is repeated.

Yes, it is true that the results ordinarily will fall off when you go back to a list after a test. But the direct-mail advertiser can take account of that in the calculations. Seasonal effects can also be allowed for.

The display advertiser, however, is at the mercy of changes in the position of the ad in the magazine, more or less competition, better or worse editorial matter and many other factors. The display advertiser never does as well on the second insertion either (all else being equal), but has more trouble estimating the dropoff than does the direct-mail advertiser.

The greater predictive power of direct-mail results means that the direct-mail advertiser can proceed more rapidly, with greater confidence, than can the display advertiser.

These two advantages are *not* reasons for choosing to use direct mail. Whether or not you use direct mail *must depend on the product*. There may, however, be reasons for choosing a *product* that can be sold by direct mail.

THE ADVANTAGES AND DISADVANTAGES OF CLASSIFIED ADVERTISING

The *advantage* of advertising in classified columns is that, for almost any product, a dollar spent in classified advertising will bring back more profit than a dollar spent in any other space unit. That is a fact, proved many times. Chapter 14 shows a comparison of the effectiveness of classified against other space units. That is why so many advertisers that use display ads—and even full-page ads—also continue using the humble classified columns. Correspondence schools almost all use both display and classified.

Furthermore, many large firms got their start with their original ads in classified columns. Fuller Brush began with classified.

You can't generate large volume and create a big business in classified columns alone, however. You may not think so at first, but the number of places in which you can run profitable classified is small, and this restricts your business badly. Few classified advertisers can invest even $1,500 per month in classified. Most of them are limited to a much smaller expenditure by the lack of media. I doubt that fifty advertisers in the country spend more than $500 a month on classified even in the best of months.

A small investment means a small possible profit. You'll have to be a very efficient and clever mail-order dealer to net an honest $750 on a $500 advertising investment.

This limitation also explains why classified advertising is not used by many firms that *should* use it. An advertising agency's 15 percent commission on $500 doesn't look very big compared with the work involved in billing and handling the paperwork. So agencies do not recommend classified to their clients. This problem can be solved profitably for everyone concerned by increasing the agency's commission on classified (perhaps as high as 30 percent), or by paying the agency on a fee basis, or by cutting the agency in for a fixed percent of the total volume on the gross profit. Until very recently, this was considered unethical by advertising and media people, but practices are changing now.

Classified is an excellent place for the mail-order novice to begin. He can test products and gain invaluable practical experience with very small amounts of capital. Anybody can afford to risk $10 for a test ad in a million-circulation magazine. The thrills and experience will be worth that much even if the first attempt, or the first five attempts, are total busts.

The novice who advertises in classified does not have to arrange for typography, layout or art work. In classified, you *can* get into the mail-order business with an ad written on scrap paper and sent direct to the magazine.

Most classified advertisements offer free information to develop inquiries. Direct sales are seldom made from the classified ad. The reason is obvious: It is rare that you can tell enough about a product in ten words or twenty words so that the potential customer (1) wants the product, (2) understands what it is, and (3) knows how much it costs and where to order.

However, it is relatively easy in a small number of words to whet a person's desire for further information. And since the reader risks no money, he or she does not need to be convinced of your reliability in order to inquire. In your follow-up letter you have plenty of time to describe the product in detail and to convince the prospect that you are honest and reliable and that the product is a good buy.

Some products are sold directly from ads *as well as* through inquiries—often next to one another in the same magazines—by different firms. And neither forces the other out of business. These are usually information manuals (employment information, how to start a credit business, etc.) that sell for $1 directly from the ad, or for $2 or $3 from follow-up letters to inquirers.

Most successful classified ads are of these types:

1. Ads for agents to sell products house to house. This is a more complicated business than other types of mail order.

2. Ads to produce inquiries for books, correspondence courses and other information. This includes all "homework" schemes.

3. Ads that sell pamphlets directly from the ads.

Few classified ads are for repeat products, or for catalog business. Catalogs of hypnotism books are an exception.

SELLING THROUGH AGENTS VERSUS OTHER MAIL-ORDER METHODS

There are two basic ways that you can use agents as part of a mail-order operation:

1. Your agents can go out and find prospects for your goods, and sell them directly. This method is used for those types of mail-order products that almost necessarily require the use of agents: men's shoes and suits, for example, and cosmetics for women. These products require demonstration before the customer will be willing to buy.

   Direct salespersons get up to 60 percent commission on their sales.

2. A second method is to build a sales force to close leads you *develop by mail*. Encyclopaedia Britannica, major insurance firms, and top correspondence schools use this method. So do smaller outfits like Enurtone (a device to prevent bed-wetting).

The salesperson can generally double the number of sales you could close by mail alone, and the commission runs from 5 to 15 percent. Usually a product must sell for at least $50 to make this method profitable.

Either method of selling through agents is somewhat more complicated than other types of mail-order methods, and it usually involves a larger investment and greater preparation. You not only have to develop the advertising to sell the final customer, but you must also develop the selling campaign to convince prospective agents that they should sell your product for you.

But don't underestimate the potential of selling through agents. Many of the largest mail-order firms work through sales agents. One expert in this field estimates that there are 350,000 agents in the country who make a full-time living selling for mail-order firms, and lots more who work part-time.[1]

The Tactical Decisions in Mail-Order Advertising

Sell from the Ad or from Follow-ups? • What Price Should You Set? • Refunds, Guarantees and Trial Offers

These are the important decisions you must make about the selling proposition:

1. Whether you will try to close the sale
   a. Directly in your ad or letter
   b. By the inquiry-and-follow-up technique
   c. Through agents

2. What price you should set

3. What kind of trial offer or credit terms you will give

These are some promotional tactics that can increase the number of orders that you get:

1. A time limit on the offer. This prevents procrastination, but may turn off the buyer.

2. Sweepstakes and contests. These are effective but expensive, and you must be careful with the law.

3. Credit terms and postponed payments, such as "Bill me only upon receipt." Credit costs you money, and increases bookkeeping and hassle.

4. Sale prices, "prepublication" prices, closeouts and so on.

5. Bonuses and premiums with large orders or for cash with order.

6. Most powerful of all is the free trial and/or iron-clad money-back guarantee.

SELL FROM THE AD OR FROM FOLLOW-UPS?

Offers priced at $50 or over usually cannot be sold directly from a display ad. For a purchase involving a lot of money, the prospect needs a longer sales pitch than you can deliver in a space ad. You need a follow-up or direct mail to do the job.

The standard technique for merchandise priced over $25 or $50 is either (1) to run display advertising offering further information, and then to follow up with direct mail; or (2) to solicit with direct mail only.

If you use the two-step display-plus-follow-up technique, don't show the price in the ad. Like a good encyclopedia salesperson, you don't want to scare the prospect away before you have had the opportunity to make the prospect want the product very badly.

Ordinarily your first direct-mail piece to a prospect will aim to make the sale. However, some products require such elaborate and expensive sales presentations that you can afford to send them only to prime prospects. If so, your first letter is just a canvass technique to obtain really hot prospects. Then you send them the full presentation. The famous Southern Roofing direct-mail campaign first canvassed for inquiries. People who returned the inquiry card then got follow-up letters containing full information.

WHAT PRICE SHOULD YOU SET?

The basic rule is that you should pick the price at which you will make the most money.

The way to find that "best" price is to test many different prices.

Prices are much more flexible in mail order than in retail businesses because potential customers have no standards of comparison. The merchandise is almost always new to them, so they have no prior knowledge about prevailing prices. And they can't shop from store to store to check for the best buy.

A manual can sell as a book for $2.95 or $6.95. Or the same information in a slightly different format can go for $24.50, $39.50, $59.50 or even $149.50. Whether you sell for $2.95 versus $6.95 or $24.50 versus $59.50 will be a matter for testing. But whether you sell the item as a book or as a correspondence course is a more basic strategic question.

The price of a mail-order item depends relatively little on the wholesale cost to you, but it depends heavily on the costs of advertising and selling it.

How to Test for the Best Price

To choose the best price, you must know how to figure the profit you make at that price. Here's how to figure the profit you make on a single ad:

1. Add:
   a. Advertising cost
   b. Cost of merchandise, including labor, postage and other incidental costs

2. Subtract from total dollars received

3. The difference is your profit on the ad

An example: Packages of a dozen ball-point pens cost you 40 cents per order to ship, including all merchandise and handling costs except advertising. You run two ads, each costing $100, which are identical except for the price advertised. Ad A asks $1; Ad B asks $1.98.

Ad A

Pulls 300 order @ $1—Total revenue	$300	
Cost—300 × 40¢ for merchandise		$120
Advertising cost		100
		$220

$300 − $220 = profit of $80

Ad B

Pulls 130 order @ $1.98—Total revenue $257.40
Cost—130 × 40¢ for merchandise $52.00
   Advertising cost   100.00
                                                  $152.00

$257.40 − $152 = profit of $105.40

The $1.98 price in Ad B is clearly the more profitable price.

This simple example shows you that the offer at almost twice the price does *not* need to pull twice as many inquiries to be more profitable. However, the cheaper price is often more profitable.

If the purpose of your advertisement is to create customers for your other products as well as to sell the product advertised, then you must figure differently. Very often you will be willing to sell at a lower price, and to take less profit directly from the ad, in order to increase the number of customers added to your list.

The correct way to figure the price in this repeat-business case is to add the future dollar value of the customers to the immediate profit of the ad. Chapter 9 teaches you how to figure the dollar value of customers.

This is how one mail-order operator broke down his costs for a "typical article," probably a printed manual, that sold for $2.98 a few years ago:[1]

Product and postage	$0.45
Overhead—5%	0.15
Shipping container	0.06
Shipping label	0.02
Instruction sheet	0.02
Order processing	0.15
Reserve for refunds—5% of sales	0.15
Bank charges	0.05
	$1.05 = Total merchandise costs

At a selling price of $2.98, any ad that brings in orders at an average advertising cost of less than $1.93 makes a profit on this article. In other words, if a $50 ad brings 32 orders (for $95.36), the average advertising cost is $50 divided by 32, or $1.56 each. The profit per order is $1.93 less $1.56, or 37 cents each.

REFUNDS, GUARANTEES
AND TRIAL OFFERS

The terms of the offer can have a terrific effect on your sales. It is very important that you choose the most *profitable* terms. And the most profitable terms are not necessarily the terms that pull the most orders.

The Refund Offer. It is a practically unbreakable rule in mail order that you must guarantee satisfaction or money back. Even if you don't want to offer a guarantee, many advertising media will accept your advertisement only if you agree to do so.

It is true that some people will return goods. Some people even are cranks about returning goods. Others will find interesting ways to sting you. And none of us likes to part with money that has once been paid over to us.

Nevertheless, you will almost surely wind up with more *profit* overall by making the refund offer. The extra sales will more than counterbalance the refunds you pay out.

Once in a while you may offer a product on which returns are so high that you lose money. If that happens, it's usually because the product is rotten, and that should be an indication for you to pull it off the market until you can improve it.

Returns can be quite high and the offer still make money. Booksellers who offer a 7-day free trial without payment of any sort expect 20 percent of the books to be returned, and 20 percent more not to be paid for. They can still wind up in the black.

Returns can be very small if customers are truly satisfied. In the 1960s I sold thousands upon thousands of a tiny sixteen-page booklet that cost under 3 cents apiece to print—for $1 a booklet. I offered an unconditional guarantee of satisfaction with no time limit. I received exactly one request for a refund—from an apologetic fellow who said he had bought another copy months before.

There are several types of guarantees you can make. You can offer money back within 7 days, within a month or within a full year. You can offer double-your-money-back, too. The strength of the guarantee will affect the pull of the ad as well as the number of returned orders. If you have a really strong product, make the strongest possible guarantee.

If the number of returned orders you get on the strongest possible guarantee is significantly large, your final decision will depend upon a *test* of the various refund-offer plans.

If you offer a full-year guarantee, you don't need to wait a whole year to find out how many returned orders you will get. How fast they come back depends upon the product and how long it takes customers to give it a real trial. But in any case, you can almost always count on more than half the returns coming back within a month of receipt.

When you make your guarantee, emphasize in your ad that if your customers want their money back, they'll get their money back. A money-back guarantee always seems a little too good to be true. And readers are suspicious that you will find some excuse not to refund. Write your guarantee as powerfully as you can to put that fear to rest. "Iron-clad." "Unconditional." "Legally binding guarantee." "No questions asked."

The Trial Offer. People like to keep their money in their hands until they have the goods. They also like to delay their final purchasing decision as long as they possibly can. The trial offer is designed to get around the reluctance that people have to commit themselves. The trial offer gives people the feeling that they have maximum freedom to return the merchandise after they have examined it.

People also seem to prefer to delay payment even when the commitment is made. Think how many times you have said "Bill me later" even when you knew the purchase was final.

Here are Stone's figures on delayed-payment offers, relative to a rating of 100 for cash with order: Cash with order and free gift for trying the product, 144; "Bill me" (open account), 177; "Bill me" and free gift for trying, 233.[2]

Naturally, what you *really* care about is the amount of *profit* you wind up with. Just because a trial offer pulls more requests doesn't mean you make more that way. It means that you must make careful calculation to evaluate whether you are better off with or without the trial offer.

Other Tactical Decisions

There are three other tactical decisions that are discussed at some length in the unabridged version of this book for which there is space only to mention here: (1) whether to accept credit cards; (2) whether to offer credit terms or to require cash on the barrelhead; (3) whether to solicit telephone orders. In each case the question is whether the tactic that gets you more orders and gross revenue also brings in more *net* revenue.

Calculating the Dollar Value of a Customer

Introduction • The Value of a Customer to Various Businesses • How to Estimate Repeat Rates • Using the Value of a Customer

INTRODUCTION

How much is it worth to you to get an additional customer? The calculation of the answer to this question is the most important calculation a mail-order merchant makes, and this calculation is what this chapter is about.

The calculation of the value of a customer may be done more precisely in the mail-order business than in any other line of business. And yet, there are many (even many successful) mail-order firms that have never made this calculation correctly, as may be seen in the interviews with mail-order firms frequently reported in *Direct Marketing*.

This chapter is not easy reading. But please don't skip it. At least read until the last example. Knowing the value of a customer is crucial because this information helps you find the break-even point for the number of responses to a space advertisement or mailing-list campaign that are necessary for you to make money rather than lose money. Once you have correctly calculated the value of a customer, you only need to estimate the number of new customers you will get from the ad or mailing (and know the cost of the space ad or the mailing) to decide if that space ad or mailing should be undertaken.

The value of a customer is the total *profit* he will bring you. Not the *volume*, mind you, but the profit. You certainly would not pay me $2 to bring you a customer who will give you $10 in volume but only $1 in profit. But if you had a high-margin business and $10 volume gave you $4 profit, you *would* pay me $2 to bring you in a customer who would spend $10. In fact, you'd be willing to pay me almost $4 for him or her.

Three elements enter into the calculation of the dollar value of a customer: (1) The dollar amount of revenue you expect to get from the customer in each year; (2) the cost to you of filling the order; and (3) your "cost of capital"—that is, the worth to you today of a dollar in net revenue next year or 2 years from now.

There are good customers and poor customers, and obviously the good customers are worth more than the poor customers. But we're talking now of *average* customers. When you first get a *new* customer, you can't tell whether he or she will be a good customer or not.

For a one-shot deal—say, a camera sold by Bell & Howell from a Diners Club list mailing—the calculation of the value of a customer is reasonably simple. The revenue from the first sale is all that Bell & Howell will get from the customer. And the costs of the camera are relatively easy to figure because they will all be incurred immediately. And you do not need to know the "cost of capital" because all the revenues and costs will occur within a short time, and there is no "interest" to be paid while waiting for your money. So the value of a customer to Bell & Howell is simply the sales price minus the cost of goods sold and the cost of servicing the order. (Notice that the cost of the advertisement that solicits the customer is *not* included in this calculation of the value of the customer.)

Even in this simple case one can err badly by forgetting some important costs, a matter which will be taken up in the next chapter. In this chapter we'll assume that the costs are figured correctly.

The main complication in calculating the dollar value of a customer arises when a substantial portion of your business is repeat business— as is the case for almost all successful mail-order businesses. When a substantial number of customers buy more than one time, the value of a customer derives not only from his first purchase but also from the subsequent purchases he is likely to make. If you ignore the subsequent purchases, you will arrive at a wrong calculation and too small a customer value. That will cause you to forgo some valuable customer volume, and in fact may lead you to decide that a whole line of business is unprofitable when in fact it is profitable. For example, if magazine publishers did not include repeat business in their value-of-a-customer calculations on subscription campaigns, they would never solicit *any* subscriptions by mail.

We'll proceed with several examples. We'll begin with the simplest possible example of a typist who solicits business by advertising. Then we'll go on to a common sort of repeat-business situation, a mail-order sewing-supplies firm. Then we'll wind up with a calculation from a magazine's subscription campaign that looks more complicated but still is fundamentally the same calculation.

THE VALUE OF A CUSTOMER
TO VARIOUS BUSINESSES

Let's begin with a very simple example—the case of a typist who wants to get typing work to do at home. The reason for beginning with such a simple case is that the method needed to handle this kind of problem is straightforward and almost obvious. Yet it is the same method needed for major mail-order advertising campaigns.

Assume that Judith, your wife or girl friend, wants to make money typing at home. She realizes that she must advertise in order to obtain jobs. The question is: Where and when should she advertise?

We must begin by collecting some information. Does Judith type fast enough to make a profit? She announces to us that if she cannot net at least $3.75 per hour from typing, she prefers to read mystery novels instead. Next we must find out whether she can type fast enough to earn at least her "opportunity cost" of $3.75 per hour. Judith wisely *experiments* to determine her cost of production. She clocks herself typing some average material and determines that she can do five pages per hour on the average. If we assume for the moment she will charge the going rate for average-quality work—$1.20 per page in this town— she can hope to gross $6 per hour, not counting any possible costs of advertising promotion.

A notice on a college-dormitory bulletin board is Judith's first advertising. In the first week she gets one call, which results in her typing a four-page paper. On this evidence, she sensibly concludes that while the bulletin-board notice may produce some business, it will not produce *enough* work to keep her busy. This is frequently the case for advertisers. A particular advertising vehicle may produce business very cheaply—in this case, at practically no cost at all—and therefore be very profitable. But one must also use less efficient advertising vehicles to get more business and increase *total profit*.

Judith now considers placing advertisements in both the college daily and the town newspaper. At this point, she must begin to think in a more businesslike way. Which of the two papers is likely to bring in the most business per dollar of cost?

One source of information about an advertising vehicle's potential is observation of what other firms—other home typists, in this case—are doing. Judith observes that there are many advertisements for home typists in the college newspaper's classified section but just one ad in the town newspaper. She therefore wisely decides to imitate the other typists, and she places a classified advertisement in the college paper.

Now that Judith has run her advertisement in the college newspaper for a week's trial, she must calculate whether the advertising is profitable or not. Judith paid out $7.50 for the week's classified advertising, and she obtained two customers from it. She can directly link the customers to the advertising for these reasons: (1) She has not publicized her services in any other way; and (2) when they called, both customers said they had read her advertisement in the paper. One customer's business amounted to $9 worth; the other's was $3. This required a total of 2 hours' typing. Judith then figured this way:

$$
\begin{array}{lll}
\text{Production expenditures:} & & \\
\quad \text{2 hours' labor} \times \$3.75 & = \$7.50 & \\
\quad \text{Advertising expenditures} & = \$7.50 & \\
\qquad \text{Total cost} & = & \$15.00
\end{array}
$$

The total cost of $15.00 exceeded her first week's sales of $12. Hence she figured that the advertising was a losing proposition and she decided to advertise no more.

But the following week one of her customers returned with another $6 worth of business, reducing the apparent loss on the initial advertising. Clearly Judith must somehow take account of the long-run effect, the *repeat* sales that the advertisement generates.

What is needed here is an estimate of how much business our home typist can expect to get from an *average customer in the long run*. But instead of waiting many months to collect this information, Judith wisely consults a friend who is experienced in home typing. Her friend tells her that on the average, a customer yields $30 worth of business before leaving town or graduating or buying a typewriter or otherwise ceasing to patronize the typist. Some customers provide less than $30 worth of business, of course, and others more; $30 is an average. Judith can now estimate that her first week's advertising brought in $60 worth of business (two customers multiplied by the $30 long-run estimate for the average customer), and she can now figure the overall profitability of the advertising this way:

Total sales (gross revenue)	$60.00
Production expenditures for $60 business:	
10 hours × $3.75	$37.50
Sales minus production cost	$22.50
Advertising expenditure	$ 7.50
Sales minus production cost minus advertising cost	$15.00

The advertising now is seen to be profitable because the sales revenue less the production cost exceeds the cost of the advertising. So the typist decides to rerun the advertisement in the next issue of the college newspaper. So we see that correct figuring leads to a decision opposite to that of her earlier naive figuring.

The value of a customer enables us to quickly determine whether any given advertisement is above or below the break-even point of profitability. The value of a typing customer can be estimated as sales minus labor expenditure. That is, $30 − (5 × $3.75) = $11.25. The labor cost is estimated at 5 hours on the basis of the experimental data which showed that Judith types an average of five pages per hour. The concept of the value of a customer is then used this way: Any unit of advertising that produces customers at a cost of $11.25 or less per customer is profitable; otherwise, it is unprofitable. For example, Judith's original advertisement produced two customers estimated to be worth a total of 2 × $11.25 = $22.50, for an advertising expenditure of $7.50. This suggests that her first advertisement was profitable.

In following weeks the repetitions of her advertisement produced an average of only one and one-half new customers per week, but since the value of one and one-half customers (1.5 × $11.25 = $16.88) is considerably greater than the $7.50 weekly cost, the advertising still is profitable on the average, indicating that she should continue to run the advertisement.

The value of a customer provides a standard against which to compare the results from any medium as well as any advertisement.

Before we leave Judith, our home-typing friend, and move on to more complex problems, a few of her other management decisions deserve to be mentioned.

Other decisions for the home typist are *how large* an advertisement to run, and *how many* advertisements to run in various media. These decisions depend on the extent to which she really wants to set up a business. If she wants to do no more than obtain work for herself for 8 hours a day or less, these questions may not arise. But if she really wants to start a business, employ other typists and job out the work, she will need to run bigger advertisements and more of them. The decision rule in every case is the same as before: Does the added unit of advertising produce enough customers so that, when multiplied by the long-run value of a customer, the cost of the added unit of advertising is exceeded?

Now let's move on to the actual (but camouflaged) case of Home Sewing, Inc., a firm that sells sewing materials by mail. Home Sewing obtains customers with a special introductory offer at $3 in space advertisements. Its records show that 30 percent of those introductory customers buy again from the line of regular merchandise. And on the average, 40 percent of customers who buy regular merchandise once then buy a second time; 40 percent who buy a second time then buy a third time, and so on. The average size of subsequent orders is $10. Home Sewing figures that the total costs of servicing a customer (the goods, shipping and everything else except the cost of advertising) amount to 70 percent of the sale price for the introductory offer, and 50 percent thereafter. The average time between orders is 6 months, and over that period the cost of money to the firm is 10 percent, so $1 received 6 months hence is worth about 90 percent of $1 (90 cents) now.

The value of a new customer to Home Sewing can be figured as follows: ($3 introductory-offer revenue $-.70 \times \$3$ cost to the firm of introductory offer) plus (.3 probability of repeating from introductory offer) times ($10 second-order revenue $-.50 \times \$10$ cost of second-order) times (.9 to allow for the cost of money over half a year) plus (.4 $\times$ .3 probability of repeat from second order) times ($10 third-order revenue $-.5 \times \$10$ third-order cost) times (.9 $\times$ .9 to allow for the cost of money over two 6-month periods), and so on for subsequent periods.

That is,

$$\text{Value of new customer to Home Sewing} = \begin{aligned} &(\$3 - \$2.10) + .3\,(\$10 - \$5) \\ &(.9) + (.4 \times .3)(\$10 - \$5) \\ &(.9 \times .9) \ldots = \$.90 + \$1.35 \\ &+ \$.49 \ldots \approx \$2.74 + \ldots \end{aligned}$$

So the value of an additional customer to Home Sewing is about $2.74. Actually, the value is considerably higher, because subsequent orders have not been figured in. But it is clear from inspection of the figures that the value now of additional future orders is really quite small—so small that their calculation is hardly worthwhile.

Now let us see how the value of a customer changes if one of the elements is different. Let's say (as actually happened) that this firm found on further inspection that the reorder rates were higher than originally thought—the reorder rate is really 40% (that is, .40) from the introductory offer to the second order, and 49% (that is, .49) for subsequent reorders. The value of a customer then is:

$$
\begin{aligned}
\text{Value of a customer} &= (\$3 - \$2.10) + .4 \ (\$10 - \$5)(.9) \\
&\quad + (.49 \times .4)(\$10 - \$5)(.9 \times .9) \ldots \\
&= \$.90 + \$1.80 + \$.80 + \\
&\approx \$3.50 +
\end{aligned}
$$

For practice, another change: Let us calculate the value of a customer to Home Sewing under a third set of conditions. Assume, the firm found that its costs for subsequent orders were only 45 percent rather than 50 percent. So:

$$
\begin{aligned}
\text{Value of a customer} &= (\$3 - \$2.10) + .4(\$10 - \$4.50)(.9) \\
&\quad + (.49 \times .4)(\$10 - \$4.50)(.9 \times .9) \ldots \\
&= \$.90 + \$1.98 + \$.88 \\
&\approx \$3.76
\end{aligned}
$$

Before the death and resurrection of *Life* a few years ago, its circulation director supplied excellent data on *Life*'s circulation advertising results, summarized in Table 9-1. Like every other magazine and like other repeat-business mail-order firms, *Life* could never have been profitable if it had depended on the revenue from the first orders. For the sample shown, the first year the net *loss* was $2,877. But by the end of 5 years, the profit was $32,685.

Assume for the moment that "fulfillment" costs of producing and distributing the magazine equaled the revenue from advertising—a pretty good assumption for mass consumer magazines. Then figure how much *Life* could afford to spend for a new customer in this way:

1. Subscription revenue from an *average* customer during the "life" of the customer equaled

$$\$46,929 \div 2,830 = \$16.58$$

2. The total cost of soliciting *renewals* for a group of customers divided by the number of original customers in the group equaled

$$\frac{\$1,698 + \$530 + \$398 + \$298}{2,830} = \$1.03$$

3. The most that the magazine should have spent to get a customer, then was

$$\$16.58 - \$1.03 = \$15.55$$

Table 9-1

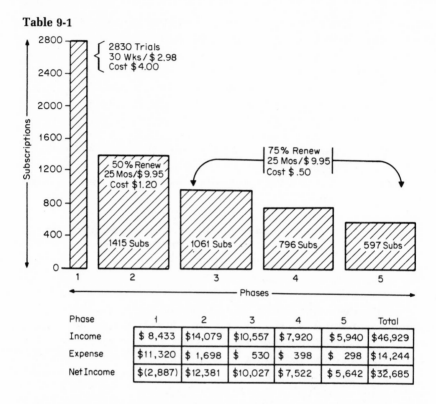

Phase	1	2	3	4	5	Total
Income	$ 8,433	$14,079	$10,557	$7,920	$ 5,940	$46,929
Expense	$11,320	$ 1,698	$ 530	$ 398	$ 298	$14,244
Net Income	$(2,887)	$12,381	$10,027	$7,522	$ 5,642	$32,685

Note how, after the trial-period renewal, customers fell away at about 25 percent *each year.* It will be true for practically every mail-order business that a constant *percentage* of a group of customers will drop out each year. Once you have estimated the customer fall-off rate for one year for your business, you have a terrifically valuable tool for future planning.

Here is a more recent report, on *Bon Appétit* magazine[1]

Mr. Knapp calculates that his advertising cost per subscription runs between $3.50 and $4.50 from magazine ads and between $7 and $8 from direct mail. Rather high for a magazine with a $7.95 annual subscription rate, you say. But you have to know that publishers expect to make their money on renewals. Bon Appétit's are running at 70 to 75 percent, Mr. Knapp says.

HOW TO ESTIMATE REPEAT RATES

But, you ask, how does one know what the repeat rates will be? Sometimes the repeat rate is very easy to learn, sometimes a bit harder. An easy example: Once I sold monthly flower subscriptions by direct mail. After the first experimental month, I immediately saw that fifteen of twenty-five (60 percent) of my introductory-offer customers signed up for another month at the regular rate. And at the end of the second month, I found that eleven of fifteen (about 73 percent) bought again. That was enough information for me to make a rough estimate of how the business would do in the future. Of course my samples were small, and at first I had no evidence yet about subsequent repeats after the first repeat. But after a few more months I had accumulated solid evidence from bigger samples, and I had information about the repeat rates after the first repeat. My initial estimates were not far off, and they certainly were accurate enough to work with.

Now let's take the case of a camouflaged fishing-equipment firm, Doog and Doog, two friends of mine that have been in business for about 4 years as of the date we are making the analysis, March 1980. Doog and Doog had never estimated their repeat rates as of the date they called me in as a consultant. But they had kept all their old orders in boxes. So we sorted out all the customers whose names started with B or R, as a rough way of taking a sample of the buyers who had first ordered merchandise in January, February and March of 1977. (We could tell which customers were ordering for the first time because they were buying the introductory offer. All the other B and R orders we put aside.) Then we checked to see how many times each of them ordered again. We found that of the 110 first-time B- and R-named buyers in January through March of 1977, the following were the re-peat-purchase records:

Total sample: 110 buyers. Of these

26 (24 percent) reordered once only,	representing 26 orders
12 reordered twice	representing 24 orders
4 reordered 3 times	representing 12 orders
3 reordered 4 times	representing 12 orders
1 reordered 5 times	representing 5 orders
Total buyers 46	Total orders 79

(You may think that it cost a lot of work and money to go back through 3 years' worth of old orders to get this information. It was a bit of a nuisance, and now the firm has learned that it makes sense to keep records in better form; in their case, the Doogs are now ready for a modern punched-card system. But even so, the total cost of studying the back orders was only a few hundred dollars, and the information gained is worth much more than that to Doog and Doog in future added profit.)

If the firm has kept good records of customer purchases in the past—say, on index cards—the job is much simpler. All one then need do is take a random sample of, say, 300 people who first bought between 3 and 5 years ago, and study their purchases over 3 years from the date of first purchase. (Use a longer period if the firm's repeat business extends a very long time, as is the case with magazine subscriptions.) If the firm's records are on punched cards or tape, the firm can even work with *all* the customers in that category with no extra effort.

The best way to take a fair random sample from index-card records is as follows:

To make things simple, we shall assume that the future ends after 3 years. Anything you take in after that is gravy, a margin for error. For several economic reasons this won't distort our calculations very much.

If you have been in business over 3 years, the figuring is a breeze. If your records are computerized, you instruct the computer to make the calculations from every customer's record. If you are not computerized yet, but are using index cards, all you have to do is take a sample of people who bought from you over 3 years ago, and see how much they purchased in the first 3 years after you first heard from them. Use a ruler to make a mark at equal intervals in your customer files so that there are *300 equal intervals*. This saves you the trouble of counting off the cards. Take the first customer's card *over three years old* that comes after each mark.

If you have been in business only a short time, you can *estimate* the same data by first figuring out how the average customer's purchase frequency drops as time goes on. Then you project the effect for a 3-year period. Better get some help from a statistician on this. Actually, this procedure is especially vital for new businesses. It is only in this way that you can accurately decide whether you are making or losing money.

IMPORTANT: You *must* sample *both* the customers who are still active *and* those who are now in your inactive or "dead" file. If, by some unfortunate accident, you have thrown away the records of inactive customers, you will need a procedure slightly more complicated than we have space to describe here. Any statistical consultant should be able to set up a satisfactory procedure for you in a few hours.

I can't tell you the *exact* size of the proper sample for your business. But 300 customers should be more than enough in most cases, and a sample a little too big won't cost you much extra.

The value of a customer then is calculated as follows:

1. Take a *fair* (random) sample of the names of 300 customers—active and inactive—who first bought over 3 years ago.

2. Add up the total amount they have purchased in the 3 years from the date of first purchase.

3. Divide by 300.

4. Multiply by your average profit margin (in percent).

The figure you come out with is the amount it is worth to you to *get a customer onto your books.* Never lose an opportunity to get a customer for anything less than that cost.

The procedure described here should not cost you more than $800 at 1980 prices including clerical time, no matter how big your list is. (And if your business has progressed to the point where the customer records are on punched cards or electronic tape, the job is even less expensive.) I practically guarantee that the information will increase your future profit by many thousands of dollars, if your business is any size at all.

USING THE VALUE OF A CUSTOMER

The most obvious point—that one *must* use the value of a customer as the criterion, and as the *only* criterion—is sometimes overlooked. For example, a successful auto dealer quit his direct-mail auto sales campaigns after a postage increase, without even checking the results of his campaign. But when he realized that the sale of even a single car would justify a good many thousand letters, he began to reconsider. The moral: always keep the value of a customer in mind.

The dollar value of a customer is used in decision making as follows: Any advertisement or list for which the expected result of this multiplication [(number of customers) times (value of a customer)] is greater than the cost of the ad or mailing should be run. But if the cost of the ad is greater than the expected number of customers multiplied by the value of a customer, the ad or mailing should not be done.

Remember that you are interested not only in the *frequency* of reorders, but also in the *dollar amounts* of reorders. Calculate the dollar size of reorders *separately* for first reorders, second reorders, etc. In the example above, the amount of the reorder is the same for each reorder, but in many cases the amount is different, averaging higher (or, less often, lower) with subsequent purchases.

Remember that from the expected *revenue* of a customer, you must subtract the *cost* of servicing these orders, or else your calculations will overstate the value of a customer. The next chapter takes up the subject of estimating those costs appropriately and accurately.

Often it is useful to refine the calculation of the value of a customer to take into account the value of his particular first order. This refinement can be worthwhile because customers tend to vary much more in the size of the first order than in subsequent orders, and because the money from the first order is received immediately and hence has higher value to you per dollar than future revenue.

Here is an example of how the calculated value of a customer depends upon the first-order size for the sewing-materials firm:

Table 9-2

If first order is	Firm can pay, to get the order
$ 3.00	$3.00
3.50	3.20
4.00	3.45
4.50	3.65
5.00	3.90
5.50	4.10
6.00	4.35
6.50	4.55
7.00	4.80
7.50	5.00
8.00	5.25
8.50	5.45
9.00	5.70
9.50	5.90
10.00	6.15

It is amazing and sad to see how much profit mail-order firms forgo by not correctly estimating and using the value of a customer. For example, a large mail-order shoe firm was asked about its mailing-list rental policy.[2]

Q. What rate of returns from your mailings do you consider a good point?

A. We happen to break even at 1.8%. We rent anything that goes over that. By break even, I mean it pays off in the first mailing. We don't rent a list that pulls less than that because it goes into a loss position and we don't like that. Although in a long test, it might be worth doing, we like to have short-term profits.

Q. In other words, you won't take a 1.5% return and hope you get repeat orders which will then make it worthwhile?

A. We do not have to do this right now. I think it might be acceptable, but not necessary.

I am absolutely sure that if this firm took into account the value of the customers after the initial order, it would greatly increase its profit by renting more lists and increasing its volume.

Another example: A firm that sells correspondence courses had been making no distinction between the potential value of future equipment and course purchases by those who had actually purchased and those who had only inquired. When these different values had been calculated, they immediately indicated changes in advertising patterns that would increase profits by a quarter of a million dollars per year.

The value of a customer also shows up in a lawsuit against a firm that stole a customer list. The thief got 4,000 customers, who purchased an average of $100 the first year, with a decay rate of 20 percent a year and a net margin of 35 percent, so the value of the stolen customers could be reckoned as:

$$(\$100 \times 4,000 \times .35) + \frac{1}{1-.20} (\$100 \times 4,000 \times .35) .85 + \ldots$$

It would be appropriate to take account of expected increases in unit sales in the future, in this case.

This chapter and the next one are not easy reading. However, it is important to read them for two reasons: (1) I think I know a fair amount about all the topics covered in this book. But I am more of a specially qualified expert on the economic calculations of mail order than on any other topic. (2) These calculations are more likely to make the difference between losing money and making money than any other mail-order decisions you will make.

Calculating
Mail-Order
Costs

The previous chapter said that knowing the value of a customer is crucial in making decisions about which advertisements and lists to run. But, to calculate the value of a customer correctly, it is necessary to know the cost of servicing the customer (*all* the costs of merchandise, shipping, and so on, but excluding the costs of the advertising itself). This chapter shows how to calculate those costs.

A small, but (to me) painful, story illustrates how the wrong cost calculations can lead to the wrong decision. One day I sat with an executive of the firm that had published a book of mine, the firm being one of the three biggest book publishers in the United States. (I consider that concealing its identity is an act of charity.) I asked why the firm did not continue with a mail-order advertising campaign that had just been tested to sell the book. The executive told me that the advertising campaign was not profitable. I was curious, and we examined the figures. The test showed that the publisher could expect to sell copies at the mail-order price of $8.95 for an average advertising expenditure of about $3. I said that in view of the production expenditures necessary for printing additional books—only about $1.25 or $1.50 per copy because the book had already gone through two printings, plus small expenditures for handling and mailing—the advertising campaign clearly *was* profitable. But the executive said no, we had to add in the "overhead" of several dollars, which meant that the advertising campaign would then be below the break-even point. When I asked what the "overhead" charge was for, he replied that it was the standard charge the firm's accountants insisted be applied to all such decisions. He said the overhead covered executive salaries, editing, physical plant, and so on. He agreed with me that additional advertising for this book, that had already been produced, would not increase the firm's need for editors, and so on. But nevertheless, he insisted on including that "overhead" charge in the calculation, and hence the campaign was not continued. The result was that both the firm and I wound up a lot worse off then we could otherwise have been—a bad decision because of bad reckoning of costs.

You estimate the costs of servicing orders as follows: You calculate how much of everything is needed for the average order: how many items multiplied by the price of the items; how many minutes of labor multiplied by the price of labor per minute; the average cost of mailing; and so on. The sum of the individual cost elements for an average order is the cost of the average order. The estimates of the physical quantities of resources used are made by actual physical examination of each of the inputs—for example, counting the number of orders each worker handles per hour.

This description applies to a situation in which you sell only one kind of merchandise—for example, only watches or only magazines—so that all the costs apply to the single line of business. In such a situation you know exactly how much building rent, say, is relevant to each watch or magazine subscription, on the average. But where you sell watches *and* books *and* fishing boots, it is difficult or impossible to know what the cost of building rent, say, is for the sale of the average watch or the average pair of boots.

The main point to remember in estimating costs by the engineering method is *not to forget any important costs*. The costs of the merchandise and the direct labor in handling and the shipping cost are obvious, unforgettable, and easy to estimate. But what about such costs as the following?

1. Returned merchandise—costs of shipping and of damage to merchandise

2. Merchandise that must be replaced because it arrived damaged at the customer's address

3. Bad debts

4. Lost shipments

You must estimate how often these events will occur and then apply an appropriate proportion of the cost to each order.

Then there are costs which apply to each order but which you may not be able to relate to any particular order. These include:

5. Bank charges

6. Management costs

7. Indirect labor, such as truck drivers and supervisors

Many a mail-order novice has figured that he was making a profit on every individual order, but then, at end of the year, has found that he had lost money altogether—usually because he did not take account of all these nonobvious costs.[1]

How to
Key Your
Advertisements

How to Key a Magazine Advertisement ● *How to Key
Direct Mail*

HOW TO KEY A MAGAZINE
ADVERTISEMENT

These are the jobs that the key and address in a mail-order ad must
do:

1. The key must indicate clearly which ad the customer is answer-
    ing.

2. *The key must be easy to identify by clerical help.* What not to do
    is illustrated by the advertisers who used to key with the material
    on the back of the coupons. The editorial or advertising matter
    was different for each coupon, all right. But the clerk who recorded
    the key had to remember the back of each coupon, or compare it
    with a sample. That was a slow, expensive process. And some
    people send in the coupon pasted to a sheet of paper!

3. *The key must make it easy for magazines to advance the key each
    month,* in order that you have a separate record for each issue.
    Some advertisers key by using only a different name in each mag-
    azine. This practice is not wise unless you already know the re-

sults from the magazines so well that you don't need a monthly record.

4. *The key must make it easy to tabulate returns* in your media records. This means that you need some sort of alphabetical or numerical code in the key.

5. For classified ads only: *the key must use minimum word count.* The best system for classified ads that include a post office box number will be a single block of numbers using one of the key systems described below.

There are many methods of keying. You can use "Drawer," "Department," "Studio," "Room" or similar words, followed by the actual code. If you sell several products, you can use a different introductory word from the list above. This will ease your keying problems and will speed the job of sorting the mail.

You can also use different street numbers if you live in a small town, and if you get the postmaster's permission. Or you can address the mail to different first names. (But if you are asking for money in the ad, you will need to stick to one name so you can deposit checks easily.)

The crucial problem is: What letters and numbers shall make up the key?

This is the solution I have found best: A typical key is "71-223" as in "Samco, Drawer 71-223, Hoboken, N.J.," the third ad in a series in *Field & Stream.*

"Drawer 71" is the number of the post office box.

"F22" stands for the magazine, and is established by referring to an alphabetical list of magazines. *Field & Stream* is the 22nd magazine alphabetically among the F's. (If a magazine is alphabetically between 1 and 9, it gets redesignated with a number from 91 to 99.) I use the *Standard Rate & Data* index list, but you can use any list.

If the magazine is not on the list, it is designated 81, 82, etc. Or you can start your list with every other number, and fill in the spaces with unlisted magazines.

The "3" is for the third issue. The fifteenth issue becomes "F2215."

The major virtue of this system is that it permits records to be kept in the order in which keys are listed, and still in nearly alphabetical order. This eases the record keeping and tabulating in a great many ways that you won't appreciate until you have tried other keying systems.

This system also meets the other requirements cited above.

It *is* possible not to key each issue separately. This procedure saves some clerical labor in tabulation. But it loses much information that is extremely valuable unless you already have several years of experience with the media in question.

The crucial things in keying are:

1. *Don't forget to key.*

2. *Key correctly.*

It is usually in the very first ads for a product that you omit the key or you duplicate keys, because you have not yet set up a complete system. And unfortunately, it is those first ads that give you the most valuable information that your records can supply. *So don't forget to key, and key correctly.*

Writers on mail order often state flatly that a post office box number produces fewer orders than a street address. But I have never seen any *evidence* on this. It is *probably* true that if you ask for money in the ad, and if the ad is small enough to look insubstantial, a *high* box number in a *big city* might reduce response. But other than that, I'll bet it doesn't matter *what* address you use.

The lower the number of the box or drawer, the better. In general, a low number sounds impressive and old, while a high number sounds anonymous. But more than that, a number in two digits makes some kinds of keying easier than three or four digits (one digit is even easier).

HOW TO KEY DIRECT MAIL

Direct-mail keying is easier than periodical keying, because the customer does not need to write down the key. You print or stamp the key on either the return envelope or the coupon that the customer sends back—a different key for each list you test. You can also code the key to show the date sent out.

An alphabetical key is still best, for the reasons mentioned above.

If you use a two-step selling system, you often want to key the follow-ups so you can know how many dollars each medium finally produces. The commonest and easiest system is to type the original incoming key onto the address label for the follow-ups. The address label is then placed on the order coupon, and arranged so that it shows through a window envelope. The date of receipt is also typed onto the address label in most cases.

As you examine samples of direct mail, you will notice examples of other types of keys.

How to Start
a Classified-Advertising
Business

*The First Steps to Classified • How to Write a
Classified Ad • How Long Should the Classified Ad
Be?*

This chapter is about advertising in the classified columns of magazines, and it does not deal with newspaper classified advertising. This topic is seldom mentioned at all in discussions of mail-order advertising, but it can be a first-rate way to get into business. The unabridged version of this book has a great deal more detailed information on this topic.

With few exceptions, newspaper classified columns will not pay off for mail-order advertisers. Some correspondence courses, books and book-finding services are exceptions to the rule, however. The classified sections of nationally distributed newspapers like the *National Enquirer, The Wall Street Journal,* the *National Observer* and *The New York Times* are good for some mail-order offers. Many weekly farm newspapers are also excellent for mail order.

The arena of classified includes far more than a few magazines like *Popular Science,* however. There are over 300 magazines that are good classified media, most of which you have never heard of.

The page from the classified section in the 1979 *Grier's Almanac* shown in Figure 12-1 and the section from *VFW* magazine in Figure 12-2 contain examples of mail-order businesses that use the classifieds,

YOURS FREE! WHOLESALE CATALOG filled with Motorcycle, Snowmobile, Small engine parts and accessories. Low. Low prices. Manufacturer's Supply, Box 157GA, Dorchester, WI 54425

RINGS, JEWELRY priced 130% below retail price. Catalog, $1.00 (refundable). Anka-GR, 95 Washington, West Warwick, RI 02893

CARNIVOROUS PLANTS

CARNIVOROUS AND WOODLAND terrarium plants. Catalog 25¢. Peter Pauls Nurseries, Canandaigua, NY 14424

CHAIN SAW PARTS

SAVE TO 40% on first quality, guaranteed, Chain, Guidebars, Sprockets, Sharpening Equipment for all makes saws. Also Small Engine Parts, Service Tools. Free Catalog. Write today. Zip-Penn, Dept. A22, Box 6329, Erie, PA 16512

COINS

INDIANHEAD & LINCOLN Cents 33 Different, 1883-1949—$2.99. Catalog—25¢. Edel's, Carlyle, Illinois 62231

SEND 50¢ for 5 "S" wheat cents and price list. Jacobs Coins, POB 532-A, Mableton, Ga. 30059

EARLY AMERICAN COINS before Nineteen Hundred—Solid investment. Half cent $15.00, Indian cent 60¢, Large cent $4.50, Two cent piece $4.95, Three cent piece $5.50, "V" Nickel 75¢, Half dime $7.00—All with clear dates. Satisfaction Guaranteed—Postpaid. Detroit Coin Co., 1764 Penobscot Bldg., Detroit, Mich. 48226

CURIOS

VAN VAN OIL—$1.00. Incense and other items. Curios, 436 Front St., Memphis, Tenn. 38103

DO-IT-YOURSELF

MAKE YOUR OWN TRAPS, CAGES! 2500 Cage Clamps. Clincher $14.95. 999 picture pet hobby supply catalog $1.00. Stromberg's, Pine River 46, Minnesota 56474

JAPANESE BEETLE TRAP. Commercial bait, milk jug. Plans $2.00. Bill Gazaway, Rt. 4, Alpharetta, Ga. 30201

EARTHWORMS

MAKE MONEY FAST raising Fishworms, Crickets. We teach you how to raise and sell. FREE LITERATURE. Breeder Redworms—1,000-$8.95, postpaid. Carter Worm Farm—9, Plains, Georgia 31780

BIG MONEY Raising Fishworms! Redworm Breeders 1,000-$6.95 2,000-$13.50 5,000-$30.00 African Nightcrawlers 1,000-$12.95. Postpaid with instructions. Seymour Sales, Bronwood, Georgia 31726

EDUCATION, SCHOOLS, INSTRUCTIONS

DETECTIVE CAREER. Rewarding, exciting. Free Information. Universal Detectives, Box 8180-GA, Universal City, Calif. 91608

UNIVERSITY DEGREES by mail! Bachelors, Masters, PhD's... Free revealing details. Counseling, Box 317-GA2, Tustin California 92680

HIGHLY EFFECTIVE Specialized Home Study Courses. Over 70 categories to choose. Advance rapidly! Diploma awarded. Our 33rd Year! Free literature. Cook's Institute, Desk 12, Box 20345, Jackson, MS 39209

CIVIL SERVICE Test Preparation home study course. Job Security may be yours by preparing for coming examinations. Write National Training Service, Inc., Box 160, Haddonfield, N.J. 08033

LEARN SEWING MACHINE repairing. A profitable trade. Easy to learn. Free details. Sewing Center, 187 GR, Rochelle, Ga. 31079

FINISH HIGH SCHOOL at home quickly! See our advertisement page 58! Academy Senior High School.

EMPLOYMENT OPPORTUNITIES

OVERSEAS EMPLOYMENT—$15,000 — $50,000+. Free information! Employment International, Box 29217-MO, Indianapolis, Indiana 46229.

FEMALE HELP WANTED

TEAR OUT THIS AD, mail with name, address for big box of home needs and cosmetics. FREE to reliable men and women. Tell and show friends, make good money spare time taking their order. Write today. BLAIR, Dept 341JA, Lynchburg, Va. 24506

GENEALOGY

ANCESTOR HUNTING? Trace Your Family Roots The Easy Way! Details Free. Lokadex Library, Box 8948-G, Rochester, NY 14624

GINSENG

GINSENG! $50 POUND. Have seeds, roots Goldenseal. For complete growing, marketing information write F. B. Collins, B16, Viola, Iowa 52350

GINSENG, SEEDS, roots, books for sale. Write for prices. Roots "O" Gold, RR2, Box 74, LeCenter, MN 56057

GOVERNMENT SURPLUS

GOVERNMENT SURPLUS DIRECTORY. Buy 250,000 different items (including Jeeps) low as 2¢ on dollar! Most complete information available—$2.00. Surplus Disposal, Box 19107-MO, Washington DC 20036

OFFICIAL UNITED STATES DIRECTORY—Unequalled!!—Tells Everything!!—Jeeps—$37.22!!—Cars—$22.50!!—Agri-Machinery!!—Livestock!!—Forage!!—400,000 Listings—Your Immediate Area!!—$2.00—(Includes G-Lands Info-Guide!) United States/Great Lakes Federal Surplus Depository, P.O.B. 807-FM, Marshfield, Wisconsin 54449 (Copyright 1979)

JEEPS—$59.30!—Cars—$33.50!—200,000 items! Government Surplus. Most comprehensive directory available tells how, where to buy—Your area—$2.00—Moneyback Guarantee—Government Information Services, Dept. GI-4, Box 99249, San Francisco, California 94109 (433 California)

GREETING CARDS

REQUEST FREE: 1979 Scripture-text Card Folder. Special Offer. Write, Box 81 (A), Roanoke, Va. 24002

HEALTH ITEMS, INSTRUCTIONS

UNDERSTAND YOUR HAY FEVER & Asthma Problems. 6 Basic Principles 25¢ for Booklet. Write Nephron Corporation, Dept. XXAA Tacoma, Washington 98401

NATURE'S ANSWER against Heart Attack, Arthritis, Diabetes, Cataract. Free information. Provoker Press, St. Catharines—223, Ontario L2R 7C9.

NERVOUS—Write for free literature how John Winters approached this problem. Address Orbacine, Dept. A-94, 2 Overhill Road, Scarsdale, N.Y. 10583

HEMORRHOIDS (Piles)? Take Melrose for permanent relief. Used effectively for 50 years. Guaranteed. An Herbal medicine. $4.75 for one month's treatment. Robert S. Moser Druggist, P.O. Box 8863, Asheville, N.C. 28804

ARTHRITIS. Please send for Paul McCoy's remarkable true life story about his complaint. It's free. Address: Norkon, Dept. A-94, 2 Overhill Road, Scarsdale, N.Y. 10583

WANT BEAUTIFUL FINGERNAILS? Simply brush on famous formula. Guaranteed. Send $1.50 Phoebe, Box 221G, New Canaan, Ct. 06840

FOR HEALTH & Happiness Send $2.00 to H & H, P. O. Box 1701-GA, Kissimmee, Fla. 32741. You'll be glad you did.

EDGAR CAYCE Recommended Products Specialists in hard-to-find herbal remedies mentioned in the Cayce readings. Current pricelist free on request. Heritage Store, Box 444-GA, Virginia Beach, VA 23458

HOW TO STOP SMOKING. Guaranteed method. $2. Path Research A107, Box 1060, Orangepark, FL 32073.

OVERWEIGHT? In controlling weight, mind-power beats dieting, pills or will-power. Amazingly easy! You simply relax, listen and lose. Two cassettes and booklet. $25.00 (Refundable). RELAXED LEARNING, INC., 30-C South El Camino, San Mateo, Ca. 94401

MY ARTHRITIS has been completely wiped out. To receive our proven, safe, money back guaranteed plan, send 15 cent stamp. Raney's Medical Research, Box 104, Drasco, AR 72530

THUMB SUCKING? If someone you know wants to stop and can't, let us help. Safe, simple, rewarding method. Proven effective. Send $8.00 for complete kit, postpaid. Thumbs Up, 70 E. 96 St., New York, N.Y. 10028

HEARING AIDS

SAVE UP TO 50% OFF comparable aids. Buy direct. 30 Days FREE Trial. No Salesman will call. Low Battery Prices. LLOYD S, Dept GLC, 128 Kishwaukee St., Rockford, Ill. 61104

FREE HEARING AID Catalog. Save ½ by mail! Write MONEY$AVER$, 9530GRA Langdon, Sepulveda, Ca 91343

HONEY

PURE, NATURAL HONEY. $14.00 gallon Postpaid. Sample jar $1.50. Ellison's, 205 Oak Drive, Belton, South Carolina 29627

INVENTIONS, PATENTS WANTED

IDEAS, INVENTIONS, NEW PRODUCTS needed by innovative manufacturers. Marketing assistance available to individuals, tinkerers, universities, companies with feasible concepts. Write for Kit-GAL, IMI, 701 Smithfield, Pittsburgh, PA 15222

JEWELRY

GENUINE INDIAN JEWELRY/Handcrafts/Findings/14K Gold Chains. Wholesale! Details $1.00 (Refundable). Lange/GA, 6031 North 7th St., Phoenix, AZ 85014

BIG PROFITS—Jewelry! Lowest Wholesale Prices. Free List. CCCC, Conover, N.C. 28613

LIVE BAIT

MAKE MONEY FAST raising Fishworms, Crickets. We teach you how to raise and sell. FREE LITERATURE. Breeder Redworms—1,000—$8.95, postpaid. Carter Worm Farm—2, Plains, Georgia 31780

SELLING ENTIRE Farm Red Wigglers! Majority Breeders' Special! 3,000-$9.95 5,000-$15.95 10,000-$26.95 African Crawlers 1,000-$12.95. Postpaid with instructions. Beatrice Worm Farms, Dawson, Georgia 31742

GOLDEN MEALWORMS, 1,000/$3.50 Giant Mealworms, 1,000/$12.00 2,000 to 5,000, $11.00 per 1,000 6,000 to 10,000, $10.00 per 1,000. Mableton Mealworms, 5539 Andrews, Mableton, Ga. 30059

GOLDEN MEALWORMS 1000—$5.00 with raising instructions. Georgia-Anne Farms 2, Plains, Ga. 31780

LOANS BY MAIL

SECRET LOANS by Mail. Borrow $100 to $5000 for any good reason in absolute privacy. No endorsers, no co-signers. Fast Service. Write Dial Finance, Dept. 3727, 340 S.W. Eighth Street, Des Moines, Iowa 50309

BORROW $25,000 "OVERNIGHT". Any purpose. Keep indefinitely! Write Success Research, Box 29263-MO, Indianapolis, Indiana 46229

MAGIC TRICKS, JOKES

FREE! World's Leading Novelty Catalog. 1600 Funmakers, Jokes, Science, Sports, Hobbies, Bargains. Johnson-Smith, C-54, Mt. Clemens, Mich. 48043

MISCELLANEOUS

CHRISTIANS, CLERGYMEN, SCHOLARS! Illustrated map of heaven! with 500 descriptive words $2. C. Brewer, 1298 Carr, Memphis, 38104

EVERYONE! VETERANS! Collect Now! From Government. Five special reports! 25¢. Guaranteed! Grandcees, GR79, Hamilton, Ga. 31811

WHO ELSE Will Be Successful? Booklet $1.00 Success, Drawer P, Lexington, N.C. 27292

NEW-CAR-TRUCK pricing wheel calculates invoice cost w/in .005! Send $3.00 Buyers Guide, 2511 SW 410, SA, TX 78227

PECAN HALVES-WALNUTS-Sliced Almonds! Three-Quarter Sampler, $9.95 Postpaid! Canecreek Farm, Box 2727-GA, Cookeville, TN 38501

FREE BAR of luxury soap each $5.00 order Catalog. Soap Source, P.O. Box 4009-K Greenwich, CT 06830

77

Figure 12-1 Classified section in *Grier's Almanac*.

though some of these offers are of less overall value than I wish they were.

THE FIRST STEPS TO CLASSIFIED

Your first step toward a classified mail-order business is the same first step we talked about in Chapter 3. *Examine the media and the competition.* Write a postcard to every medium you can find that carries classified, asking for a sample copy of the magazine and rates for *classified* advertising. Rate information on classified is omitted from some rate cards and from some *Standard Rate & Data* listings.

Then get hold of the back issues of magazines from back-date magazine shops. Or, you can examine the back files of *Popular Science, Workbasket, Popular Gardening, Popular Photography* and others at your nearest public library.

Clip the classified pages out of the magazines and file them alphabetically. At the same time, make up a 3 × 5 inch file card on each magazine, noting on the card the products and firms advertising in it that interest you. Don't spend much time thinking about what you're doing until you have looked at the classified pages of at least fifty different media. Then you can begin to consider what looks good and what doesn't. You are, of course, looking for the ads and products that appear in many media and over a long period of time. Those are the *successful* products.

Pay most attention to the magazines whose cost is *highest* per word. That's where the gravy is. If you can't use the expensive magazines successfully, your operation will be tiny potatoes at best.

Your product need *not* appeal to everyone; it need *not* be able to run profitably in all media. If you have an offer that will be successful in most of the farm magazines, you are in good shape. On the other hand, if your offer will be profitable only in the automobile-magazine classifieds, the volume will probably be too small to justify your investment of time.

Prices

As a very general rule, $1 is a better price than either 50 cents or $2— in *classified,* and for printed products whose cost is low. From my own experience I have found that you will not make twice as many sales at 50 cents as at $1 and in that case $1 is more profitable than 50 cents. I have also found that $1 gets considerably *more* than twice as many sales as $2, enough more to make the $1 price best.

CAUTION: My experience should be only a *suggestion* to you. The opposite results will occur for some kinds of products. You must *test* various prices for your own product and offer.

Remember that the more the product costs you to make and mail, the more you must get for it. But the price does *not* go up in proportion to the costs. See Chapter 8 for a full discussion of how to set the best price for your product.

When reckoning your costs and revenues, don't forget the value of the names of your customers or inquirers. Satisfied customers can later be sold other products, and each customer's name then comes to be very valuable. And even if you yourself never try to sell anything to the customer again, or even if the prospect has never bought from you, the name has value and should *never, never* be thrown away. You can convert names into money either by renting the list or (more likely for beginners and small businesses) selling the names. See Chapter 17 for a discussion of lists, list brokers and how to sell or rent lists.

HOW TO WRITE A CLASSIFIED AD

What is true of *all* advertising copy is *especially* true for classified writing: the copywriter must be absolutely precise and economical with the words and language he uses. Every fuzzy or useless word takes a chunk out of potential profit. A single word that is not true to its mark and completely clear may turn potential customers away from the ad.

These are the actual steps that I follow in writing a classified ad. I can only recommend them to you as one man's method. Your approach may be different but just as good.

1. Study the ads of your successful competitors.

2. In the order in which they come into your head, scribble down every word or idea or group of words that would help you to sell the product if you had all the space you wanted. In addition to all the words about your product, include all the classic selling words: "News," "New Discovery," "Bargain," "Free," "Save," etc. Include every important word that is in your competitor's ads.

3. Write down your lead word (or words). Your first ads will have the best chance of success if your lead words express the same *idea* as your most successful competitor's ads. (But make your words *different* from his.)

4. Using your list of important words and phrases, write the best ad

you can, without trying to make the ad short or concise. Just make sure that you have in the ad everything you think must be in it, in the correct order. Include every "selling idea" that your successful competitors have in their ads.

5. Then hone and polish the ad. Try for the most powerful and evocative words you can find. It is amazing the difference that a single word can make. I found that the words "Manual" and "Book" brought in *twice as many* orders as did "Instructions" in an ad for a how-to-do-it booklet I was selling. Every experienced mail-order dealer has at least one story like this.

6. Squeeze out every single *extra* word. Keep in mind that one extra word can cost you $500 in a year's time. Use figures instead of words ("50¢" for "fifty cents"). Leave out "the," "a," "an." But don't abbreviate, because a short word costs you as much as a long word. Long words help because they make the ad look bigger.

Use as much punctuation as possible to make the ad look exciting and big. Use quotation marks ("New Discovery"), dots ("Quick . . . Cheap . . . Powerful"), exclamation points (Now!!!).

Remember that publishers generally count each letter or group of letters as a word. ("Department J" is two words.) Hyphenated words usually count as two words, also. ("Do-It-Yourself" is three words.)

7. After that, you're on your own. You will have to test new words and new ideas to see if they increase your returns. Test action words like "Write today." Test extra description words. Test new lead words. Test leaving out various words and ideas. Test everything, and keep testing till you have really profitable copy. Then test some more. See Chapters 4 and 27 of the unabridged edition of this book for instructions on how to test.

HOW LONG SHOULD
THE CLASSIFIED AD BE?

When asked how long an ad should be, people in advertising like to paraphrase A. Lincoln's famous remark: The ad should be long enough to do the job. The advice is sage, but not very helpful except to point out that the best length for an ad must differ from situation to situation.

Properly, the length of an ad is determined by these two factors.

1. *The ad must be long enough to tell the basic story.* If any crucial element is left out, the ad will fail completely. For example, if you do not include enough description of the product so that readers understand what it is you are selling, you make no sales at all. Telling the reader what the product will do *for* him or her may be a crucial element. Telling him or her the product is new may also be crucial.

2. *"The more you tell, the more you sell."* Assuming that all the crucial elements are present, further sales talk will increase sales to *some* extent. The problem is to determine *how* much more than the crucial elements it is profitable to pile into the ad.

Not only does each extra sales word increase your sales somewhat, but the sheer size of an ad affects its selling power. In other words, even if you just added neutral dummy words like "the," "and so forth," "Now Now Now Now," etc., you would probably increase sales somewhat. But dummy words seldom or never increase sales *sufficiently* to make them profitable.

You can find the best size of your particular ad only by actual testing. Try an ad 50 percent longer than your basic ad. Try another ad 100 percent longer. Try a third ad that leaves out some of the elements in your basic ad. Then calculate which ad is most profitable. Then and only then will you know the best size.

If you find that the bigger ad is more profitable, try an even bigger ad. If the smaller ad is more profitable, try an even smaller ad.

This is how you *calculate* which is the most profitable advertisement:

1. Figure how much you net on each *sale,* exclusive of advertising cost. Take everything into account, including labor, *but exclude advertising cost.* If a pamphlet sells for $1, and printing, binding, etc., costs 10 cents, outgoing postage 6 cents, clerical labor (including your own) 5 cents, reserve for refunds 3 cents, labels, envelopes, and other costs 8 cents, adding to 32 cents, then $1 less 32 cents equals 68 cents net, exclusive of advertising cost.

2. Determine how many *more* orders the bigger ad brings in than does your basic ad, and multiply by the 68 cents net. (In other words, if the big ad brings in 80 more orders than the little ad, multiply 80 × 68, which equals $54.40.)

3. Calculate how much more the bigger ad costs than the basic ad. (In other words, cost of big ad minus cost of small ad.)

4. If the cost in step 3 is less than the extra net in step 2, then the bigger ad is profitable. Otherwise, run the basic smaller ad.

You should understand very clearly that an ad twice as long (and therefore twice as costly) as your basic ad definitely does *not* have to bring in twice as many orders to be more profitable. Wrong figuring will lead you to lose much profit. The *only* correct way to figure is the way set forth above.

Display-Advertising Procedure and Testing

How to Place an Ad • Exploratory Testing of Your Offer • How to Estimate Results Quickly • Where to Advertise • When to Advertise

So you have a product and an offer that you think will do well in magazine display advertising! You think you're ready to get into print and into business. This chapter will guide you in your next steps.

We shall not discuss the arts of writing copy and laying out ads. Constructing display ads calls for competent professional skill. Amateur dabbling just won't get by. One solution is to use the services of an advertising agency. (It is crucial that it be an agency whose main business is *mail-order* advertising—avoid ordinary advertising people like the plague.) Or else you must make yourself into a copywriter of semi-professional skill. More about that in the unabridged version of this book.

HOW TO PLACE AN AD

If you use an agency, and if your account is sizable, an advertising agency will handle many or all of the technical problems for you. But the beginner—who needs help the most—has only a small account to offer an agency, and hence gets little service from the agency. Therefore, whether you set up your own house agency, or whether you have an outside agency, you must know how to produce and place an ad.

Getting to be an agency is simple in principle, and not much harder in practice. All you need is a supply of insertion orders and stationery, plus recognition and credit from the media.

Remember to choose an agency name distinct from your mail-order firm name, in order to maintain the fiction of a separation. The media have no desire to ferret out the connection, because it might cost them business. But everyone concerned must join together in maintaining the phony appearance.

(Actually, there is some question whether media have the legal right to deny the same discount to direct advertisers as to agencies.)

Gaining recognition and credit with media is a bootstrap operation; if one magazine thinks that other media have given you credit, it will, too. So you have to develop a list of references. The newspapers are toughest on credit, perhaps because they have to wait longer for their money.

Start by merely sending off your ads, on regular agency forms, to the media you choose. If the magazine questions you, offer to pay in advance. That will almost surely end their squawks.

Once you have placed ads in several media, either on credit or with cash on the barrelhead, you can use those media as references. Just tell other magazines the names of the media in which you have placed ads. In a relatively short time, you will be able to satisfy all but the toughest credit managers.

I do not suggest that you seek recognition from the various media associations because I assume your assets are too limited to make a good showing. But if you can deposit a chunk of money in a separate checking account, and if you can claim some experience in marketing and advertising, you might try for formal recognition.

To place an ad you must know how to read a rate card. Reading a rate card and the *Standard Rate & Data* listings is confusing at first, but really quite easy. Two rate cards are shown in the following figures.

The *Spare Time* rate card in Figure 13-1 practically duplicates its *Standard Rate & Data* listing.

These are the items of special interest to you:

The Cost per Agate Line. There are fourteen agate lines to the inch. Notice the decreasing cost per line as you take larger units of space. Some magazines offer much greater discounts than others do.

The price of space is theoretically the same to all comers. However, "distress covers"—covers that remain unsold at the last minute—are

SPARE TIME 5810 West Oklahoma Avenue, Milwaukee, Wisconsin 53219 414/543-8110

1 PERSONNEL

Publisher and Advertising Manager—
Harvey R. Kipen
Editor—Stan Holden
Production Manager—Betty C. Hinz

2 REPRESENTATIVES and/or BRANCH OFFICES

Chicago, Illinois 60611
Harvey R. Kipen
919 N. Michigan Avenue
Telephone (312) 787-4545

3 COMMISSION AND CASH DISCOUNT

a. 15% to recognized agencies.
b. 2% cash discount 10 days from date of invoice, net 30 days. No commission or discount on bills covering creative and mechanical services.
c. Bills rendered date mailing of an issue begins.

4 GENERAL

a. Rates subject to change without notice except on contracts which have been accepted and acknowledged by the publisher.
b. Advertising which is objectionable or misleading in the opinion of the publisher is not accepted.
c. Orders with special conditions such as positioning or editorial are not accepted.
d. No frequency discount.

5 DISPLAY ADVERTISING RATES

1 page (429 lines)	$2,450.00
2/3 page (286 lines)	1,845.00
1/2 page (214 lines)	1,590.00
1/3 page (143 lines)	1,150.00
1/6 page (70 lines)	595.00
1 inch (14 lines)	126.00
2 pages facing	4,765.00
2 pages facing, black and standard red	5,075.00

Advertisements other than standard units charged for on the following basis:

7- 69 lines	$9.00
71-142 lines	8.50
144-213 lines	8.00
215-285 lines	7.40
287-428 lines	6.45
Over 429 lines	5.70

6 COLOR

Red, per page, extra	$185.00
Red, smaller units, extra	155.00
Special color, per page, extra	250.00
Special color, smaller units, extra	225.00
Four colors, per page, extra	600.00

7 INSERTS

Post card	$3,950.00
First post card and ad page facing	6,550.00
Other post card positions with ad page facing	6,200.00

Add $155.00 for second color, standard red, page facing.

Post card inserts are 5" deep x 6" wide, printed in two colors, both sides.

8 BLEED

Bleed requirements: 8¾" wide x 11¼" deep. Type matter must be at least ¾" away from edge. No extra charge.

9 COVERS AND SPECIAL POSITIONS

Bigger space users get special positions on a rotating basis. No extra charge.

Split runs available. Information on request.

10 CLASSIFIED

$2.50 per word. Minimum 15 words—$37.50. First line set in Caps. All copy set solid without display, leaded or blank spaces. Name, address and numbers must be included in word count. Zip code does not count as word. Cash with order unless placed by recognized advertising agency.

11 CONTRACT AND COPY REGULATIONS

a. Advertisers and advertising agencies assume liability for all content of advertisements including text, representation and illustrations and also assume full liability for any claims against the publisher arising therefrom.
b. Cannot guarantee proofs for correction if copy is not received by closing date.
c. Publisher does not assume responsibility for errors in key number and no allowances or deductions are given should such errors occur.
d. Cash with order unless credit has been established.

12 MINIMUM DEPTH—ROP

1 column, 7 lines; double column, 14 lines.

13 MECHANICAL REQUIREMENTS

a. Publication trim size: 8⅛" x 10⅞"
b. Standard units in inches:

	Width	Depth
Full page	7½ x	10¼
2/3 page	5 x	10¼
1/2 page (vertical)	3⅝ x	10¼
1/2 page (horizontal)	7½ x	5
1/2 page (double column)	5 x	7½
1/3 page (vertical)	2⅜ x	10¼
1/3 page (double column)	5 x	5
1/6 page	2⅜ x	5

c. Width of column: 2⅜"; double column, 5".
d. Depth of column: 143 lines.
e. Pages are 3 columns, 429 lines to a page.
f. Kind of printing: offset.
g. Publisher assumes no responsibility for materials uncalled for 6 months after date of insertion.

14 ISSUANCE, CLOSING AND CANCELLATION DATES

a. Published nine times a year: January, February, March, April, May, August, September, October, November (monthly except June, July, and December).
b. Issued 1st of month.
c. Closes 1st of month preceding. For example: March issue closes February 1. Mailing begins March 1.
d. Cancellations not accepted after closing date.

15 CIRCULATION INFORMATION

a. Character of circulation: Men and women known to be interested in income opportunities; interested in selling (spare time or full time), starting a business of their own, franchise openings, profitable sidelines. Current respondents to a wide variety of Direct Selling and Start-Your-Own-Business offers.
b. Sources of circulation: names drawn for each issue from carefully selected lists of persons who have answered specific ads.
c. Locality of circulation: national.
d. Rates based upon a circulation of 300,000 copies per issue.
e. Publisher will provide copies of postal receipts upon request.
f. Subscription: 9 issues (one year) for $3.00; single copy, 50¢. Mailed free to selected readers.

16 MISCELLANEOUS

a. Established 1955.
b. Published nine times a year by The Kipen Publishing Corp., 5810 W. Oklahoma Ave., Milwaukee, Wisconsin 53219. Harvey R. Kipen, president.
c. Member: Direct Selling Association; Direct Mail Marketing Association.

SPARE TIME

Money Making Opportunities

RATE CARD NO. 13A

Issued June, 1979 Effective August, 1979 Issue

Published Nine Times A Year

**January
February
March
April
May
August
September
October
November**

Monthly Except June, July and December

300,000 copies per issue mailed to selected readers

5810 West Oklahoma Avenue, Milwaukee, Wisconsin 53219 414/543-8110

Figure 13-1

sold at a cut price to major mail-order advertisers. Other special deals are also made from time to time.

There are discounts for repeated insertions in many magazines.

Theoretically, the price of space also remains the same all year round. But the publishers are well aware that mail-order results drop off drastically in the summer, and many of them offer special summer rate reductions. Three insertions for the price of two is a common inducement to advertise in the poorer months.

Size of the Circulation. Usually you will decide about a magazine without considering the circulation, solely on the basis of the other ads it carries. If, however, your product requires merely huge numbers of readers, examine the ratio of cost-per-line/circulation. Fifty cents per line per 100,000 readers is the going price for totally unspecialized, low-class magazines, good for many mail-order products. Specialized magazines may get as much as $3.20 per line per 100,000 (*Popular Photography*, for example) as of 1974—but astonishingly, this rate has not changed in more than 10 years.

Type of Circulation—Newsstand or Subscription. Magazines whose circulation is almost entirely by subscription distribute almost the same number of copies every month, whereas newsstand magazines sell fewer in summer. The readers of subscription magazines are the same people, month after month. Different people buy at newsstands from month to month, increasing the relevant circulation for the mail-order advertiser who advertises in consecutive months. Still another difference is that returns come in slower for newsstand magazines.

Method of Printing. *Spare Time* is printed letterpress and requires a plate, or you can send copy. *Complete Women's Group* specifies offset, and requires reproduction proofs or material "ready for camera."

Width of Column. The column width determines the layout you must send. But it also affects how much you pay per inch. The wider the column, the fewer the inches of space you require to tell your story.

Editorial Mention. Item 4 on the *Spare Time* card in Figure 13-1 is interesting. It suggests how prevalent is the practice of making deals for editorial mention along with the advertising space purchased.

Advertising Representatives. Many mail-order magazines solicit advertising through independent agents known as publishers' representatives. Work through them whenever possible.

Closing Date and Publication Date. The actual publication date is important because it determines whether the month will be good or poor for mail orders. The lag between closing date and publication date is the period you will have to wait for results from the medium.

If you have a small ad, you can sometimes get the ad into a magazine after the listed closing date. Call the representative to find out if the issue is still open, or send the order in, specifying the exact issue you want to be in, even if it is past the closing date.

EXPLORATORY TESTING OF YOUR OFFER

Even though you know that a competitor is making money with an offer, you can't be sure that your ad will make money until you try it. Even if you run in the same media that he does, you may not make money if (1) your ad is inferior to his, or (2) the market is too small to support both of you.

Ideally you will run your first ad in a medium that (1) is used by your competitor and (2) has a short closing date so that you can get quick results. The time of the year doesn't matter much because you can use the information in Table 13-2 to predict how the ad will do in other months of the year on the basis of any month's results.

How do you find the media in which the competition runs ads? By intensive study of mail-order media, of course.

The competition may not run in any short-closing medium, however, and you still need a quick test. So you will run a test in a short-closing medium anyway. The results will still give you a good idea of how effective your ad is.

The best short-closing media for your product will depend on the offer, of course. If the product is a novelty or style item, the magazine sections of the Sunday papers will be a likely bet. The Sunday magazine sections of *The New York Times, Family Weekly* and the *Chicago Tribune* are the standard test media for such outfits as Spencer Gifts, Sunset House and Walter Drake, *Family Weekly* is a favorite test medium for many mail-order firms. See *Standard Rate & Data* for the names of other Sunday newspaper magazines. The closing date for these magazines is 2 to 4 weeks before publication.

Other kinds of offers will do better in the regular mail-order sections of the Sunday papers, *Capper's Weekly* (which has a special low test-rate), *Grit* or the *National Observer*.

The *National Enquirer* is the favorite testing place for off-color or "private" offers related to sex, hypnotism, patent medicines, etc.

The Sunday papers are extremely discriminating about the ads they accept. They find many mail-order propositions objectionable and refuse to carry them. However, if *The New York Times* accepts your proposition, most of the others will, too. So sometimes it pays to try the *Times* first and convince them. Then you're in.

Your first ads will probably be bigger than later ads because you don't want to risk leaving anything out of the ad that might cause a flop. After you have found a successful combination you can sharpen up and compress your copy, find the most economical layout and generally refine the ad.

Your first ad should be *approximately* the size of the competing ads. In other words, if the competition runs 4-inch, one column ads, you will probably run 3- to 6-inch ads, rather than a full page or a 1-inch ad.

Your exploratory ads will probably be all type and no artwork if the product is a book, or a course or anything else that doesn't absolutely require a picture to sell it. All-type ads can almost always do a *satisfactory* job, though artwork may make the ad much more profitable. Your test media usually will set all-type ads for you without extra charge. Artwork, plates and typographer's type for a fancier ad often cost more than it pays to spend while you are still in the experimental stage.

HOW TO ESTIMATE RESULTS QUICKLY

If you had all the time in the world, mail order could be almost a sure thing for you. At each step along the way you could wait until you were absolutely sure you had enough information before taking the next step. Of course you would always take the risk that just when you were finally about to go ahead full steam, a faster-footed competitor would swing in and pick up all the marbles.

The mail-order professional doesn't wait to proceed until he is sure. He can't afford to. He has to get plenty of ads running in a short time so that he can produce volume and profit. He therefore must take risks by acting on insufficient information.

A person's ability to take risks smartly *and* boldly determines how well he or she will do in mail order. The person with no guts doesn't have to be so shrewd to make money, but will only make peanuts. The person with guts and bad judgment will lose his shirt. Only the operator with courage *and* good judgment can make a pile. In this respect mail order is like all other businesses, but much more so.

This gives an advantage to the beginner who enters the mail-order business in his spare time. The beginner can take much more time between steps than the person who depends on mail order for bread and butter. The extra information you gain by taking plenty of time offsets your lack of knowledge and experience—at least partly—and gives you a fighting chance to make money (a little bit, anyway) while you serve your apprenticeship.

First you must estimate, when a small part of the returns are in, how well an ad will have pulled when *all* the returns have come in. Then you must estimate how well the ad will do in future insertions in the same medium and in other media, based upon the guess in the first part of the estimate.

Now we shall talk about how to guess the total results on the basis of the early results. Remember that, like any other scientific estimate, the estimate must be only approximate. The accuracy of the guess will depend upon the amount of information you have available, and upon how shrewd you are at considering all the pertinent circumstances.

Table 13-1 summarizes the prediction tables given by several writers on the mail-order business. The elapsed time in each case dates from the day the first inquiry is received, except as noted. The numbers indicate the total percentage of responses received by the end of a time period.

Baker says that many of his clients report faster returns than the figures he shows. By my findings he seems very slow, too. Cates's data are old, so don't rely on them very much.

Sumner says that the method of distribution has a particularly large effect on return rates in the women's service-magazine category. He shows these data:[1]

	10 days	30 days	60 days	90 days	1 year
Subscription	32.9	66.5	82.0	88.3	98.4
Newsstand	13.3	51.4	81.7	87.0	97.8

In each of the schedules in Table 13-1, the figure given for "First week" means the number of returns in hand on the seventh day that returns came in.

But things are not so simple. The "first day" can mislead you. Frequently, an employee of a publication writes for the offer weeks before the magazine has been distributed. Many mail-order people believe that when this happens, it is an infallible omen of good results. Maybe, but it certainly fouls up your prediction schedules. You can ignore returns that come in prior to magazine distribution. But remember that

Table 13-1   Time Rates of Returns—Cumulative

Media	1st wk.	2d wk.	4th wk.	8th wk.	26th wk.	52d wk.
TV						
Baker[2]	82	96	99	100		
Radio						
Baker[2]	80	94	99	100		
Daily newspaper						
Grant[3]	90					
Baker[2]	42	78	95	98	100	
Cates[4]	70	95	99	100		
Stone[5]	74	90	96			
Sunday news supplement						
Baker[2]	35	65	79	89	99	100
Graham[6]			(33% in first 4 days)			
Sumner[1]			(50% in first 4 days)			
Stone[5]			(90% by end of third week)			
Sunday predates (preprints)						
Graham[6]			(50% in first 10 days)			
Sunday comics						
Stone[5]			(90% by end of second week)			
Weeklies						
Baker[2]	21	41	65	82	96	100
Graham[6]	33					
Simon (H. K.)[7]	30					
Cates[4]	41	78	96	100		
Segal (Alexander)[8]			(20% in first 2 days, 33% in first 3 days, 50% in first 4 days)			
Biweeklies						
Baker[2]	15	30	60	77	93	100
Fraternal monthlies						
Baker[2]	7	28	61	83	99	100
Simon (J. L.)[9]		35	67			
Monthly magazine shopping section						
Baker[2]	7	33	65	85	100	
General monthly magazine						
Grant[3]			60	75	96	
Baker[2]	5	18	45	68	91	100
Graham[6]			(50% in first month)			
Kestnbaum[10]	11	35	55	81		
All-newsstand monthlies						
Baker[2]	4	13	26	57	87	100
Segal (Alexander)[8]	25		(50% in 30 days)			
All-newsstand bimonthlies						
Baker[2]	1	4	12	36	80	100
3d-class direct mail						
Segal (Alexander)[8]	33	66	80	91		100
3d-class direct mail to business firms						
Stone[11]	49	81	(87% in third week)			

the distribution date varies from month to month by as much as 10 days. Remember also that some magazines mail their subscription copies over a period of many days. The magazines that go to direct salespeople (*Spare Time,* for example) mail over a 15-day period.

Returns vary by *type of product.* John Moran asserts that the higher the unit of sale, the slower the returns,[12] but I've seen no statistical evidence of this.

Returns may vary by *size of ad.* I have observed that classified returns come in faster than display ads. A possible explanation: The bigger the ad, the easier it seems to be to clip it out and save it.

I'd suggest placing little faith in a prediction based on other people's schedules until you reach the point that should produce 50 percent of the returns. Once you have run ads for your own product, you will have the most accurate information for your purposes. The second time you run an ad in a magazine, you should know within the first week or two how well the ad will pull. Another good trick is to compare the highest-return days of the two insertions. This high day will occur fairly early for non-newsstand media, usually. The comparison is usually not as accurate as a comparison of several weeks' totals, because it is based on relatively few returns. But it avoids the problem of when the "first day" is.

WHERE TO ADVERTISE

Are Your Chores Done? Long ago you should have written to every mail-order magazine for a sample and a rate card. You should also have made a card file containing an entry for each magazine. The card should show how much mail-order advertising the magazine carries and the kinds of products advertised there. Soon you'll be using that file very hard, so check that it is complete.

Which Categories of Magazines Will Make Money for You?

The general answer to picking categories is the same as the answer to everything else in mail order: Go where the competition is, because that's where the profit is. Read through your sample copies again, looking for the ads of your competitor.

Here is an illustration of how being a copycat can help you and why you should not fear the presence of competition in media: As I was writing the first edition of this book, I was in the midst of developing a correspondence course for the mail-order market. My thinking was as follows:

> Right now I'm in no rush to market the course. One competitor has come a little way into the market. And I am glad to see him, because he is thoroughly professional and will do much of the job for me. He will test out media and product offers, and find out just how much of a market there is. If he does very well, I'll speed up my project. If he does poorly, and gets completely out of the market, I'll take stock again—perhaps run a few tests—with an eye to dropping the project. If I didn't want to write this course for the fun of it, I would have waited to start it until I saw how the competition did.

The rest of this section discusses the situation when you can't just follow your competition—either because your product is somewhat new or because your competitor hasn't developed his media schedule fully enough. (Be suspicious, though. The competitor is smart, too, and likes profit. If the competitor is not advertising widely, there may be good reason for it.)

Look at the mail-order magazines on the newsstand and elsewhere. Quite a few, aren't there? Some will produce a profit on your particular offer; some will not. Your problem is to find out which will and which won't.

Testing the magazines one by one would be difficult and time-consuming. What you can do, instead, is to consider the various *categories* of magazines, one by one, using one magazine to test a category.

When we talk about categories, we shall use the *Standard Rate & Data* classification.

First you select the categories in which your offer has the best chance of success, using your judgment. Then you run your ad in the best prospective medium within each category. (That is, within each category you would probably pick the medium with the most mail-order advertising.)

After the results are in, you will know which categories *will* work for you. Then you will place ads in every magazine in the categories which test out profitably. You will probably also place ads in a few of the magazines in more questionable categories, and if they pull well, you can then try the others.

For the time being, place no more ads in those categories that did not show a profit. But don't forget about them entirely. You may later come back to one or more of them successfully, either because you have improved your copy, or because the magazine you tested was not representative of the rest of the group, or because your original test went astray by chance.

Remember that you cannot infallibly choose categories for your product by the names or readership of the categories. Men's products have been sold profitably in women's magazines, and vice versa.

In each category, some magazines will produce better for you than will others. And it makes sense to try the best prospects first, because that way if your test is not successful, you will lose as little as possible. You can't know in advance which magazine in each category will be best for your product. But as a general guideline, it makes sense to try the magazine that carries the most mail-order advertising. In addition, here is Stone's list of the best prospects in a few important general groupings, as of a few years ago:[13]

DUAL AUDIENCE:

General and entertainment—*TV Guide*
News—*Time*
Intellectual—*Saturday Review*
Ethnic—*Ebony* (choice of pilot publications depends upon specific ethnic categories desired)

MEN'S:

General—*Esquire*
Entertainment—*Penthouse*

WOMEN'S PUBLICATIONS:

General—*Redbook*
Fashion—*Mademoiselle*

SPECIAL INTEREST PILOT PUBLICATIONS:

Dressmaking and needlework—*McCall's Needlework*
Fraternal and clubs—*Elk's*
Music—*High Fidelity*

During this second stage of testing, if you wish to test the largest magazines, you should consider running in only one of their *regional editions,* to reduce the possible loss of the test. If your product has any regional appeal (for example, camping in the West), by all means test that region. But you should recognize that aside from special regional advantages, your test is likely to produce somewhat poorer results than will running in the entire national edition, because regional ads tend to be placed in the back of the magazine where ads produce less well than in the front. And regional ads cost 10 to 50 percent more per thousand readers than the national rate.

All decisions described above should be considered in the light of seasonal variation, of course.

Most of the time you will stick to media on our list. There may be times when you have a very specialized product (i.e., by definition, a product that appeals only to a narrow group of people). In that case you may successfully go into magazines that carry little or no mail order. An example: Electroplating kits appeal to the hot-rod set, and they are sold successfully from some automobile magazines that carry no other mail-order advertising.

What About Newspapers?

In some countries, such as Great Britain, newspapers are the main display mail-order medium. But in the United States, newspapers have only been a very secondary medium, except for Sunday supplements. Recently, however, Media Service Corporation of Cleveland has announced a plan to reduce the cost and increase the flexibility of national newspapers' mail-order campaigns. And it is certainly fast-acting. If you're interested, you'll have to check on this.

Do All Magazines in the Same Category Pull the Same?

In general you can expect magazines in the same category to be more like one another than like magazines in other categories. But there can still be great differences among magazines that are listed together and that seem similar.

Here is an unusual (and perhaps unbelievable) example of different results in the same category. These are the results of the same ad in three similar salespeople's magazines, as reported by publication Z, of course:

Publication	Ad cost	No. orders	Volume
X	$520.00	106	$1,002.50
Y	487.50	88	511.50
Z	422.00	1,132	7,772.05

When prospecting for new media, or shopping among media for the best magazine for your test, keep an eye on the cost-per-agate-line per 100,000 readers. For many kinds of offers, you want just circulation and more circulation. One dollar per 200,000 circulation is a basic, low-line rate.

But don't forget to look at the width of the column. A wide column means you get more advertising space per inch.

For low-class magazines especially, space is generally bought through publishers' representatives rather than directly from the magazines. It is preferable to work through them in order to gain their goodwill, advice and assistance.

WHEN TO ADVERTISE

Remember this principle first and always: The best months for your product may run entirely contrary to the general findings for most products. Of course you won't be enough of a darn fool to advertise bathing suits in the winter. But other products have less obvious, but just as significant, seasons that have nothing to do with general buying trends. Every month in the year is the best month for some types of offers.

Whether or not your product is the gift type will affect its seasonality. Gifts hit a peak before Christmas, of course. Products that do not serve as gifts don't do so well just before Christmas. And money-making offers do wonderfully well in January.

Just as soon as you have seasonal data on your product, use your own data as a guide rather than refer to the general results. Your own data are always much more accurate for your purposes than anyone else's data can be.

Table 13-2 compiles data from several reports that rank the months for general display advertising from best to worst.

I hope you're a little confused at the differences between the various rankings of the months. Your confusion should teach you this: While there are some general seasonal principles, eventually your decision must depend upon your own product and your experience with that product.

The frequency of appearance of newspaper preprint inserts, which are expensive and on which the advertiser usually keeps very close‘ records, tells us something about the amount of response in various seasons. Stone kept track of the number of inserts, one year. In January there were six preprint inserts, in February six, March two, April none, May none, June one, July seven, August five, September seven, October fourteen, November six, and December one.[14]

Over the years, International Correspondence Schools has amassed a wealth of advertising statistics. Their seasonal fluctuation is consid-

Table 13-2 Month Rankings for Mail-Order Advertising

Month	Baker[a] (mostly novelties, probably)	Moran[b]	Fate Magazines[c] (book advertisers)	Stone[d] (direct mail)	Grant[e] (mostly money-making offers, probably)	O. E. McIntyre, Inc.[f] (from magazine and book publishers)	Stone[g] (space advertising)
January	3(96)	3	1(100)	1	1 (100)	1 (100)	2 (98)
February	4(92)	1	9(76)	3	24(98)	3 (85)	1 (100)
March	7(83)	2	8(77)	2	44(96)	8 (78)	4 (91)
April	8(79)	7	4(80)	6	104(67)	10 (71)	8 (80)
May	9(69)	9	12(65)	10	12 (58)	11 (70)	10 (77)
June	12(60)	10	11(68)	11	9 (71)	12 (69)	12 (71)
July	11(65)	11	5(79)	12	8 (75)	64(80)	10 (77)
August	9(69)	8	3(82)	9	64(83)	2 (86)	64(83)
September	4(92)	5	6(78)	5	24(98)	44(81)	10 (77)
October	1(100)	4	2(87)	7	44(96)	9 (76)	4 (91)
November	1(100)	6	6(78)	4	64(83)	44(81)	4 (91)
December	6(87)	12	10(74)	8	104(67)	64(80)	64(83)

Note: Index numbers for relative pull are given in parentheses. Highest = 100.

[a]From Robert A. Baker, *Help Yourself to Better Mail Order*, Printers' Ink Publishing Co., Inc., New York, 1953, p. 71.

[b]From John Moran, *The Mail Order Business*, MBA Business Associates, Syracuse, N.Y., 1949, page not known.

[c]From *Fate* Magazines, promotional literature, undated.

[d]From Robert Stone, *Successful Direct Mail Advertising and Selling*, Prentice-Hall, Englewood Cliffs, N.J., 1955, p. 59.

[e]From Paul Grant, L. W. Mail Order Survey, page not known.

[f]From O. E. McIntrye, Inc., "Best Seasons for Direct Mail," *Media/Scope*, September 1963, p. 27.

[g]From Robert Stone, "Where to Start, How to Test, in Direct Response Magazine Ads," *Advertising Age*, Oct. 22, 1973, p. 119.

erably greater than indicated in any list shown above. International Correspondence Schools' advertising boss has said that "during the best month of the year our inquiry cost is one-half that of the worst month of the year."

Yet International Correspondence Schools advertises the year round. Why? Because they and the other large correspondence schools are not pure mail-order organizations. Their direct-mail literature is not expected to close the sale. The inquiry names are sent on to salesmen in the various localities, and it is they who close the sale.

Salespeople have to eat and to work, summer as well as winter. So even though summer inquiries cost twice as much to obtain, the correspondence schools are willing to pay through the nose anyway, in order to give the salespeople work year round, and hence maintain their organization intact. (But don't weep for the correspondence schools. They make it up in winter.)

The extent of the seasonal fluctuation also depends on the type of circulation a magazine has. The more copies it distributes by subscription, the less we expect the mail-order sales to fluctuate from month to month. Like readers of subscription magazines, readers of newsstand magazines purchase less by mail during the summer. But the *number* of newsstand readers *also* drops during the summer, whereas the number of *subscription* readers stays much the same.

Remember that we are *not* talking about sales in *calendar months*. We are talking about total returns to issues that appear in particular months. It is easier to understand why May is so relatively poor and August so relatively good if you understand that the May issue is in readers' hands in June, July, etc. (the summer doldrums). The August issue has much life left in the lively fall. The fact that direct mail does worse in June and July than in May supports this reasoning.

However, my own data suggest that the general seasonal patterns shown above indicate something about calendar-month sales as well as about issue months. In other words, May is a poorer calendar month than September, which is just as summery.

Not only the seasons of nature can affect the pattern of sales. Human events can make a dent, too. During the first month of the Lindberg kidnapping, returns were reported to slump 30 to 70 percent. Pearl Harbor also reduced sales volume drastically. There isn't anything you can do in advance about cataclysms. But understanding their effect can help you interpret your test results.

It would make sense for magazines to drop their advertising rates during the summer, and some do. (You will get offers of one-third off for summer issues.) But too few magazines show the good sense to drop their rates, or perhaps they believe it is important to be a one-price store.

Effect of Size of Ad on Repetition. A small ad can be rerun more frequently than can a big ad. Schwab estimates that a second insertion of a full-page ad within 30 to 90 days of the original insertion will pull 25 to 30 percent less than the original insertion. The third insertion within a short period will drop to 45 to 50 percent of the original insertion. Schwab claims that a wait of 6 months to a year is required before the repeat insertion will do as well as the first insertion.[15] Note that these estimates apply to *identical* advertisements and not to different copy.

The same *small* ad can run month after month in *some* media and continue to be profitable. However, even classified ads can suffer a dropoff, too. I ran a classified ad in *Western Farm Life* in two consecutive issues of the little all-subscription twice-monthly. The second insertion pulled just 80 percent of the first insertion. A third insertion a month later pulled less than 50 percent of the first insertion. A fourth insertion 2 weeks later pulled 37 percent of the first insertion. Until I stopped them, subsequent insertions took a beating, ranging from 32 percent to 4 percent of the original insertion. We were bucking a seasonal trend, but the trend could account for only a small part of the effect.

However, the same ad in the *Saturday Review* ran almost indefinitely, week after week, changing only its classification. After an initial not-too-sharp dropoff that coincided with the seasonal trend (I can't estimate the dropoff accurately because there was a copy change), the ad hit a plateau and pulled the same gratifying results week after week.

Neither *Western Farm Life* nor *Saturday Review* is typical of classified sections. *Western Farm Life* is all-subscription, twice a month. *Saturday Review* is also almost all subscription, biweekly. Therefore, their results are not samples of classified advertising generally. The differences *between* them might be explained by the greater amount of classified carried by *Saturday Review*.

It is easy to understand why big ads should suffer greater dropoff than small ads, if we consider the difference in the number of people who "notice" the ads. About 4 percent of the readership of *Popular Mechanics* will "notice" a 1-inch ad, while anywhere from 20 to 60 percent will "notice" a full-page ad. The second month it runs, the small ad can put itself before the eyes of 96 percent of the prior audience who never saw the ad before, and almost 4 percent will again "notice" it (assuming no change in readership). But the big ad has used up a very substantial chunk of its audience.

Furthermore, except for completely subscription magazines, far more than 4 percent of the readers of any issue will not have *read* the previous issue. (But keep in mind that the people who "notice" an ad are not a random sample of the readership. Rather, they are those people who have the highest perception for a product and the greatest likelihood to buy.)

Subscription versus Newsstand Circulation. It stands to reason that if exactly the same people see every issue of a magazine, the dropoff must be greater than if there is a turnover of readership. The more newsstand copies sold, the greater the turnover, and hence the less the dropoff.

This effect will be greater upon big ads than upon small ones, of course.

Number of Media Used. The pool of magazine readers in the United States is huge. But it is not limitless. If you insert a big enough ad often enough in enough magazines, you can certainly reach the point where the returns will decrease. This is akin to the saturation concept of general advertisers.

It is unlikely that the returns to a *small* ad will be much affected by the number of magazines in which it runs.

Competition. Competitors move in if they sniff the pungent aroma of a golden goose. The competitors can kill your goose if they deluge the media with ads. Their potential customers are your potential customers, too.

But the appearance of competition does not automatically mean that you must fold your tent and quit. Sometimes competitors will try to enter your business, then fail and leave you in peace; this may happen because they cannot learn to operate as efficiently as you do, or because they do not discover some essential aspect of the business (see the example of the collection stickers). Another reason why the arrival of competitors may not be a disaster is that they may not affect your sales as badly as one would expect. For example, one firm I have worked with introduced an old but never mail-ordered product to the market. I did not believe it would succeed—and it did, anyway, going from nothing to $1.4 million yearly gross and $160,000 yearly profit in the first 5 years. Then, when the firm did succeed, I worried about competition. And competition did enter and has remained. But the effect on the response to this firm's ads has not been disastrous, even when a competitor's ad ran on the same page.

In most mail-order situations, moreover, you are competing mostly against inattention and inertia in your audience rather than against other advertisers.

Fads and Repeat Items. Some products are of interest once in the lifetime of a customer. A book on karate is an example. Other products are repeat sellers—clothes, for example. Still a third type are products that people are likely to get interested in only at special times in their lives—specialized correspondence courses are one such item.

It is more likely that you can "force" the market for karate books than for clothes or correspondence courses. And once you have forced the market, it takes a couple of years for the market to recover. Products that you can "force" are like fad products. This is the only possible explanation for the waves of saturation ads for such commodities as karate books that roll in for a year or two, then disappear for a while. (However, many propositions that disappear drop out because the government muscles them out, and not because the market is temporarily exhausted.)

How Profitable Is the Ad? Just as with classified ads, you should repeat a *very* profitable display ad more often than a borderline ad—despite the continuing drop in returns to the profitable ad. As we proved in the classified discussion, you will almost always make more total profit by running two insertions at less than maximum results than you will by running one insertion that gets you maximum results.

Not only will your own profit be greater, but you have a better chance of keeping competition out if you run your ad more frequently. The competition may be attracted by apparent success as shown by your frequency of insertions. But when the competitors run a test ad, the results will be lower under the frequent-insertion plan, just as yours are. And so the results appear less attractive to them, and they are not so likely to continue competing.

What about running *different* ads instead of the same ad, in an attempt to foil the dropoff effect? If you run full-page ads, it certainly pays you to follow the example of such experienced advertisers as International Correspondence Schools, who run several different ads each season. But the advertiser who runs small ads or classified ads will find it too costly and too time-consuming to work with several ads. Instead, you will run the same ad at such intervals as you find profitable.

Customary repetition intervals for small ads are (1) every issue in monthlies that are largely sold on newsstands; (2) not quite so often in all-subscription magazines; and (3) every month or every 2 months in Sunday supplements.

Shryer gave us the sound rule of thumb that the interval between insertions should be long enough for the earlier ad to pay out its break-even costs. This is on the conservative side.

Before we leave the subject of repetition, here are a couple of inspirational notes:

- The full-page Sherwin Cody ad pulled 225,000 inquiries, 11,000 orders and $328,500 in a 10-year period. This ad has never really been changed in over 30 years, though many ads have been tested against it.[16]

- La Salle Extension University's basic 1-inch ad occupied $300,000 worth of space and produced $3 million in sales over 25 years. (Several years after those figures were collected, the ad is still going strong.)[17]

The Display Advertisement

What Almost Every Good Ad Contains • *Appeal and Copy* • *Layout and Artwork*

You must either learn mail-order copywriting from experience plus one of the top-notch books referred to earlier, or use an agency. There are no short cuts to the vitally important art of creating ads. That's why this book makes no attempt to teach you how. But we will provide some facts and figures to aid your judgment.

WHAT ALMOST EVERY GOOD AD CONTAINS

Here are some *facts* about mail-order ads and their selling power:

1. *The power of a single word can be incredible.* In an eleven-word classified ad, the offer of a "book" or "manual" pulled nearly twice as many dollar bills as did the offer of "instructions" (as mentioned earlier).

2. *Never write a classified ad without a guarantee in it. And never forget to play up the guarantee in a display ad.* The extra word may up your cost almost 10 percent in a classified ad, but in my experience it ups the returns perhaps 20 percent—even when no one uses the guarantee.

Don't be afraid of refund demands even if the product is information that can be read and then returned—as long as the merchandise is good and customers don't feel gypped. Charles Atlas offered to return the first payment after 7 days, or to return payment in full plus 6 percent after completion, to dissatisfied customers. Only 1 percent are reported to ask for their money back.

On the other hand, I know of a firm that sold a shoddy money-making manual for $2 and offered a money-back guarantee. The 20 percent who wanted refunds made the operation a losing venture.

3. *Always offer the customer a chance to trade up* to "deluxe" models and/or an opportunity to purchase accessory merchandise. Schwab quotes these results of comparative split-run tests:[1]

a. Choice of three types of products did better than one model by 19.7 percent and 30.4 percent in two tests.

b. Choice of six did 52.6 percent better than choice of four, and 261.8 percent better than one model.

c. Choice of two did 52.9 percent better in number of orders and 25 percent better in dollars than one model.

Maybe the effectiveness of choices is that they lead people to ask, "Which one?" rather than "Should I?" A classic closer of face-to-face salesmen is "Which model would you like?" or "What size, please?" However, such speculation is unnecessary, even though it is fun. What counts is the oft-demonstrated useful effect of offering the choice.

4. *These are ways to encourage quick action:*[2]

Time limit

Limited supply

Prices about to rise

Combination offers

Cut-price leaders

Copy technique

Incentives to quick action get more total orders. If the potential customer waits awhile, his desire to buy very often cools off.

If you use any of these devices, keep them truthful or the Federal Trade Commission may get you.

5. *Harold Preston gives us this quote on colorful language:*[3]

Victor O. Schwab, a leading authority on mail selling, advises you to use words in your headline that the public doesn't expect, "words that *stop* the casual reader—startle him—grip his eyes and his interest."

Mr. Schwab cites such words as "Pushover," "Ain't," "Don't Belly-Ache," "Scatter-brain," "Weasel," "Hog," "Skunk," as eye-arresters that substantially increased the returns from advertising in which they were used. Words like "Bunk," "Bosh," "Gee," "Phooey" are in the same class. . . . By changing the conventional salutation of a letter to "Yousah, Yousah," I tripled the returns of a subscription campaign.

6. *Use as many testimonials as you can.* People must believe before they'll buy.

Testimonials are a powerful means of inducing belief. If you wait around for completely unsolicited testimonials, you'll be gray before you have a handful of testimonials, even if you're giving gold nuggets away free. You can obtain "unsolicited" testimonials by writing to your customers some time after the sale, saying that you appreciate their patronage and asking if you can help them further. This kind of courtesy and conversation stimulates some of them to write you chatty letters in which they will say nice things about your product.

But remember that you can't stretch the truth by using testimonials. Any statement in a quoted testimonial must be as true as if you yourself make the statement. Recheck Chapter 6 on what you can and can't do with testimonials. (While I'm talking about testimonials, I'd appreciate hearing from any of you who are willing to write me comments—even criticism. It won't be for quotation, unless you so indicate, but rather to help me when I again write about mail order. You can address me in care of the *publisher.* As I said in the preface to this edition, the many letters I received from the previous editions have been a great satisfaction to me. And I have been able to help some of the people who wrote me about their mail-order problems. So I will welcome hearing from you.)

Here is evidence of the importance of belief and trust from a split-run test: Using an unknown firm name brought in 77 orders to each 100 orders pulled by the identical ad *signed* by a well-known company.[4]

APPEAL AND COPY

"Appeal" is what advertising men call the basic selling idea of an ad. If the ad emphasizes how the product will make money for the purchaser, money-making is its appeal. If the ad suggests that the product will make a woman devastatingly beautiful, the appeal is sex. And so on.

The best way to pick an appeal is the same as the best way to pick a product and a media schedule. Use the same appeal as your successful competitor—at least to start with.

Gather all the information you can on the words and ideas other people use to sell the product. Before I sat down to write copy for a book on hypnotism, I not only read the competitor's ads, but also examined hypnotists' listings and displays in the classified phone directory, read book jackets and pored over hypnotism catalogs and brochures. I jotted down every selling idea I could find in all that reading and used it for my material.

Following the competition will take you a long way, but to make the most money, you must also be a leader. Like any other kind of a leader, however, you must not leap too far from where the pack is at any one time. Instead, you make changes gradually on the basis of your analysis and your hunches about which appeals can be emphasized. Of course, there are occasional exceptions to this rule—the stories of Al Sloan and Joe Sugarman that were told earlier in the book. But such exceptions do not disprove the rule that most successful mail-order operations develop from well-established trade practices.

The only way to determine which appeal is best for a product is to test. Testing methods are described in Chapter 18.

The headline "How to Fix Cars—quickly, easily, right" sold 20 percent more books than exactly the same headline with the word "Repair" in place of "Fix"[5]—which already was a very successful ad.

Schwab's split-run tests for his clients produced these results:[6]

- "Reducing" did 138 percent better than "Relieving Nervous Tension," and 266 percent better than "Improving Your English." (However, this was a test of three *different books* as well as different appeals, which makes the test less conclusive.)

- "Sex" did 211 percent better than "Succeed in Business," and 223 percent better than "Selection of Vocation."

- "Newness" improved an ad 75.4 percent and 79 percent in two tests.

How to Qualify Prospects

To "qualify" prospects means to weed out poor prospects who cost you money for catalogs and direct mail, but at the same time to keep the attention of the good prospects.

Here is a list of ways Moran suggests for qualifying prospects:[7]

1. Make headline selective.
2. Reduce emphasis on free offer in headline and copy.
3. Charge for booklet.
4. Ask for age, sex, occupation, etc.
5. Make it obvious that booklet is a sales piece.
6. Show that product has limited use to a special few.
7. Eliminate coupon.
8. Insert stipulations, restrictions, etc., in coupon.
9. Show the price.

LAYOUT AND ARTWORK

Coupons

A coupon is a crucial part of almost every mail-order ad that is big enough to contain one. The only time the coupon is omitted is when the advertiser wants to qualify prospects very strictly, and not make it too easy for them to respond.

Notice that most advertisers who run even a 4-inch ad find it profitable to spend *one-quarter of the advertising cost* just for the coupon area. That's how important the coupon is in increasing response!

The coupon makes it "easy to order." The prospect doesn't have to think what to say or how to write it. All he does is fill in his name and address, and perhaps check a box or two. That's why 70 to 85 percent of responders will use the coupon.

The coupon suggests *action*, and it also seems to suggest getting something free or at a bargain rate. The coupon itself attracts many readers to the ad. Many years ago general advertisers suffered a fad of testing their copy by couponing ads for free booklets and other giveaways. They soon quit the practice when they found that the rate of response depended as much on the size of the coupon as it did on the excellence of the copy.

Some advertisers use a coupon that is too small for anyone to use. Nevertheless, it has much of the effect of a coupon in increasing response and it saves space. Inquirers write their names and addresses in the margin of the page next to the coupon.

Some advertisers use a heavy dashed border around the entire ad. "Tear Out and Mail Today" at the bottom of the ad is also used frequently. The whole ad looks like a coupon even though there is no room for name or address. I have found that this device gives a good boost to small ads composed entirely of type.

The list below is Henry Musselman's checklist of important items in the coupon for a *direct-mail piece*.[8] The list is just as valid for display ads.

Leave room for complete name and address.
Require only a fill-in for sizes, colors, etc.
State the proposition clearly.
Tell prospect just what to do.
Convenient size and shape.
Keyed to denote source.
Re-state the guarantee.
Stand out from rest of ad.
If premium is offered, the offer is included in coupon.

In full-page ads, put the coupon at the outside bottom of the page. Some advertisers who drive terrifically hard for inquiries—e.g., the Duraclean rug-cleaning franchise ad—seem to have success with making the coupon the dominant element in the ad's layout—either at the top, as shown in Figure 14-1, or by turning the coupon sideways, or by similar gimmicks to make the coupon stand out visually. (In his recent best seller, David Ogilvy triumphantly trumpets as a recent Madison Avenue discovery this well-known mail-order device.[9])

Points of Interest about Layout and Art

Readers usually pay more attention to editorial matter than to advertising, and they have more faith in it. The "reading notice" tries to take advantage of that fact by making the ad look like the adjoining editorial columns. The headline must also look like "news." Figure 14-3 illustrates a reading notice.

Some media charge extra for "readers." Others do not accept them because they regard them as undesirable.

Figure 14-1 Example of a prominent coupon.

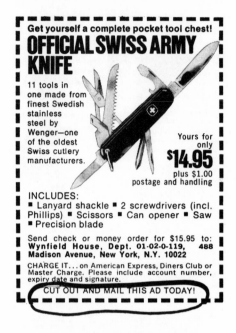

Figure 14-2 Example of saving coupon space.

General advertising strives for an esthetic quality in advertising, and perhaps wisely so. The general advertiser aims at a huge audience with whom its reputation is precious. The general advertiser therefore cannot afford to irritate its potential customers with unpleasant ads.

But mail-order firms have different requirements for an ad. Many successful mail-order ads look crowded, vulgar and garish—called "buckeye" by the trade. The buckeye format creates "excitement" and uses space to the utmost.

Split-run tests comparing a "busy" layout to a balanced and artistically unified layout showed that the "busy" layout did 111 percent better, 68 percent better and 30 percent better than the artistic layout, in three tests.[10] (But Bruck Holocek tells me that in the hobby field, busy ads do not do best, in his experience.)

Baker points out that the "busy" layout technique uses lots of gimmicky "spot art": scissors on top of the coupon, a hand pointing at the guarantee, one-sentence claims thrown all around the page.[11] Figure 14-4 is a good example.

So—don't let any "fine artist" sell you a bill of goods about how your ad is ugly and should be beautified. You're liable to find that as artistic satisfaction increases, profits sink.

Artwork can often be obtained cheaply and efficiently from "clip books" that contain a variety of standard artwork elements. One such book is *Instant Art for Mail Order Operations,* sold for $15 (1979 prices) by Crain Books, 740 Rush Street, Chicago, Ill. 60611.

et to Be Feb. 3

k at Council Event.

ther-
ly re-
Day
67th
the
Feb.
will
aken
meet-
p.m.
hool.
from
peech
her
illikin
d re-
grees
ovid-

ed by The Mothersingers.

Committees for the banquet are:

Arrangements, Mrs. P a u l Bricker and Mrs. Tracy Stevenson; program, Mrs. Walter Chaplin and Mrs. Harold Walker; decorations, Mr. and Mrs. Thomas C. Buschbach; reservations, Mr. and Mrs. Robert Jacob; program books, Mrs. George Anderson, Mrs. Donald Cupp, Mrs. Morris McCarty, Mrs. Richard Schmall, Mrs. Richard Spitz and Mrs. Murray Outlaw, and publicity, Mrs. Roy Michael Jr. and Mrs. Willis Busch.

General chairman for the affair is Mrs. Joseph Grimsey.

Shrinks Piles Without Surgery —Relieves Pain

al) —
has
ance
ty to
itch-
hout

after
rove-
veri-
tions.
ptly.
ving
r re-
place.
all —
nain-
ctor's
nued
nths!
hor-
able
tate-

ments as "Piles have ceased to be a problem!" And among these sufferers were a very wide variety of hemorrhoid conditions, some of 10 to 20 years' standing.

All this, without the use of narcotics, anesthetics or astringents of any kind. The secret is a new healing substance (Bio-Dyne®) — the discovery of a world-famous research institution. Already, Bio-Dyne is in wide use for healing injured tissue on all parts of the body.

This new healing substance is offered in *suppository* or *ointment form* called *Preparation H®*. Ask for individually sealed convenient Preparation H Suppositories or Preparation H Ointment with special applicator. Preparation H is sold at all drug counters.

---

been delivered.

school all this week.

It was suggested that those parents interested in seeing the exhibit might go a little early to the PTA meeting scheduled for 7:30 p.m. Thursday, or stop by at their convenience during the week.

Mrs. Fred Omer, dance teacher, will hold a demonstration class at 3:30 p.m. Friday at the school. This will follow the procedure of a regular class. Parents are invited to attend to see what their children are learning to do.

Mrs. Johanna Braunfeld currently is making recordings of the German speech of her pupils. Parents are to be notified later of a time when they can hear those recordings and have an evaluation of their children's progress.

All the classes have met since October under the supervision of a Yankee Ridge PTA committee headed by Mrs. Bruce McCormick.

Could This Be You?

Well, probably not, but thousands of such accidents do occur every year. And when they do the accident insurance coverage that you have comes in mighty handy. Courier subscribers* receive free extra Travel & Pedestrian Accident Insurance coverage underwritten by The Washington National Insurance Company with their subscription Accidental death benefits ranging from $500 to $11,000. And it costs you no more than the subscription price of the Courier.

*Except students living on campus.

You're Automatically Insured

Champaign-Urbana COURIER

---

the quality of patient care."

Why Can't You Remember

A noted publisher in Chicago reports there is a simple technique for acquiring a powerful memory which can pay you real dividends in both business and social advancement and works like magic to give you added poise, necessary self-confidence and greater popularity.

According to this publisher, many people do not realize how much they could influence others simply by remembering accurately everything they see, hear, or read. Whether in business, at social functions or even in casual conversations with new acquaintances, there are ways in which you can dominate each situation by your ability to remember.

To acquaint the readers of this paper with the easy-to-follow rules for developing skill in remembering anything you choose to remember, the publishers have printed full details of their self-training method in a new book, "Adventures in Memory," which will be mailed free to anyone who requests it. No obligation. Simply send your request to: Memory Studies, 835 Diversey Parkway, Dept. AO31, Chicago, 14, Ill. A postcard will do.
ADV.

Figure 14-3   Example of a reading notice.

147

Figure 14-4 Example of a "busy" ad.

Special inserts into magazines cost more than ordinary full-page ads, but some are worth the added freight. According to Stanley Rapp, reply cards increase returns by 3 to 6 times for some advertisers, 2 to 3 times for others of his clients (probably including record clubs).[12]

About *color* in ads: Split runs indicated that color outpulled black and white by 182 percent, 83 percent, 224 percent, and 26 percent for a *home-decoration* product.[13] So for *that* product, color was worth the usual 50 percent surcharge. But a marriage book would undoubtedly not get the same benefits from color as a home-decoration product.

HOW BIG SHOULD AN AD BE?

Mail-order advertisers figure the size of an ad in this way: They increase the size of their ads in each medium until a further size increase would cost more than the revenue it would produce.

There are some types of mail-order products that *demand* large space. For example, a 4-inch ad may pull *more* than 4 times as much as a 1-inch ad for *some* products. This usually occurs when it is impossible to tell a full advertising story in less than the 4 inches. Four inches may be the "natural" space unit for that product. A half-page may be the "natural" unit for other products. The famous Charles Atlas course found that the ad had to be at least one column by 98 lines (7 inches) in order to show Atlas' picture effectively. Small space was no good for that offer.

Generally speaking, however, the published evidence is overwhelming that increasing the size of an ad will *not* increase the returns in proportion. For almost every mail-order advertiser who cares to use them, classified ads are far and away the most productive medium— often 3 times as productive, dollar for dollar, as the most effective display space. A full-page ad will practically never pull twice as many orders as a half-page ad. La Salle Correspondence University has never found *any* display ad that performs as well as its thirty-year-old 1-inch ad.

Seventy years ago Shryer found, when selling his correspondence course on starting and managing a collection agency, that the cost of inquiries went like this:

Classified 5 lines	30¢	per inquiry
7-line display	53¢	per inquiry
16-line display	70¢	per inquiry
56-line display	76¢	per inquiry
half-page display	92¢	per inquiry

In many cases the five-line classified ad made more *total profit* than did the fifty-six-line ad in the same medium.[14]

This effect still holds in our day, and for many kinds of products. An agency expert who serves many mail-order clients writes: "Many small space users find their most efficient use of space ranges between 28 and 50 lines."[15]

But it *is* economical and rational to increase the size of the ad as long as the profit from the increased orders is greater than the increased cost of the space. If a quarter-page costs $400 and returns *net* a profit of $200 on sales of $800, a half-page ad *may* net a profit of $250 on sales of $1,400. If that is the case, it pays you to run the half-page ad.

The advertisers who run large ads are those who pull very success-fully in small space. They are the advertisers who (by definition) face a large potential market. The large ad demands that a large percentage of the medium's audience have an active interest in the product.

John Caples wrote:[16]

If the reader of a publication does not have a corn, your full-page ad, no matter how attractive, will not sell him a corn remedy. On the other hand, if the reader does have a corn that is bothering him, he will be stopped by the one-word headline, CORNS, in a small ad. Since you cannot predict when the readers' corns will be troublesome, you are better off with a small ad in every issue of a publication than with a big ad once in a while.

And Robert Baker ventured to qualify the relationship, saying: "If the item is of genuine interest to 25 percent or more of a particular medium's readership, you can effectively use as much as a full page. But if your item is of limited interest, probably you should confine yourself to small units."[17]

Mail-order advertisers cannot increase their total profit by running more small ads instead of fewer larger ones. There are always too few media that will pay out a profit, and the trick is to use each of them to the limit. That is why, unlike general advertisers, the mail-order person does not fix a budget and then spread it over the various media. Instead, you will keep spending as long as it is profitable to do so. If medium A will make more with a big ad than a small one, then the big ad will run in that medium. That decision will stand independent of decisions about media B through Z. (This principle also explains why you sometimes will also advertise in months that are half as pro-ductive as the best months.)

As a practical matter, then, you will begin with the smallest ad that can do a complete selling job, and gradually increase the size of your ads until your profit begins to diminish.

Some magazines give discounts for larger space units that make it profitable to run larger ads. The discounts are huge in some magazines. You can sometimes purchase a whole page of a three-column magazine for little more than two columns would cost. On the other hand, the discounts in other magazines are not worth bothering about. The smaller the discount, the smaller the ad you will run.

The discounts almost always mean you should use even units of space, however. Use a full column instead of almost a full column. You get more space and actually pay less.

"But then," you say, "why do some of the biggest and smartest firms in the country run full-page ads in *Reader's Digest* and *Time?*"

There are several parts to the complicated answer. This is one of the possible reasons: Repeated surveys have shown that a half-page gets 55 to 60 percent as many *readers* as does a full page. But in a huge study, Rudolph found that a half-page produced almost 70 percent as many *coupons* as a full page.[18]

National advertisers want *readers*. Mail-order firms want *coupons* (and money). That's part of the reason why mail-order firms advertise differently than auto and soap manufacturers do.

Furthermore, the biggest advertisers are not always the smartest advertisers. A big firm can often get away with stupidity that would break a small, competitive producer. And a big national advertiser can't measure its successes and failures as accurately as a mail-order firm can.

Writing Mail-Order Advertisements
by John Caples

[*John Caples may be America's most experienced advertising man. His mail-order ads include such classics as the best-known, most-quoted ad of all time, "They Laughed When I Sat Down at the Piano." He has written four valuable books on advertising.*]

About Headlines • About Pictures • About Copy • About Sales Boosters • Summing Up

ABOUT HEADLINES

1. *The headline is the most important element in most advertisements.* Headlines make ads work. The best headlines appeal to people's self-interest, or give news. Long headlines that say something outpull short headlines that say nothing. Remember that every headline has one job. It must stop your prospects with a believable promise. All messages have headlines. In TV, it's the start of the commercial. In radio, the first few words. In a letter, the first paragraph. Even a telephone call has a headline. Come up with a good headline, and you're almost sure to have a good ad. But even the greatest writer can't save an ad with a poor headline. You can't make an ad pull unless people stop to read your brilliant copy.

Reprinted with permission from the Sept. 22, 1975 issue of *Advertising Age*. Copyright 1975 by Crain Communications, Inc., Chicago.

2. The best headlines appeal to the reader's self-interest or give news. Examples: "The secret of making people like you." "Do you have these symptoms of nerve exhaustion?" "Announcing a new fiction-writing course." "How a new discovery made a plain girl beautiful."

3. Sometimes a minor change in a headline can make a difference in pulling power. A mail-order ad for a book on automobile repair had this headline: "How to repair cars." The pulling power of this ad was increased 20 percent by changing the headline to read: "How to fix cars."

4. Recasting a headline can make a big difference in response. Here is the headline of a couponed ad selling retirement annuities: "A vacation that lasts the rest of your life." Here is the headline of an ad that pulled three times as many coupons: "A guaranteed income for life." The losing headline attempts to be clever by calling retirement a vacation. The winning headline is a straightforward promise of a benefit.

5. Long headlines that say something are more effective than short headlines that say nothing. A book publisher had difficulty selling a book with the title, "Five Acres." The book was transformed into a best-seller by changing the title to: "Five Acres and Independence." Another publisher had a book titled "Fleece of Gold." The sales of the book were more than quadrupled when the title was changed to "Quest for a Blonde Mistress."

6. Writing headlines, the copywriter should try to break the boredom barrier. "How I became a star salesman" was the headline of a successful ad for a course in salesmanship. The pulling power of the ad was increased by changing the headline to "How a fool stunt made me a star salesman."

7. Attract the right audience. Do not use a headline or opening sentence that merely shouts "Hey You" or "Attention Everybody." Be selective.

Use a headline that attracts prospects—prime prospects—persons who will buy your product or service if your copy is convincing.

I recall two ads I wrote for a retirement income plan. Both ads were designed to get coupon leads for salesmen. One ad had a selective headline "How we retired on a guaranteed income for life."

The other ad had a more general headline "A vacation that lasts the rest of your life." I thought: That vacation headline is clever.

It has a poetic sound. It may do well.

Both ads were tested in the New York Times Sunday Magazine Section. I learned a lesson.

The ad "How we retired on a guaranteed income for life" pulled more than twice as many coupons as the ad "A vacation that lasts the rest of your life."

Here are two more examples of successful headlines. Note that the very first words reach out and grab prime prospects.

(a) Car insurance at lower cost if you are a careful driver.

(b) The deaf now hear whispers.

Here are two prospect-grabbing headlines that were printed on direct-mail packages:

(a) If you are eligible for Medicare . . . here is important news.

(b) Now, at last—a brand new magazine exclusively for apartment dwellers like you.

8. Ads that involve the reader are effective. For example, the best-pulling ad for a book of etiquette showed a picture of a man walking between two women. Headline: "What's wrong in this picture?" A successful ad for a course in interior design had this headline: "Can you spot these 7 common decorating sins?"

9. Straightforward ads usually outpull "cute" ads. Two couponed ads soliciting subscriptions for a daily newspaper were tested by mail-order sales as follows:

First ad—headline: "Take it from me, this is the newspaper for you." Illustration: Picture of a smiling newsboy offering the reader a copy of the *Los Angeles Times*.

Second ad—headline: "How to get the *Los Angeles Times* delivered to your home." Illustration: None. Just headline and copy.

Results: Ad No. 2 outpulled Ad No. 1 by 190 percent.

10. A book could be written on the subject of appeals but it is safe to say that *self-interest, news,* and *curiosity* always have been, and continue to be, powerful motivators.

Here is a successful correspondence-school headline that combines both news and self-interest: "Announcing a new course for men who want to be independent in the next 10 years."

Here is a famous curiosity-arousing headline for a book on etiquette: What's wrong in this picture?

Here is a successful headline that combines both self-interest and curiosity: How I made a fortune with a "fool idea."

11. You can sometimes combine two successes to make a super success. For example: Seven ads for house paint were tested for pulling power. Here are the headlines of the two most successful ads:

● "New house paint made by (name of manufacturer)."

● "This house paint keeps white houses whiter."

These two headlines were combined as follows: "New house paint made by (name of manufacturer) keeps your white house whiter."

A campaign with this theme sold more house paint than any previous campaign.

ABOUT PICTURES

12. Use pictures that sell. Avoid far-fetched pictures that fail to identify your product or service. I recall an ad for air travel in which the main illustration was a picture of a camera.

Another time I saw an ad for a camera which featured a picture of an airplane. The writers of these two ads should have exchanged illustrations.

13. As a rule, a good picture is one which shows your product or service in use. For example, the best-pulling illustrations in Retirement-Income ads are pictures of happy couples sitting on a beach.

In an ad for a bicycle, a picture of a boy riding a bicycle shows the product in use.

The winning illustration in a series of tests for house paint ads was a picture of a man painting a house.

14. Don't forget the pulling power of a picture of the product itself. Book club ads show pictures of books.

Record club ads show pictures of records. Jackson & Perkins, rose growers, show pictures of roses.

ABOUT COPY

Hold the Audience

15. After you have stopped your prime prospects with your headline or picture, you must find a way to hold their interest. One way to do this is to use a first paragraph which continues the idea expressed in your headline. Example:

(Headline) Learn Piano
(First Paragraph) Play popular song hits perfectly. Hum the tune. Play it by ear. No teacher—self-instruction. No tedious practice. Just 20 brief, entertaining lessons, easily mastered.

Another method is to quote an authority. Example:

(Headline) HOW TO WIN FRIENDS AND INFLUENCE PEOPLE

(First Paragraph) John D. Rockefeller, Sr., once said: "The ability to deal with people is as purchasable a commodity as sugar or coffee. And I will pay more for that ability than any other."

Ad writers can take a tip from magazine article writers who often hold the readers' interest with a dramatic opening paragraph. Here is the beginning of a recent article on fat reducing:

One of the heaviest patients I ever treated was a 360-pound man who had to squeeze sideways through my office door.

Here is the opening sentence of an article on deodorizers:

The hit of the annual Chemical Show held in New York City a few months ago was a pair of skunks housed in a plastic cage.

16. In a direct mail letter, your opening sentence can perform the function of a headline by making an attractive offer. Here is the opening sentence of a direct mail letter selling hospital insurance: You are cordially invited to apply for the first 30 days of coverage for only 25¢.

Body Copy

17. Write your copy to the sixth-grade level. Simple language is not resented by educated people. And simple language is the only kind that most people understand. When you read over your copy, say to yourself: "Will this be understood by my barber or by the mechanic who fixes my car?"

18. What you say is more important than how you say it. Mail-order advertisers do not use expensive artwork or fancy language.

19. Two forces are at work in the minds of your prospects. (1) Skepticism, and (2) the desire to believe. You can do your prospects a favor by giving them evidence that what you say is true. Your client will also benefit by getting increased response.

20. Specific statements are more believable than generalities. An example of a specific statement is the famous slogan for Ivory soap: "99 44/100% pure."

21. When writing copy, don't merely tell your prospect the benefits he will get by buying your product or service. You should also tell him what he will lose if he doesn't buy.

22. Put your best foot forward in your copy. A copywriter asked my opinion of an ad he had written. He said, "I saved the best benefit till the end and used it as a punch line in the last paragraph." I said, "Put your best benefit in the first paragraph. Otherwise, the reader may never get to your last paragraph.''

23. Avoid humor. You can entertain a million people and not sell one of them. There is not a single humorous line in two of the most influential books in the world—the Bible and the Sears, Roebuck catalog.

24. If you want to drive home a point, you should say it three times. For example, suppose you are making a free offer. At the beginning of your copy, say, "It's free." In the middle of your copy, say, "It costs nothing." At the end say, "Send no money."

25. Long copy sells more than short copy. The more you tell, the more you sell.

26. *Write long, boil it down.* Write more copy than you need to fill the space. If you need 500 words of copy, begin by writing 1,000 words. Then boil it down to a concise, fact-packed message.

27. Your ad must not only be truthful, it must be believable. Here are ways to accomplish this:

(a) Tell how long the company has been in business. A recent ad said: Our 100th Year . . . 1883–1983.

(b) Include testimonials from satisfied customers.

(c) State approval by experts—(Examples: Good Housekeeping Seal of Approval. . . . Won Gold Medal Award).

(d) Give proof of popularity—(Examples: More than 12,000 sold. . . . 700 letters from delighted customers).

Testimonials Increase Sales

28. Include testimonials in your ads. Two ads for a financial publication were split-run tested in *Reader's Digest*. The ads were identical except that one contained four brief testimonials buried in the copy. The ad with the testimonials produced 25% more sales. Some of the most successful mail order ads have been built entirely around testimonials. Examples: "I was a 97 pound weakling," "How I improved my memory in one evening."

29. Localized testimonials in local media are especially effective. Seven couponed ads for a public utility were tested in New Haven newspapers. One ad featured a testimonial from a New Haven woman. This ad outpulled all the others. A newspaper campaign featuring local testimonials for a packaged laundry soap raised the sales of the soap from fourth place to first place.

ABOUT SALES BOOSTERS

Offer a Guarantee

30. Offer a free trial or a money-back guarantee. And spell out your guarantee. The word guarantee has been used so many times that it has lost much of its force. Here is a classic example of a spelled-out guarantee:

"This is my own straightforward agreement that you can have my coaching material in your hands for 10 days examination and reading before you make up your mind to keep it. You are to be the sole judge.

"You can return the material for any reason, or for no reason at all, and your decision will not be questioned. Your refund check will be mailed to you in full by the very next mail. This agreement is just as binding as though it had been written in legal terms by a lawyer."

Prove It's a Bargain

31. If the facts warrant, you should prove that your proposition is a bargain. Examples:

(a) A recent Doubleday Bargain Book Club ad contained a certificate with this heading: This Value Certificate is worth up to $63.25 in Publishers' Editions.

(b) A recent Columbia Record Club spread in TV Guide said: Any 14 records $2.86.

(c) One advertiser dramatized his low price by saying: Only 15¢ a day. Another said: Only 10% above wholesale price.

(d) Some advertisers build up the value of their propositions. The publisher of a business periodical said: $20 spent for a year's subscription may save you $2,000. A manufacturer said: One gallon of this floor wax covers the average kitchen floor about 30 times.

Give a Reason to Act Now

32. You can often improve the pulling power of an ad by setting a time limit. Retail advertisers increase sales by setting a cut-off date. *Reader's Digest*, in selling subscriptions, frequently uses such phrases as, "Return this card before Oct. 31."

33. If the price is going up, say so. If the supply is limited, say so. Use action words (Examples: Act at once. Don't put it off. Delay may be serious. Order today.)

Offer a reward for promptness. For example, in a current Book-of-the-Month Club ad featuring a 10-volume set "The Story of Civilization," there is a small picture of a book entitled "The Lessons of History by Will and Ariel Durant." The text alongside the book says: A copy will be included free, with each set sent to new members who enroll at this time. Pub. price $5.

34. You should ask for action at the end of your ad. Tell the reader what you want him to do. Sometimes it pays to offer a reward for action. In selling a 10-volume world history, the Book-of-the-Month Club offers a free book "to new members who enroll at this time."

Make It Easy to Act

(a) Offer a booklet or sample.

(b) Offer a free trial.

(c) Offer a free cost estimate.

(d) Offer an easy payment plan.

(e) Tell how to order or get information by telephone. A Finance Company increased telephone replies by including in their newspaper ads a panel containing a picture of a telephone and these instructions: For quick information on loans, telephone MAin 2-4500 and ask for Miss Miller and just say, "Please tell me how I can get a loan."

The name "Miss Miller" was changed to a different name every time a new ad ran. This made it possible to tell which ads pulled best.

(f) Use a coupon or business reply card. Make the coupon or card easily accessible. Not long ago, *Reader's Digest* in their subscription ads, started using reply cards which are lightly held in place by a sawtooth, die-cut edge.

This device gives the reader the easiest-to-tear-out reply card in the world.

SUMMING UP

The next time you write a direct response ad or letter ask yourself these questions:

1. Does the headline (or envelope copy) attract prospects?

2. Does the illustration attract prospects?

3. Does the opening paragraph hold the prospect's interest?

4. Does the ad contain news? Does it appeal to self-interest? Does it arouse curiosity?

5. Is the copy believable?

6. Does the copy prove it's a bargain?

7. Is it easy for the prospect to act?

8. Has the prospect been given a reason to Act Now?

The Direct-Mail
Piece, Postage and
Results

*The Mailing Piece • General Principles of What to
Send • The Letter • Coupons, Order Cards and Reply
Envelopes • Catalogs • Types of Postage*

By now you have found a product or a line of products that you have chosen to sell. And you have tentatively decided the terms of the offer you will make: price, credit, etc.

As in other media, in direct mail the offer is most important of all in bringing about success or failure. The choice of good lists is next most important. Copy and the "letter package" are the third important factor in success or failure. Despite this order of importance, most mailers spend a disproportionate amount of time preparing and testing copy and the physical characteristics of the mailing, when they would do better trying to improve their offers and the lists they use.

This chapter is about "cold" mailings that offer your product to rented or purchased lists, or to your own list of customers.

THE MAILING PIECE

So you have decided to try direct mail with your offer! This is a quick summary of how you proceed. Each step is spelled out in detail later.

First, you must select a list to test (usually with the help of a list broker). The test list will be your guess as to the best possible list available. More about that later. Second, you work up a mailing package—a good, standard type of copy and package—also discussed on the next few pages. And next you mail your package to a test portion of the list you selected. Read Chapter 18 to determine how big a test you should use.

Then you sit back to await the results. A section in this chapter teaches you how to predict the total results before they are all in. Compare the *predicted* returns against your costs, to establish whether you have a success or a failure. Another section discusses the proper accounting techniques for this comparison.

A success? Go back to the list you tested, and mail either a much larger test, or the entire list. Chapter 18 helps you make that decision. And start testing other lists, in order to widen your scope and increase volume.

GENERAL PRINCIPLES OF WHAT TO SEND

Many of the principles of display copy apply to direct-mail copy, of course. Testimonials improve results. Premiums improve results. Time limits improve results.

The results you get *can* be influenced *very greatly* by what you write in the letter and brochure. And it is difficult to identify good copy without testing. As an example, consider this experience of Bringe's:[1]

WHAT YOU SAY FIRST MAKES A DIFFERENCE

An eight-way test of 2,000 mailing packages, identical except for the lead line, mailed on the same day to the same state, brought some interesting variations. With the winning mailing as 100, the rest pulled 93, 90, 88, 84, 81, 78 and 62. Of course tests of 2,000 pieces do not give a very high predictability factor. But in this case 38% fewer orders from the worst of the lot compared with the winner could be the difference between a successful business and bankruptcy.

It demonstrates how a small difference in presenting an idea can make a big difference in results. Nine people tried to rank the packages before they were mailed. Three put the worst letter first. Four put the best letter last. None guessed the second or third correctly. Which demonstrates that the customer who pays for the product is the only reliable judge of effective copy.

This section will try to give you some *facts* about direct-mail packages that apply for mail order. Many of them come from tests run by the National Research Bureau.

The Elements of the Best Direct-Mail Packages

There are no hard and fast laws about what elements will make up the best direct-mail package. But subject to innumerable variations and exceptions, most direct-mail experts agree that the best direct-mail piece will consist of either (1) letter, reply card (or coupon and reply envelope), outer envelope; or (2) letter, brochure or circular, reply card, outer envelope.

The letter is the single most crucial part of the package. No salesperson would ever walk into an office, slap down a presentation, and expect the prospect to do the rest of the selling. Sending a brochure or circular without a letter does just that—and it isn't good enough.

Brochures and circulars work best when your product requires illustration.

Other Offers in the Package

Every direct-mail seller eventually gets the idea of increasing revenue by adding extra offers in the package. And with that idea comes the dream: "If it costs me no more to mail ten offers than one. . . ."

Sometimes you can increase revenue in this fashion. In fact, a catalog is just a big bunch of offers. But sadly, your original offer will never pull quite as well when you include other offers in the package.

Whether or not it is profitable to add further offers to your offer is a question you must test for yourself.

You must test everything important, of course. Chapter 18 tells you how to make the tests. But you must also be discriminating about *what* you test. Don't waste your time testing hand-sealed versus machine-sealed envelopes, or Remington versus IBM typewriter face. Save your testing energy for the big and important things: price, extra offers, presence or absence of a brochure, etc.

THE LETTER

Write as much copy as you need to write. Never cut your sales argument short because you think the prospect won't read that much. Successful sales letters have run to four and six pages, outpulling shorter letters. In general, a two-page letter outpulls a one-page letter.[2]

But don't be wordy. Say only what you must say, and nothing more.

A good *letterhead* is very important. The best letterhead fits the spirit of the letter. The National Research Bureau found that a letterhead specially designed to fit the offer usually outpulls a "standard" letterhead, and that two-color letterheads outpull one-color letterheads.[3]

The quality of the paper *may* matter, but sometimes does not. Moran reports a *Standard & Poor's* test in which cheap paper pulled the same number of returns as expensive paper.[4] (This test, unlike so many others, was large enough to be reliable.) Usually 20-pound stock is quite satisfactory, except for letters to professional groups.[5]

Make the letter as interesting to read and look at as possible. Avoid any repetitive regularities in style. Use plenty of subheads, indentations,[6] underlinings, capitalization of paragraphs, handwritten interjections and even spot art to jazz up the appearance. But never make the letter so jazzy that it cheapens the product. Good taste, experienced taste suited to the market, the price and the product, is your only guide.

A two-color letter usually will outpull a one-color letter.[7] Furthermore, B. M. Mellinger says that the second color almost always proves to be worth the extra cost.[8]

A long time ago a *Forbes* magazine test showed that colored paper would outpull white-paper letterheads very substantially.[9] The best colors were, in this order: pink (260), gold (210), green (160), corn (140), white (90). (I don't put much stock in the figures. The differences are far too big to be believable.) Several writers say that canary, goldenrod and pink pull better than blue and green. I have seen no definite figures, though.

But nowadays big mailers find that colored paper is seldom worth the extra cost. Instead, they frequently use colored ink.

The same *Forbes* test showed that two small illustrations on the letters raised the response considerably (400 to 210). (Again the differences are not believable.)

A two-page letter on two separate sheets is better than two sides of the same sheet.[10]

Automatically typed letters are used more and more. The purpose is to make each letter seem individual. Of course you can't fool people. But at least, as Paul Bringe says,[11]

> [D]on't let the repairman keep your machine in too good shape. If your letter is perfect it defeats the personal touch you want to create. Try to make your automatic letters look as though Sadie the Steno labored over them. If your machine *is* perfect you will help your cause by slipping a small error in somewhere. People make mistakes and personal letters should look as though they came from people.

COUPONS, ORDER CARDS AND REPLY ENVELOPES

The most important fact about coupons and reply envelopes or reply cards is: *Always* include one or the other in *every* mailing. The theory is, "Make it easy to order." Evidence is abundant that return envelopes and order cards increase returns substantially, far more than their extra cost. Baker estimates an average 5 to 10 percent increase for the reply envelope.[12] Musselman says a coupon "increased sales 22%."[13]

CATALOGS

Catalogs really are much more than direct-mail pieces. They are more like stores assembled in a book and (usually) delivered by mail. The world of catalogs ranges from mimeographed eight-papers of tiny firms selling used books to the fantastic productions of Sears, Roebuck and the other giants, from consumer-novelty catalogs like those of Sunset House to those of major industrial firms selling generators and tractors. Catalogs really deserve a whole chapter to themselves. Maybe they will get one in the next edition of this book.

Many of the decisions about a catalog are similar to decisions about direct-mail pieces: how much color, what kind of artwork, what kind of gimmicks (free gifts and contests, for example), delivery methods (parcel post, United Parcel Service, truck, etc.), coupons and rider forms, whether to include a letter (always yes, and make it "wrap-around," a four-page piece that goes outside the catalog) and, of course, copy.

But there are also some decisions and characteristics that are special to catalogs. One such decision concerns the placement of merchandise in the catalog; generally it makes sense to put the best sellers up front. Another decision is the length of the catalog; the general answer to this question is to include all those items—and *only* those items—that more than pay their own costs of paper, printing, artwork and postage. The same answer applies to the question of which merchandise to include.

The most important special characteristic of catalogs is that you can measure with perfect accuracy the relationship between the advertisements in the catalog and the sales of each product. The smart catalog firm takes full advantage of this information, checking closely and keeping tabs on each item to see which to drop or give less space or move to the back, which to move to the front or give bigger space. This is the heart of catalog management.

TYPES OF POSTAGE

Very few mailers find that first-class postage pays for itself. Many find that third class even pulls just as many orders, at a lower cost.

Metered mail generally does just as well as, or better than, stamped mail. Prospects are not as much against business mail as many observers think. A "designed imprint" pulls as well as metered mail.

Here are the results of an interesting test of the effectiveness of different types of postage, as quoted by Paul Bringe.[14]

Four groups of 75,000 pieces each were mailed. Group A—No. 9 colored window envelope with bold teaser line on face, printed third class indicia. Group B—same but with third class stamp rather than indicia. Group C same but with first class stamp. Group D—No. 9 white window, return address on flap, "First Class Mail" printed on face, commemorative first class stamp.

	Orders pulled	Relative cost per order
Key D (equals 100)	100	100
C	89	112
A	75	101
B	70	110

The first class mailing that *looked* like first class (D) brought the most orders at the lowest cost. But it also brought back 3,962 non-deliverables. The first class mail that *looked* like third class (C) brought only 204 non-deliverables at a 12% higher cost per order.

Replies to *inquiries*, however, are generally sent first class. A prospect's enthusiasm cools off quickly if he doesn't hear from you soon after writing. Grant states that inquiries "lose 1 percent" for each day not answered.[15]

Direct-
Mail
Lists

List Brokers • Types of Lists • How to Choose Lists •
Duplication of Names on Lists • List Building and
Maintenance • Extra Revenue by Renting Your List

This fact bears repetition: The choice of lists is absolutely crucial in direct mail. A winning offer in a winning package will fall flat on its face when sent to the wrong list. If you ever sell mail-order products by direct mail, you'll learn this lesson for yourself sooner or later, and the lesson will be expensive.

LIST BROKERS

List brokers are of vital importance to almost every direct-mail mail-order firm. It is their function to bring together the owners of lists and the firms that want to rent lists. They usually get a flat 20 percent commission on the rental, and it is to their advantage that each test you rent be successful, because you will then use the whole list and boost their fees. The broker is unlikely to make any money on a test that fails.

Brokers have a wide knowledge about choosing lists, which they pass on to you as part of their service. But brokers, like other people, are fallible. Don't be afraid to let your judgment override the broker's judgment on ocassion.

Brokers also may *own* compiled lists, which they rent to you outright for their own account. There are other firms that specialize in compiled lists, too.

Don't ever consider buying or renting the cheap lists of names offered direct by tiny, unknown firms to anyone who runs a classified ad or small display ad. Even if the lists were satisfactory, they are far too small to do you any good.

Consult a broker about future rentals of *your* list, today. Do this *before* you have a big list because the broker's advice may affect the way you maintain your list.

Rental Means Rental. You use the names once and that's all. The owner of the list is protected by the criminal law against your stealing the list. He guards against stealing by placing "decoy" names on the list, made-up names which you couldn't know of unless you use his list. Decoy names are evidence in court.

The use of decoy names is absolutely crucial. It is legally-binding evidence against anyone who might steal your list. For example, I was called as a witness by a firm whose sales manager had photocopied their entire list of industrial buyers, and then moved over to a new competitor. The mail received from the competition at the old addresses were the basis for a legal settlement that ran near $100,000. (In that case the firm did *not* have coded names on the list but by a lucky accident there were some catchalls and a "COD account" with the firm's own address on the list, and the post office delivered the criminal firm's mail to that address!)

Not only must you put coded names and addresses on your customer file, but you must not reveal which ones they are to your employees. For example, in a case now in the courts, a top-salaried executive became disgruntled and took the customer list with him to a new employer.

To arrange to rent lists, call or write one or more list brokers. Tell the broker what you are selling, and if possible, include a mailing piece. The broker will recommend lists by sending you cards with full information about the lists he recommends. Figure 17-1 shows sample pages from a list broker's catalog.

The mechanics of renting lists vary, but they are always simple. The two most usual arrangements are: (1) You send your envelopes to the renter or to the renter's letter shop, which then returns the addressed envelopes to you. (2) The list owner sends you gummed labels to affix to your envelopes.

Code No.	Quantity	Description	Dollars Per Thousand
HORTICULTURE, con't.			
Ht 14	17,000	rose bush buyers	15.
Ht 15	95,228	garden supplies, seed and nursery item buyers	15.
Ht 16	40,000	plant food, planters & garden supply buyers	15.
Ht 17	82,000	seed, ornamental shrubs, and fruit plant buyers	15.
Ht 18	2,067,100	buyers of lawn care magazine, supplies	15.
Ht 19	209,000	women buyers of dutch bulbs (home owners)	15.
Ht 20	10,000	buyers of water plants, lily pool supplies	19.
Ht 21	17,000	former subscribers to famous horticulture magazine	17.
Ht 22	150,000	members of horticulture groups and societies	17.
Ht 23	30,000	persons interested in raising orchids	15.
Ht 24	7,725	subscribers to Tropical Homes & Gardens (Florida)	15.
Ht 25	40,000	90% women who sent money for iris bulbs	15.
Ht 26	1,689,290	bought products for lawn care (in central states)	14.
Ht 27	22,500	retail florists	20.
Ht 58	75,000	bought rose bushes or	15.
Ht 59	37,500	buyers of geraniums, violets, ivy plants	15.
Ht 60	11,850	bought tree & shrub seeds	15.
Ht 61	50,000	bought nursery products	15.
Ht 62	23,077	buyers of quality seeds	15.
Ht 63	30,000	seed, bulb, plant buyers	15.
Ht 64	56,000	75% are repeat buyers of fruit trees	15.
Ht 65	15,000	leading female flower growers & gardeners	15.
Ht 66	140,000	buyers of trees, roses, evergreens, shrubs, etc.	13.
Ht 67	125,904	buyers of fruit trees and other nursery items	14.
Ht 68	95,000	buyers of pompon, mums, azaleamums	15.
Ht 69	140,000	above average income home owners who bought fruit trees, berry plants, seed	15.

Page 72

Code No.	Quantity	Description	Dollars Per Thousand
Ht 70	12,000	members of Plant of Month Club, buyers of shrubs	15.
Ht 71	25,000	subscribers to Popular Gardening	15.
Ht 72	24,000	buyers of flower seeds, bulbs, rock gardens	15.
Ht 73	180,000	fine seed buyer list	15.
Ht 74	44,700	buyers of nursery items	15.
Ht 75	39,000	buyers of choice flowers (glads, etc.)	15.
Ht 76	32,000	women buyers of Hawaiian good luck plant	14.
Ht 77	14,200	hobbyists who purchased orchid plants	15.
Ht 78	29,117	orchid fanciers who bought catalog and growing instructions	15.
Ht 79	90,103	U.S. florists and nurserymen	15.
Ht 80	10,930	80% public spirited men, members of American Forestry Association	17.
Ht 81	30,000	buyers of horticulture supplies, violets	15.
Ht 82	13,000	catalog requests (50% women) for seeds, garden supplies	13.
Ht 83	135,000	buyers of perennial plants, lawn seeds, etc.	15.
Ht 84	50,000	buyers of grass seed, shears, garden hose	14.
HOUSEWARES			
Hs 1	25,900	buyers of aluminum cake molds	13.
Hs 2	100,000	buyers of electrical appliances	15.
Hs 32	117,000	bought thermal salad bowl	13.
Hs 33	119,000	buyers of personalized door mat	15.
Hs 34	49,000	99% women who buy household cutlery	15.
Hs 35	100,000	buyers of colorful plastic dinnerware	13.
Hs 36	69,900	buyers of many household items	14.
Hs 37	64,000	buyers of top quality home accessories, toys	15.
Hs 38	1,500,000	buyers of kitchen gadgets	15.
Hs 39	50,000	buyers of colored burlap	15.

Page 73

Figure 17-1

TYPES OF LISTS

There are three basic types of mailing lists: (1) compiled lists, (2) lists of mail-order buyers, and (3) the "house list." They are very different, but all have their important uses.

Compiled lists are lists of people who have some characteristic in common. The common characteristic may be as simple as that the addresses are in the same area. (For example, the crisscross telephone directories that list people up and down the street, "occupant" lists and "rural box holder" lists.) Or the common characteristic may be that the addressees all belong to the Interplanetary Study Society.

Compiled lists are derived from many sources—mostly records of trade organizations, professional organizations and publicly available records. But even if the original material is available to you, you will usually find it cheaper in the long run to use the services of a list broker.

Mail-order buyer lists are lists of people who have bought from particular mail-order firms. People on mail-order buyer lists have *two* things in common:

1. They have bought or expressed interest in a particular type of merchandise.

2. They are inclined to buy by mail.

The importance of 1 is obvious; 2 has been *proved* crucial, time after time. All else being equal, it is tremendously harder to sell by mail to people who have no record of buying by mail than to mail-order buyers.

The house list is the list of people who have bought from you in the past. Paul Bringe gives this example of the tremendous power of the house list.[1]

The Republican Party is having good results with its fund raising by mail effort. First mailings last year brought an average 3% response of $11 each at a cost of 174 cents per dollar collected. "Renewals" this year from last year's donors brought a 50% response at a cost of 14 cents per dollar.

This is a good demonstration of the great difference between a qualified list and a non-qualified list. The first year the Republican mailing was probably made, with the aid of census tract information, to upper income groups suspected but not known to be Republican.

The second year's mailing went to known customers who, if they did not contribute, would have to admit to themselves that they made a mistake the first year. Such an admission is difficult for anyone to make. Doesn't this indicate that in many cases an outright loss the first year could prove mighty profitable thereafter? Magazine publishers have known it for years.

HOW TO CHOOSE LISTS

These principles may help you to analyze lists for your offer:

1. Use the same lists, or the same types of lists, as your competition does. This is our old key principle, of course, of following along wherever success has been proven.

2. Use your competitor's lists themselves, if you can get permission. Many competitors exchange lists.

3. Among the likely lists, test the *biggest* lists first. Only a big list can give you the big volume that makes a heavy profit. (On the other hand, there is some tendency for smaller lists to be of better quality.)

4. Use *fresh* lists, or *well-maintained* lists. The Direct Mail Marketing Association estimates that *each year* changes in address or name include 22 percent of householders, 23 percent of merchants and 39 percent of advertising executives.[2] Stone estimates 20 to 30 percent annual changes on buyer lists.[3] And there was a 25 percent change in a single year in job addresses from a McGraw-Hill list.[4]

The meaning of these statistics is clear: Because of the "nixie" undeliverables, a one-year-old list can give you up to 25 percent less revenue than a new list, a difference bigger than your probable profit margin.

5. The longer the time since the customers on a list last bought from the list owner, the less likely they are to buy from either the list owner or another firm that rents the list. Stone estimates the deterioration as follows: If this year's customers will buy at a rate of 100 units, last year's customers will buy at a rate of 80 units, and two-years-ago customers will buy at a rate of 60 units.[5]

6. Compiled lists are seldom good for consumer items. But they are invaluable for commercial and industrial sales.

7. Inquiries versus purchasers: Purchaser lists will always do better because there are no "curiosity seekers" among them. The interest of a purchaser is bound to be higher than that of an inquirer.

8. Price of item bought: The higher the unit sale, the more money the customers obviously had to spend—and the more they are able to spend for your products, too.

9. "Class" of lists: High-class lists do very well for a variety of customers. The Diners' Club list is a favorite. Leslie's gift list is another "high-class" example.

10. Moran says that these are the lists rented most often:[6]

(1) Business executives

(2) Buyers of luxuries

(3) Men purchasers

(4) Buyers of health specialties

(5) Book buyers

(6) Woman buyers

(7) Psychology book and course buyers

(8) Buyers of beauty specialties

These further principles may help you:

1. Ask yourself, "Are these the kind of people who will be interested in this offer?" There is no replacement for sound intuition, experience and knowledge in answering that question.

2. Rely on your list broker. He or she is on your side. The very nature of your financial transactions means that his or her interests are your interests.

3. Consider whether you can use only *some of the states* on a list, or consider dropping out the cities. Often you can greatly increase the average results from a list in this way, because you are weeding out the areas that would drag the average down.

4. Mail to businesspersons' homes may pull better—but it may annoy some customers who prefer to get business mail at their offices.

Direct-mail experts disagree on many points, but on this they are unanimous: *The best list is the list of your old customers.* It will pull 2 to 10 times better than any list you can find. The people on your list know you and patronize you as they would patronize an old friend.

Second-best to the house list is a list of people who have purchased similar goods by mail. Third-best is a list of people who have purchased *anything* by mail. Next is a compiled list of people with some special characteristic to which your goods will appeal. Poorest of all is just any old list, such as the alphabetical telephone directory. Few and far between are the offers so good they will make money on such "cold" lists.

Exceptions to these rules:

1. *Commercial venders.* If you sell steel in 10-ton lots, no list of mail-order buyers will do you any good. What you need is a list of manufacturers that use steel.

2. *Retailers.* The delicatessen around the corner in a big city can *only* use the crisscross phone book (in which the listings run up and down the street, rather than alphabetically). And many a retailer has done well with this kind of direct mail. (Retailers can use other local lists, too, on occasion.)

It is prudent to get as much information as you can about the lists you consider renting. For consumers lists, find out exactly what was the offer that generated the list, and how the names were acquired. For compiled lists, find out how the list was compiled. And in every case, find out enough to ensure that you're not renting a list you've rented before through a different broker (it happens).

Above all, don't rely on your judgment. Test! Often the results contradict your intuition, as in this experience of Bringe's:[7]

A fund raising letter for a girls college was sent to three groups: A-parents of previous students, B-parents of present students. C-people who had paid admission to public fund raising entertainment program the previous year.

Response: A-6½%, B-12½% and C-25%. The group with the weakest connection with the school responded the best. I have my own ideas about why this happened but it illustrates a point—don't be too sure a list will not respond to your offer. Too often our own unsupported notions of what people will do stop us from testing. Uncle Remus says: "The answers always come after the askin'."

DUPLICATION OF NAMES ON LISTS

Some names appear on many lists, of course, and it is to your advantage not to send six appeals to the same fellow on the same morning.

You can reduce duplication by mailing similar lists at different times. That way, your duplicated letter has several chances to sell the customer. The second and third letters are not completely wasted as they are if they arrive on the same day.

Sometimes the avoidance of duplication is more costly than are the wasted letters. But now that most lists have been put on computer cards and tape, in many cases it is possible to automatically eliminate duplication between the lists. This is done with what is called a "merge and purge" program, carried out by the computer-service organization to whom the lists are sent for processing. Ask the list broker about this when you order the lists.

Duplicates are not just a sign of waste, however. Duplicated names are likely to be particularly good prospects. In fact, if a list that is a candidate for rental has a high degree of duplication with your house list, that is a sign that the list is a particularly good prospect for you to use.

LIST BUILDING AND MAINTENANCE

You *must* have as big a house list of active customers as possible. You must build this list in any way you can and maintain it in tiptop shape. Your list is vital for rental income as well as for your own use. For some firms, list rental accounts for 25 percent of their annual gross, and list rental has a terrific profit margin.

The post office helps you maintain your list, though their help costs you money. The most important help is informing you of new customer addresses. And you *must* keep up to date with accurate addresses.

To obtain this list-correction service, your third-class mail should bear the imprint "Return requested." The post office employees will return your third-class mail to you with the forwarding address marked on it, charging you 10 cents per letter. Another part of keeping your list clean is to scratch off the first-class nixies that are returned as unknown.

The post office helps in other ways, too, depending on what you request on the envelope. Check with your postmaster and use your *Postal Manual*, because procedures change from time to time. (By the way, a *Postal Manual* should be your first investment in your mail-order business, even at $40.)

It is sometimes helpful in building a list to ask your customers for the names of their friends who may be interested in your products. Satisfied customers are glad to cooperate, especially if you offer them a small free gift.

EXTRA REVENUE BY RENTING YOUR LIST

Not only is your house list worth a great deal to you in repeat sales, but you can boost your income greatly by renting your list to other mailers.

You can rent your list yourself by offering it to other mailers. Or you can use the services of a list broker to help you rent your list. The list broker usually takes a 20 percent commission, and he is almost always worth it.

An advertisement for *Moneysworth* magazine provides interesting information about list rental. This is a list of firms that rented that firm's list:

USERS OF THE MONEYSWORTH LISTS

Alden's	Columbia Record Club	GEICO Insurance	Mother Earth News	Research Inst. of America
Ambassador Leather	Comml. Travelers Ins.	General Nutrition	NAACP	Rodale Press
Amer. Civil Liberties	Common Cause	Gulf Travel Club	National Wildlife Fed.	Saturday Review
American Express	Consumer Reports	Hammacher-Schlemmer	Nation's Business	F.A.O. Schwartz
American Heritage	Cosvetics Labs	Harper's Magazine	Nationwide Auto Ins.	Simon & Schuster
American Mngmnt. Assn.	Crown Publishers	Highlights for Children	Newsweek	Ski Magazine
Amoco Travel Club	Cue Magazine	Holt Executive Advisory	New West Magazine	Smithsonian Magazine
Amsterdam Printing	Danbury Mint	Hudson Vitamin Co.	New York Magazine	Southern Living Mag.
Atlantic Monthly	De Beers Diamonds	Instant Learning	Jay Norris Corporation	Spencer Gifts
Automated Learning	Democratic Natl. Comm.	ITT	Oklahoma Monthly	Spiegel, Inc.
Baxter International	Diners Club	Joseph Karbo	Oui Magazine	Standard & Poor's
H&R Block	Doubleday & Company	Kidney Foundation	Penthouse Magazine	Sunset House
Boardroom Reports	Dow Jones & Company	Kiplinger Letters	Philadelphia Magazine	Texas Monthly
Book Digest	Dow Theory Forecasts	Ladies Home Journal	Planned Parenthood	Thompson Cigar
Book-of-the-Month Club	The Dreyfus Corporation	LaSalle Extension Univ.	Playboy Book Club	Time-Life Books
Business Week	Dun & Bradstreet	McCall's Magazine	Prentice-Hall	Time Magazine
Calhoun Collectors Soc.	Esquire Magazine	McGraw-Hill Book Co.	Prevention Magazine	The Tog Shop
CARE	EXXON	Mason Shoes Company	Psychology Today	United Business Service
Carte Blanche	Figi's	Master Charge	Publishers Central Bureau	US News & World Report
Changing Times	Forbes Magazine	Mellinger Company	Pblshrs. Clearing House	Valley Forge Insurance
Cheeselovers Intl.	Fortune Magazine	Meredith Corporation	RCA Record Club	Value Line
Chilton Bock Company	Friends of the Earth	Money Magazine	Reader's Digest	Volkswagen Auto Ins.
Collier Publishing	Funk & Wagnall's	Montgomery Ward	Republican Natl. Comm.	J.C. Whitney & Company

Figure 17-2

To get some idea of the extra revenue to be obtained with a list rental, consider that a representative list of 100,000 to 500,000 names had a rental fee of $16 to $30 and a rate of rental as high as two or three times a month. The Jay Norris general-merchandise catalog firm took in $700,000 yearly in *list rentals alone* on rentals to forty-two other firms in 1973. (Eleven firms used over a million names from the Norris list; twenty-five rented more than 500,000 names; and the rest rented between 250,000 and 500,000.) Norris generated about 125,000 new buyer names per *month* as of 1974.[8]

One of the side benefits of renting your list to other firms is that you get new ideas about what *you* can sell to your customers. (For the same offer, the response *you* get from your list will be higher than the response to another firm.)

CHAPTER 18

The Vital Brain of Mail Order: Testing

What Is Testing All About ● *Testing in Periodical Advertising* ● *Direct-Mail Testing Techniques*

WHAT IS TESTING ALL ABOUT?

Mail order is something like poker. In poker you try to maneuver into a position where you have a really good hand, and then you play it to the hilt. In mail order, you try like the dickens to find a big-winning proposition, and then you try to milk it for all it's worth. (But don't get me wrong. Mail order is much less of a gamble than most other types of business—at least, once you are established.)

Testing tells you whether or not you have a big winner and how much you can try to milk it for. Important? Testing couldn't be more important. If you don't understand testing, you'll never make a good buck in mail order.

(But you *don't* have to understand some of the more complicated stuff I discuss in this chapter. Lots of successful mail-order people won't know what I'm talking about. I'm convinced, though, that they would be far *more* successful if they did understand and use all these ideas.)

Sometimes you will try a loser. Either it is a brand-new product and people don't want it, or it's an established product whose market is not big enough for you *and* the competition.

You would obviously prefer not to wind up with any costly stock on your hands in a situation where you can't sell it. The fear of this keeps many people from testing good products.

But there is a partial answer. Large industrial manufacturing companies test a product—perhaps a new type of steel—by asking their customers in advance whether they can use it. Their customers are likely to give accurate answers.

Major concerns that sell direct to household consumers find that they cannot rely on their customers' answers. Consumers just cannot predict their own behavior in advance well enough to give you accurate information. So these concerns resort to many other stratagems, including motivation research.

The mail-order advertiser is less interested in the way that people react to the goods and more interested in the way they react to the advertising. What you *can* do, then, is to advertise before you have any merchandise, to find out how great the response will be.

This practice never really feels very good ethically. But on the other hand, it is not really bad, either. The worst that happens is that a customer wastes time and a postage stamp in writing to you. If you do put the product on the market, he merely has to wait awhile until you are ready. Whether or not the practice feels right to you, you should know that the late Bennet Cerf of Random House (one of America's largest publishers) asserted that this practice was a necessary and common trade practice, when he was in a discussion of the ethical relationships of publishers to booksellers.[1]

The Science of Mail Order

Mail-order selling is the *most* scientific business in the world. By that I mean that *figuring* and *calculating* can control a firm's decisions more than in any other line of trade. Aside from the selection of the offer and the creation of copy, the "human factor" and other imponderables have a smaller effect in mail order than in any other business, no matter how large the business is.

For example, the split-run test (more about that later) is the most perfect experiment ever devised in the social sciences. Its accuracy and validity are fantastically greater than any psychologist, sociologist or economist ever hopes to achieve in his work.

It would seem, then, that mail-order people would respond readily to improvements in methods of figuring. But alas, no, they're just not very much interested. Like everyone else, mail-order people are satisfied to get along. They're convinced that their knowledge is basically pretty complete.

"Buying Information"

When you spend a dime to call the Weather Bureau for the latest report, you are buying information. When you lay out $300 for an encyclopedia, you are also buying information—not books, mind you, but *information*.

Testing is also a way of buying information. You spend a little extra time and energy to obtain some factual data that you can then use to increase your profit. A test is good only if it costs less than the information is worth.

Here is an example. You have a proposition that has proved to be a winner in four out of the five magazines in which you have run. Now you are in a hurry to find the greatest number of magazines that will pull a profit for you.

In this situation, you should not be too cautious in your testing. You should take a chance on every magazine that has even a *reasonable* chance of paying out. Here's why. If you think you have a one-in-three chance of making a profit on a magazine, you should test in it. Based on your test of the five magazines above, you know that you won't lose your shirt. The most you can lose is some small part of the cost of the ad and the merchandise. If you *make* money, you can rerun the ad far more than three times. And more than two insertions in a paying magazine will more than cover the losses in two nonpaying magazines.

So it pays to think of testing as buying information that will allow you to build a profit in the future. Don't think of the test as an investment all by itself. If you understand this principle, you will test more freely and you can pyramid your profits remarkably fast.

What to Test

All through this manual I've been saying, "Test this" and "Test that" or "You'll have to test this for yourself."

But test *only* the important things. Don't test petty things. Mail-order people have spent huge amounts of time and energy testing such picayune items as exact shades of color, one type face versus another type face, etc., ad nauseam. Such tests spend more to buy information than the information is worth. The results don't make enough difference to matter much.

To paraphrase Victor Schwab:[2] Test for differences that *scream*. Don't test for differences that whisper. . . . Test for differences in headlines that could double your profit. Test for a price that could increase your take by 40 percent. Test a brochure that could increase sales 15 percent.

When you first put an offer on the market, your testing will be very different from the testing that you will do later on in the product history. Your first advertisement tests the offer, but it *also* tests the medium and the copy. If any one of those elements is bad, the whole test fails. That's when you have to exert judgment to decide whether to drop the whole thing, or to repair what you think is the faulty element.

Later on, after you *know* what your offer and copy will do, you can compare one magazine against another, and your test results will give you information purely about the magazines.

Or, you can change the copy but keep the same offer, and run in a medium where you ran the old ad. In that case, the results give you a straight answer about the copy.

Testing has different meanings at the various stages of your mail-order campaign.

Does Scientific Testing Work?

People who don't understand testing don't trust its results. As an eye opener to direct-mail people, William Doppler and the Book-of-the-Month Club tested random sampling on over *a million* letters. The results were just exactly as predicted by sampling theory.[3]

(Of course, any statistician would have known that any such test was totally unnecessary. He would know that the results *had* to be the way they turned out.)

Is Testing Just Theory and Not Practice?

The practical person may wonder if scientific testing is not just ivory-tower stuff, a theoretical nicety not really done by businesses in a hurry to make profit. Not so. In the mail-order business one *has* to test, and the most profitable firms tend to do a lot of testing. For example, the vice-president of J. C. Penney, the second largest merchandiser in the United States after Sears, said this about Penney's catalog testing:[4]

> Which media alternatives are best for a particular item or promotion—mail, broadcast, print, telephone? We find out through testing. Which distribution alternatives are most efficient—mail, parcel post, united parcel? Which is more productive, color or black and white, for which categories of merchandise? Again, the answers come through testing.
>
> Decision-making is aided importantly by testing. Judgment, based on accumulated experience, will never go out of style, but in direct marketing, at

least, it is not enough. Too often I have seen our best judgments overturned by a simple test result.

The most important thing in testing is to keep good records.

TESTING IN PERIODICAL ADVERTISING

A true split run is a perfect test for two pieces of copy. In a split run, two different ads are set up for a single issue of a publication. The test is arranged so that each ad is in exactly half the copies, appearing in every other copy in each pile of magazines or newspapers that leaves the printing plant.

The split-run ads are keyed differently, and the number of returns is a perfect test of whichever copy or price is better.

Several magazines and newspapers have true split-run facilities, for which there is an extra charge. *Standard Rate & Data* lists these publications.

There are also some publications that offer *regional* "split runs." In this setup all the copies going to the West, perhaps, have one ad, while all the copies going to the East have another ad. The results are not perfectly reliable because readers in different parts of the country may have different tastes and needs. This is not a true split-run test. Nevertheless, it can sometimes be useful.

Split runs test only copy and various offers against each other. And split run is only available to the large advertiser. The small advertiser must use other testing techniques.

Problems in Testing

You need plenty of good judgment to interpret display-ad tests. As a matter of fact, how good your judgment of tests is may decide how successful a display advertiser you are. And I think that the trickiest job in mail order is to estimate, on the basis of one or more ads, how other ads or other media will pull.

These are some of the problems in judging test results:

1. If you test two different ads in two consecutive issues of a magazine, you must take account of the difference in pulling power in different months.

2. Two ads may appear in different positions in different issues. Good position can pull twice as well as poor position.

3. A given issue of a magazine may be especially attractive and sell extra copies on the newsstand, giving an extra boost to ads in that issue.

4. National events, such as a war scare, can affect results.

5. One issue may carry more competitive advertising than another issue.

These are some of the reasons why you must evaluate the results of a particular test very closely. Chapter 13 on display advertising gives you information that should help improve your judgment of test results.

General Methods of Testing Ads and Media

1. If you have a piece of copy that you have used in many media before, you can use that copy to test new media. La Salle Extension University has used one piece of copy to test new publications for over 35 years.

2. You can get a fair comparison of two ads in the "crisscross" method. In this method you run Ad A in Medium X and Ad B in Medium Y the first issue. The next issue, Ad A goes into Medium Y, and Ad B goes into Medium X. The ad which pulls more total responses should be better.

   However, different conditions can still distort the picture, even though the crosscross reduces the likelihood of that happening.

3. If you have plenty of time you can alternate ads from month to month. After 4 or 6 months your results should be satisfactorily reliable.

4. Mail-order people are fond of saying that you can test only one thing at a time. That saying is not always true. Let's say that you have run your first test ad, and the results are highly satisfactory. Now you are in a great hurry to test out perhaps eight new media and perhaps eight forms of offer, price and copy.

I am convinced that your best bet is to put a different ad into each different medium. The insertions that pull the very best suggest to you that *both* the ad and the medium are strong. The insertions that pull worst suggest the opposite.

On the next time around, place the ads from the better-result insertions into many media, including the media whose insertions pulled only middling well on the first test. But place no ads in the media where the first insertions did poorly. After this second round, by a simple and obvious deduction, you can say with much greater accuracy which media are best and which ads are best.

The advantage of this approach is that you get a lot of information rapidly. The rationale depends on the fact that your offer is generally quite profitable, and for that reason it is possible and profitable to buy the further information.

And don't forget: Keep good records, *faithfully*.

One of the disadvantages of display advertising is that it takes a long time to get results. Some media give you a quick test, though.

Television and Radio Testing

Television and radio testing is not very difficult in principle from testing in periodicals. You should first try a few stations that usually seem to produce rather well and consistently for your prior offers. Then, if they show results that are good compared with prior tests and are profitable in absolute terms, you repeat in those stations and also go on to other stations. As Lawrence Crane, head of a large television record-seller, Dynamic House, describes it:[5]

> We have five or six markets that we usually test in. They vary from time to time because we know from past experience what good results and what bad results come from that particular station. We look back at our previous records to see how well that package did. The key question I usually ask is how does it compare to a particular winner in that particular market. We can gauge just how well that package would do. And then we roll it out very slowly before we ever get to the 600 stations.

DIRECT-MAIL TESTING TECHNIQUES

Every self-respecting direct-mail tester should ask these two questions each and every time a test is run:

1. How do I design the best test for this particular direct-mail problem? Usually—but not always—this question boils down to: How big a test sample should I use?

2. How do I evaluate the results of the test after the returns are in? This question *always* breaks into two subquestions:
   a. What is my *best guess* about what the test shows?

  b. How *accurate* is that best guess likely to be, given the test-sample size?

The answers to these questions will be different from test to test. There is no cheap and easy set of rules you can follow blindly. There is no 2-dollar board into which you can plug your jack for an automatic answer.

But even *before* those questions, as a direct-mail tester you must consider:

1. What you are trying to find out from the test

2. What decisions will be influenced by the test results

3. How the test results can guide you in the decisions you have to make

4. How much money is involved.

Depending on these considerations, the testing situation will fall into one of three major categories:

1. Will this new offer make a profit?

2. How should I test a *list*?

3. How do I test one piece of copy against another?

We shall consider these major categories one by one.

Will This New Offer Make a Profit?

You want to know whether your product or offer is attractive enough for further investment. Commonly you tackle this problem by selecting a potentially excellent list, writing the best possible copy and mailing at a good time of the year. (You might mail in an off season if you know how much to upgrade the results you get.) You figure that if you have a winner, further experimentation will improve the techniques and unearth even better lists.

How big a test? How many tests? There is no stock answer. Are you selling a $5.95 product or one that goes for $5,950? Is it a one-shot solicitation, or is it a repeat-business operation?

Let's try an example. You want to sell an auto accessory priced at $15. For simplicity we'll say that it is a one-shot offer, though a sound analysis should include the future value of having the customers on your list for future solicitations. You figure that a 1.125 percent return will return your investment and leave something for overhead and profit. In other words, 1.125 percent is the break-even point you choose. If your offer pulls that well or better over the long haul, you'll consider the offer a success rather than a failure.

How big a test sample should you mail? Let's say that you want to be 85 percent sure that chance will make your test results no more than 25 percent higher than repeated mailings. You obviously don't care at all if follow-ups would be *higher* than the test results. You merely want protection against test results that are too high, leading you into unwise further investment.

(NOTE: When we say "85 percent sure," we mean that the right betting odds in a horse race would be 17 to 3. Note also that at this point we are discussing the variation in results due only to chance factors. We shall discuss the falloff effect later.)

You estimate that the offer will pull 1.5 percent. The difference between your estimate of 1.5 percent and your break-even point of 1.125 percent is 0.375 percent, which is 25 percent of 1.5 percent.

To find the correct sample size to satisfy your specifications, refer to Table 18-1. Go along the horizontal top line until you find 25 percent, the dropoff percentage you want to guard against. Then proceed down the 25 percent vertical column until you reach the 85 percent degree of surety you demand. The number in the box will be the number of returns you must set up your test sample to obtain. To find the correct sample size, divide the number of returns in the box (14 in this ex-

Table 18-1

		Percent of Dropoff* (The percentage difference between the estimated return and the break-even point; or the dropoff percentage you wish to guard against)			
		50%	25%	12½%	62%
The degree of surety. (How	75%	1.8	7.3	29.2	116.8
sure you wish to be that	85%	3.5	14.0	56.0	
the result will be over the	90%	6.6	26.2	104.8	
break-even point.)	95%	11.0	42.8		
	99%	21.7	86.9		

*The numbers within the table represent the number of returns the test must be arranged to obtain in order to meet the dropoff requirement and the degree of certainty required. Note that this table, like the other tables in this chapter, is approximate. Note also that it holds only for return percentages under 10 percent.

ample) by the percent of return you expect (1.5 percent in this case): 14 divided by 0.015 equals 933. So try a test of 933, or around 1,000.

Perhaps you are selling a higher-priced product like kitchenware. Your experience leads you to expect a return of 0.5 percent. As in the previous example, you desire to guard against a dropoff of 25 percent from test results to continuation results, and you demand a surety of 85 percent. You therefore would need to get the same number of returns as in the previous example (14), and your sample size therefore is 14 divided by 0.5 percent, or 2,799. You would probably test-mail 2,500 or 3,000.

But if you expect 0.5 percent return and are willing to settle for 75 percent surety against a later dropoff of 25 percent or more, you need a test sample of 7.3 divided by 0.5 percent, or roughly 1,500.

Let us return to the auto-accessory example.

So you run a test, expecting 1.5 percent on a test sample of 1,000, and you get results of 1.3 percent. Your *best guess* is that future mailings will pull 1.3 percent, provided the copy, list, seasonal conditions, etc., stay the same. (Don't snicker at this apparently simple-minded statement. The "best guess" is not always so obvious, and many a mailer has run into difficulty because he made a wrong "best guess.")

But how sure are you that future results will be above your break-even mark of 1.125 percent? Certainly you are not sure as you hoped to be after the test. But such are the vagaries of testing.

The difference between what you obtained (1.3 percent) and your break-even point (1.125 percent) is 0.175 percent, which is roughly 13.5 percent of 1.3 percent by my dollar slide rule. Use the figure of 13.5 percent to enter Table 18-2. Go across the horizontal top row to the column headed "15%," closest to 13.5 percent. Then run down the

Table 18-2

		$\dfrac{\text{Observed return \%} - \text{break-even return \%}}{\text{Observed return \%}} \times 100 = \%$				
		10%	15%	20%	30%	50%
Degree of surety that	60%	6.5				
future return	70%	27.6	12.4	6.6	3.1	
percentage will be	80%	67.2	30.0	16.8	7.5	
above break-even	90%	163.8	73.0	40.9	18.2	6.6
percentage	95%		121.2	63.1	30.3	11.0

Each number in the table is the number of returns a test produced—irrespective of the sample size.

Note: Tables 18-1 and 18-2 contain the same type of statistical material. We include Table 18-2 only for the convenience of the different headings.

column to 12.4, which is closest to the 13 returns you obtained. In the vertical column to the left you can read that you are roughly 70 percent sure that repeated tests will bring home an average return of better than your break-even point. (Actually, since the 13.5 percent figure you were working with is less than the 15 percent, you are even less than 70 percent sure.)

Given that information, you are probably *not* satisfied that your test results will support further heavy investment without further testing. Run another test, then, perhaps the same size as the first, or somewhat larger. Then *combine* the results of the *two* tests as if they were just one large test, and go back to Table 18-2, following the previous instructions. By this time you should have sufficiently unambiguous answers to either push forward with confidence or drop the project. (This combination technique is probably not logically waterproof, but it is simple, easy to communicate and free of serious error.)

For the situation where your test results fall *below* the break-even point and you wish to know the chances that repeated mailings would be *above* the break-even point, you can still use Table 18-2. Substitute break-even and test results for one another, and subtract the degree of surety in the table from 100 to find the desired figure.

How to Test a List

Assume that your product offer is already fixed, as is your copy. You are committed to selling the product, and you have been successful with other lists. What you want, then, is to mail to every list that gives you even a dollar of profit.

Note that in this situation you will compute overhead in a manner different from that used for the problems in the section above. When you are just *considering* a product, you must take *all* costs into overhead—including setup and organization costs—and apply them to each unit you mail. But when the question is, rather, "Do I or don't I mail *this* list?" you should only load your overhead calculations with the cost of the overrun of stock, postage, addressing and direct handling costs. This is important, because you may otherwise pass up mailing chances that would increase your total year-end profit.

How large is the entire list you want to test? The size of the list *should* affect the size of your test sample. But, contrary to popular notion, the size of the list does not affect the *accuracy* of your test, but only the *economics* of the test. On a test of 2,000, it matters little for accuracy whether the entire list is 10,000 or a million. As long as your test sample is less than one-fifth of the total list—as it always will be—the accuracy will be almost the same no matter what the list size.

To repeat this difficult-to-believe but absolutely true statement: The accuracy of a test depends only on the size of the sample and not at all on the size of the list—as long as the list is more than, say, 5 times bigger than the sample.

But—the larger the total list, the more *valuable* your test information will be, and therefore the more you should be willing to lay out for the test, i.e., the higher the degree of surety you should demand. If the entire list is 10,000 and you expect a profit of 5 cents per piece mailed, the most you can make from the list after your 2,000 test is 5 cents times 8,000, or $400. But if the list is a million, your potential profit is 5 cents times 998,000. So errors are much more expensive if the list is very large. *That's* why a larger test may be warranted for a larger list.

Next you must decide the break-even point with which you are going to work. Then estimate the percent of return you expect and how sure you want to be of your results. Example: You estimate the return will be 2 percent, and your break-even point is 1.5 percent. (The break-even estimate should be accurate, but the estimated return estimate can be off considerably without harming the calculation.) You state that if you *do* get a return of 2 percent on the test, you'd like to be 75 percent sure that subsequent mailings will be above 1.5 percent.

To find the proper sample size, read Table 18-1 down to 75 percent (because that is the surety you have chosen to demand), read across to 25 percent [because (2.0 − 1.5) divided by 2.0 equals 25 percent], and the number in the block (7.3) tells you how many returns you need to get. Then divide the number in the block by the percent of return you expect. The result—365—is the sample size you need.

If you expect a 1 percent return, and you still don't want to fall below 25 percent of your expected return (i.e., your break-even point is 0.75 percent), you will work with the same block in the chart. You will still set your test up to get 7.3 returns, but the sample size will be twice as large—730.

But we all know very well that much more must go into this than straight statistics. With most lists you face the problem that when you go back to the list after the test, the returns will fall below the test mailing. We usually assume that this phenomenon results from tests that are not random samples of the whole list. Lewis Kleid's report "Importance of Stipulating Test Samples" gives excellent directions for obtaining random test samples.[6] If you follow those directions, you can prevent falloff from this cause. However, Orlan Gaeddert suggests that when many lists are mailed in large blocks, the probability of duplication increases, and this may cause dropoff in results when you go back to lists.[7]

If you expect that follow-up will fall below the test results, there are two possible solutions:

1. You can go back to the list in several successive mailings. Each mailing should do worse than the last, and you keep mailing till you fall below your break-even point. The first remailing will be close to the test results, and you may use the technique above to predict what you will obtain. Or,

2. If it is inconvenient for you to mail to the list in several sections, and if you can't bludgeon the list owner into giving you a random sample, your only recourse is to guess how much the entire list, on the average, will drop below the test. If you figure that the list will average 80 percent of a fair test, then reduce the test returns by 20 percent and go on from there in your calculations.

(A seller of professional books turned the falloff effect to good advantage. He mailed test samples of 5,000 each to fifty different lists—with no intention of ever going back to any of the lists—and his overall results were pleasantly high. The same firm estimates that a mailing indirectly sells 3 times as many books in bookstores as through direct replies.)

To evaluate the test results *after* they are in, go back and use Table 18-2 in just the same way you did when testing a product offer. Find the blocks that contain numbers close to the total returns you received. Each block gives you a combination of a degree of surety and a boundary to your guess. If you received seven returns, you can be 60 percent sure that follow-up mailings will not fall more than 10 percent below the test average; or, you can be 80 percent sure that the follow-ups will not fall more than 30 percent below your test average. (Pay no attention to the coincidental sequencing of numbers. The two figures cannot be added or subtracted.)

How to Test One Piece of Copy against Another

In the simple copy-testing situation the *costs* of both letter units being tested are the same. All you care about, then, is which letter unit pulls "better." And you need no calculations to tell you that you should go with whichever package shows up better on the test, no matter how small the margin between the two. Post-test calculating will only help you to decide whether your first test was conclusive, or whether you need to test further.

When the costs of the two letter units are different, the situation is more complex. Then you must balance the margin between them against the extra cost, using test results as your guide. The solution to that problem is beyond the scope of this discussion.

For the simple case, begin by asking yourself: How big a difference am I interested in? You obviously don't care if one letter unit is 1/10,000 better than the other, no matter how large your mailings will be. But you certainly do care if one mailing piece will bring in twice as many returns as the other, no matter how small your mailing will be. You must ask yourself at what point you cease caring, given the particular requirements of your situation.

As an example for discussion here, let's say that you wouldn't bother to test if you thought that the difference between the two proposed letter units would be less than 10 percent (of the average return).

Next you must ask yourself: If the difference is as big as, or bigger than, I care about, how sure do I want to be that the test will indicate which is the better letter unit? In other words, how sure do you want to be that the test will not mislead you? For example, here, let's say that you want to be 85 percent sure that the test indicates the better letter unit.

With those two values in mind, refer to Table 18-3. Read across to "10%," then down to "85%," and you find that you would require 424 returns to satisfy your requirements. You immediately decide that that would be too expensive and you decide to scale down your demand for surety to 75 percent and to concern yourself only with differences of 20 percent or more of the average return. You then find that you need to get 45.5 returns. If you expect an average return of 2 percent for the two test samples, each test sample must then be 45.5 divided by 2 percent, or 2,275. In total, you need to mail 4,550 letters to satisfy your requirements in this case.

Table 18-3

		The difference you care about: Percent return, letter 1 minus % return, letter 2 (Average percent return, letters 1 and 2)				
		4%	10%	20%	35%	50%
Degree of surety (How sure you want to be that the test results indicate the better letter.)	75%	1,237.5	182	45.5	14.3	7
	85%		424	106	34.7	17
	90%		656	164	53.0	26
	95%			272	86.7	43.5

Each number in the table shows the number of returns you must expect from the average of the two test samples. To obtain the sample size for each test sample, divide number of returns by estimated average return.

If the *real* difference between the letter units is even greater than you are testing for, you stand an even better chance of the test being right. If the real difference between them is less than you care about, you stand a greater chance of the best being wrong. But you have said that if the latter is the case, you are not concerned.

After the test is over and the results are in hand, you will probably *not* want to determine *how sure* you are that the test is right. If the difference between the mailing-piece returns is great, you need no further test. If the difference is slight, there isn't much point in further testing. Shoot the works with the letter that does better—no matter by how little it does better.

The fallacy has somehow gone abroad that you can test only one variable in a mailing. Not so. You can, in the same mailing, test headline, and colors, and copy and other variables. Testing more than one variable at a time does require extreme caution and attention lest you go astray. But it also can give you a great deal of information at a relatively low testing cost.

Let's say that you want to test two headlines against each other, and you also want to test a pink versus a blue reply envelope. You will mail four equal-sized random test samples: headline 1, pink; headline 2, pink; headline 1, blue; headline 2, blue.

How big a test should you make? My recommendation is that you should use test samples just as large as if you were only testing headline 1 versus headline 2, pink versus blue. (See preceding pages for guidance on that problem.) So you are getting two tests (almost) for the price of one.

To analyze the test, look at the *total* numbers of pink versus blue, and headline 1 versus headline 2. See the example in Table 18-4.

Blue is the color that pulled the greatest total number of returns, and it is probably better. Similarly for headline 2 that pulled the greatest total number. But which *combination* is best is a difficult question. Apparently the combination of headline 2 and pink did better than any other combination. However, that could be a fluke of the sample. Unless you think that there is likely to be some *interaction* between the

Table 18-4

(Hypothetical data)

	Headline 1	Headline 2	Color totals
Pink	40	60	100
Blue	50	58	108
Headline totals	90	118	208 (Overall total)

Table 18-5

Headline	Return (in percent)
1	2.3
2	1.8
3	2.7
4	2.9
5	1.9
6	1.9
7	2.0
8	2.2

color and the headline, then you would disregard the highest-score combination. I do not think such interaction is likely, and hence I would bet that the combination of the best headline taken by itself and the best color taken by itself—headline 2 and blue—would be the best combination.

Proceed with great caution in multiple testing. You *cannot* use the tables shown here to help you with tests of three or more letter units that vary on the same dimension, i.e., when there are three or more different headlines, or colors, or what have you. It is crucial to understand that the more variations you test on the same dimension—eight different headlines, for example—the more the variability you must expect in your results, and the larger the tests must therefore be. An analogy may help to make this clear. The more evenings you play poker, the more likely you are to come up with a royal flush—even though the chance of drawing it in any individual evening will remain the same. To test eight different headlines, *each* of the eight test samples will have to be *much* larger than *either* of the test samples when only two headlines are being tested.

Furthermore, if you test eight headlines, the percentage of returns for the *best* test sample is not—repeat, *not*—your best guess about what that headline will pull in the future. In Table 18-5, headline 4 is your best bet, but chances are that subsequent retests of the headline will not pull as high as 2.9 percent. I can't prove that statement here, and the body of theory is weak on this issue, but take my word for it anyway.

Conclusions about Direct-Mail Testing

1. The more willing and able you are to make follow-up tests, the smaller your original samples can be.

2. The higher the unit sale price (the smaller the percent of return needed to break even), the bigger the test sample you need to obtain the accuracy you choose to get.

3. Ever-larger test samples are not the necessary answer to your search for reliable information. Careful thought, together with *proper* test-sample sizes, is the answer. Very small samples can yield a great deal of information. An expert can often come to very important—and sound—conclusions on a test large enough to produce only ten or twenty-five responses.

4. The size of the list does not affect the accuracy of the test, hard as this is to believe.

5. Extremely precise statistical methods are not necessary in direct-mail testing. This is true partly because test samples are often badly unrepresentative, and partly because a mailer wants the *big* indications that make a big difference in the pocketbook. (Listen to differences that scream, not the differences that whisper.) Nevertheless, the *theory* of statistics plus crude rule-of-thumb approximations can be tremendously helpful in making and saving you money.

6. If you are testing many different variations of headline, of color, etc., you must look for differences much bigger than if you were testing just one variation against another. (Just *how* much bigger is a tricky question.)

7. We have said nothing about the mechanics of splitting test samples "randomly." Most direct-mail people are aware of how easy it is to foul up a test by sending all one sample to one state, all the other sample to a second state; or by splitting so that the first half of the alphabet gets one letter unit, the last half of the alphabet the other letter unit. The surest guarantee of a fair test, of course, is to send one letter to every other name on the list—no matter what the original order or disorder of the list. In any case, don't forget that if your lists are not reasonably randomly selected, all other technique is for nought.

The purpose of this section has been to give *some* of the benefits of statistical theory to direct-mail testers who don't wish to study statistics or the philosophy of science. But the wise will recognize the risks in this shortcut, and will not look upon it as a substitute for expert advice when tricky problems arise.

How to Lose Money with Mail-Order Franchises and "Deals"

I'm sure you have seen those fascinating ads for "mail-order franchises," for "catalog mailing" and for "cooperative" deals of all kinds. Those ads make powerful promises indeed. And the literature the advertisers send you has headlines like "We Will Set You Up and Back You in a Profitable Mail-Order Business of Your Own" or "Get Rich by Mail." What about them?

Catalog-Mailing Deals

Arrangements to mail other firms' *catalogs* probably have no chance at all to make money for you unless you already have a customer list and are in the mail-order business. This goes for the best as well as the worst of them. No firm has yet presented any *facts* to show that the average individual comes anywhere near breaking even, or that *any* of its "dealers" makes a significant profit—unless the dealer started out with a list of customers from prior mail-order or retail operations.

The basic reason for the failure of catalog-mailing plans is this: If there really were money to be made in mailing the catalogs to "cold" lists, the supplier would do the mailing. You might have some advantage in mailing to your friends (like an insurance agent who contacts all relatives first). But the number of such friends and acquaintances that you can mail to is very limited. After that, you are just pouring money into the supplier's pocket.

Or, at the very best, it may be possible to make money in the long run by mailing to *some* rented lists. But you can be sure that the supplier will mail to the best lists under his or her own name, and only the "dogs" will be left for you.

Don't get the idea that the "catalog-mailing" scheme is new. It isn't.

It has been kicking around almost since the mail-order business began. This is what the author of a 1906 *Encyclopedia of the Mail-Order Business* wrote over 75 years ago:[1]

THE EVILS OF THE STOCK CATALOG

Lest the term "Stock Catalog" be misunderstood, let us explain that this phrase is used when speaking of a catalog that is issued in immense quantities by certain supply houses who carry or pretend to carry all the goods in stock that is listed in this catalog. These catalogs are offered to beginners with their own name and address printed on them, so that the recipient of the catalog would be led to believe that the beginner was really the publisher of this catalog. The argument of the promoter is that the beginner could not publish a catalog of this description unless he spent a great deal more money for this individual printing. Again they argue that the beginner need not carry goods in stock, but can forward the orders to the supply house, who in turn, would fill the order and ship the goods direct to the customer, in the beginner's own firm name. This all sounds very nice, but in all these years during which time countless thousands have been "started" in this way, the writer cannot find more than three or four who actually built up a little business by the use of this catalog, and these injected some originality of their own, to come out ahead of the game. Another inducement some of these promoters offer, is the furnishing of "a list of names" to whom to mail the catalog, or to place some "advertising" for them in "pulling" mediums. But all these schemes are failures. The writer has personally interviewed mail-order customers, he has travelled through the rural districts, stopped over in farm houses, and saw with his own eyes, no less than seven identical "stock catalogs" in one house. The difference was the imprint on the different catalogs. As these promoters advertise everywhere for victims, the people in the rural district know all about the stock catalog, and do no more than bestow pitying glances on this literature—and either throw it into the fire, or give it to the baby to play with, as was the case in the farm house where I was stopping.

In debating with yourself the arguments for and against the use of the common and moss-backed stock catalog, just for a minute consider what sort of a reception it is likely to meet with at the hands of the people to whom it is mailed; particularly when as is often the case, the catalogs are sent to the list of names and addresses of "buyers" furnished by the same firm who sell you the catalogs. The result is that at some remote farmhouse day after day there will be copies of the same cheaply gotten up catalog coming by mail, the imprints of the senders being something like this: One day, The Royal Novelty Co., Squedunk Corners, Me., next day, Imperial Crescent Supply Co., Box 9, Frogs' Hole, Wis., the day following, The Associated Mail Order Manufacturers and Merchants, of Lock Box 12, Hoboes Landing, Perry Township, Fayette County, Mo., and so on and so forth in ridiculous repetition.

To sum up, your aim should be to get out of the beaten track and strike out a path to success for yourself. And of all beaten tracks the stock catalog is the one that stinks loudest in the nostrils of honest men and real Mail Order dealers. It is a track strewn with the bones and rotten carcasses of business hopes and mail order ideals that have been killed and strangled by the nefarious stock catalog and it is heavy with the smoke of money that has been burned in the vain hope of achieving success under the direction of the fakirs who operate under the guise of promoters who will point out the way to success to you. Keep away from that veritable Death Valley and don't let your hopes and your money be destroyed together in the burnt offerings of the misguided fools who in spite of countless warnings continue to keep the misplaced confidence game alive.

The stock catalog *can* be useful and profitable to you if you already have a list of people who buy other goods from you by mail. Gimbel's is said to purchase and mail millions of a stock catalog each year, evidently at a solid profit. The reason why stock catalogs can work if you have an existing list is this: between 2 and 10 times as many people will buy from you if they have done business with you before as will buy if they have never heard of you. This is the difference between success and abysmal failure. So, if you are already in the mail-order business and if you have a mailing list of satisfied customers, you might well make money by sending them a stock catalog imprinted with your name.

In previous editions I gave the names of some organizations that supply catalogs and who either drop-ship or supply the names of individual drop-ship suppliers, and do not extort "franchise" fees. But since then I have had the impression that even these organizations actually solicit unwary beginners, and hence I'll not mention them here. Their direct-mail piece says "Yes, X has put *thousands* of individuals like yourself in the profitable and fascinating mail-order business overnight and with fantastically small capital outlay and risk." But they continue, "TESTIMONIALS ARE PLENTIFUL—but we do not publish them or ask permission to do so. This would be a violation of business privacy." That's garbage. If someone gives permission to use a testimonial, there is no invasion of privacy, and the deal therefore stinks. There are listings under "Mail Order Drop-Ship Catalog and Merchandise" in the classified section of *Direct Marketing*. Chances are pretty good that they are on the up-and-up.

There are many other reputable firms that supply catalogs that you can use to sell *in person* but that will not work at all by mail.

It is very, *very* unlikely that you can mail imprinted catalogs to any "cold" list of people who have never done business with you, and make money at it. Many "suckers" have reported substantial losses, and *Direct Marketing*—a leading trade magazine—has run article after article on the dangers of this practice.

Mail-Order "Setup" Plans

A sure-profit business is a very valuable commodity. A business that will earn $10,000 a year for your full-time effort is probably worth $15,000. So why should anyone sell you the "setup" for $5 or even $500?

Furthermore, it is certain that no one can crank out "setups" on a mass-production basis, as must be the case if those who advertise them for a small sum are to make money.

Geniuses like to be rich and famous, too. I can guarantee you that there is no genius with an almost magical inside knowledge of mail order, in Salt Lake City, or Fandango, Maine, or anywhere else, who will "put you into" a profitable mail-order business for a small price. If there ever was such a genius, he or she is now selling his or her schemes to large companies for perhaps $25,000 per proposition.

"Cooperative Setup" Deals

Another scheme: You put up the capital for an already-developed ad, then purchase the products from the firm that developed the ad.

In other words, you "rent" the ad from the firm, and run it in a magazine at your expense. Any profit over and above your "rent" would belong to you.

In theory this plan sounds OK. If the ad pulls enough returns, you *could* make money. But the nature of the one-shot mail-order business forces your chances to be small because your "rent" is too high.

One firm that offered this deal took the first part of its rent in its advertising-agency commission. They argued that you would pay this commission even on your own advertising, but that is not necessarily true. When the firm runs the ad for its own account, it pays no commission, and that commission is an important part of its revenue.

The second part of the rent is the amount, much greater than cost, which you pay them for the merchandise.

But there is an even greater danger. It stands to reason that the firm will run the ad for its own account whenever it is relatively sure the ad will pull enough to be profitable. (And if it would be profitable for you, it will be even more profitable for them!) But they can rent you the ad to run in magazines that will *not* be profitable for them, and that way they take their profit out of your hide.

I come down hard on this plan not only because it is theoretically so bad, but also because the firm in question has shown no proof that there are people who have profited by the deal. If firms had such proof, they would certainly show it. (And I would not believe any proof except *consistent and repeated* successes. They could manufacture "proof" by letting a couple of their customers make money on choice media.)

Another firm, operating now, sells you packages of direct-mail materials at prices ranging from $63 to $340. This outfit has the unbelievable effrontery to demand that "your order must accompany signed honesty pledge." And the sales piece says:

> "A few know it all characters" have written asking this same old worn out question, "If my method is such a fantastic money maker then why would I want to share it"? Now for those who consider this to be a reasonable question here is a reasonable answer, I need letter handler collection agents in the same manner that General Motors need independently franchised dealers to sell their cars—Surely you know that General Motors, a billion dollar corporation, does not sell direct-to-the-public, also for the same reason that such giant manufacturers as Pepsi Cola, Coca Cola, MacDonalds, Howard Johnson Restaurants, General Electric and virtually every other major firm in this country prefer to use local independent wholesalers, dealers and retailers to sell their merchandise.
>
> Then why don't these giant companies sell their own products? Simply because they as well as practically every prosperous business person knows that the easiest and quickest way to increase sales is by offering a hefty chunk of the profits to their independent agents.
>
> It's a known fact that for years this proven selling technique has worked profitably for General Motors and other billion dollar biggies and you can bet your boopy that I intend to let it work for me too. Obviously this is why I'm so interested in sharing my big money success only with agents who don't mind giving up some time and extra effort mailing out my tested advertisements.

If you believe that, you'll believe anything.

Then there are a couple of promoters who offer ready-made mail-order "plans." They promise to furnish you with a product (almost always a booklet) and advertising copy for display and/or direct-mail advertising.

If the "plan" really could make money for you, it could make much more for the promoter. One could make more with it than any inexperienced person, and also save the fees. Furthermore, the promoter usually sells you the product itself at a steep price, and this makes it even less likely that you can make any money with the scheme. This should persuade you that you will only lose more hard-earned money in that kind of deal.

Beware of anyone who offers you the opportunity to sell his mail-order-tested product through the mail. If you can sell it profitably, why can't he or she sell it even more profitably, because he or she keeps the markup on the sale to you? The mailing lists available to you as a beginner are available to him, and so on. The most recent offer of this sort I've seen is an outfit that sells debt-collection forms by mail, and offers to put you in the business of selling those forms by mail. Once again, I'll believe that you have a chance to make money with this deal only when I see proof that a fair sample of people have done so—and this offer doesn't even cite *one case* of a "distributor" making money.

Chain Schemes

One of the oldest mail-order rackets is the deal by which someone sells you the materials to make money in mail order by selling the same deal to someone else. Not only is this out-and-out illegal, but it doesn't even make money for anyone except the originator, who sells you the phony material at a very high markup.

Mail-order racketeers are ingenious, however. I just received a chain-letter offer which may (or may not) escape the law by offering a "report" in addition to the chain-letter scheme, which they claim makes the deal legal. The "deal" was shown in Figure 6-2, for your edification. Fascinating? Yes. And disgusting.

A Summing Up

It all adds up to this: There is no pie-in-the-sky scheme that will get you started profitably in mail order. You will just have to study and learn the business, follow the methods and instructions I give you in my book—which should give you a better chance in mail order than anyone ever had before—and take your chances like the rest of us. If you win, you will have a glorious and valuable prize. If you lose, most of what you lose will be your time, because mail-order money investments are characteristically small. And you'll have a great experience in any case. Good luck again!

Types of Successful Mail-Order Businesses

The purpose of this appendix is to list and describe for you a good many *specific* lines of mail-order businesses which might be profitable for you to compete with.

It is very important for you to understand that this appendix is not about mail-order *items*. There are literally millions of items sold by mail order, but very few of these items are a business in themselves. What I am trying to describe in this appendix are *lines of items*, or *lines of business*, that will constitute a real business year in and year out.

Let me try to explain the difference. One of the most successful mail-order items in recent years was the flat-tire inflator can. It still sells by mail and will continue to sell, but in the catalogs of a dozen different firms. It may still be an entire business to its manufacturer, but it is only one item in a line of items for mail-order firms that sell it. The *line of items* may be automotive accessories, or novelties. We shall talk only about *lines of items*.

Of course, many items do constitute a business all by themselves; e.g., correspondence courses.

Here are some other examples of *products* that sell well by mail order, but are not likely to constitute a business unless you combine them with a line of similar goods. Note how many of them appear in novelty catalogs, sooner or later.

Blackhead remover	Confederate money
Cuckoo clock	One-way-glass formula
Address labels	Shrunken heads
Closet organizer	Magnets
Cleaning cloths	Supermarket cost counter

Huge balloon	Hand vacuum cleaner
Needle threader	Pocket calculator
Paper playhouse	

This appendix is far from inclusive. If it even scratches the surface, I shall be satisfied. Where I describe one firm, there may be twenty. You will have to do most of the searching for yourself. These are some places to look:

1. The advertising media. Chapter 3 gives you full instructions about how and where to look.

2. The lines of products listed in mail-order list brokers' catalogs. Chapter 14 tells about those catalogs.

3. B. Klein's *Directory of Mail-Order Firms* gives some information on what firms sell.

4. The *Standard Directory of Advertisers* and *Standard Directory of Advertising Agencies* at your local library or a nearby advertising agency. Look under "Mail-Order," "Books," "Correspondence Courses" and similar listings.

5. Lee Mountain, Pisgah, Alabama, issues a catalog of used books and correspondence courses he sells by mail. This is a helpful source of ideas.

It is often helpful to have some idea of the size of firms in a business you are interested in. It is difficult to find out the size of a business. Publishers' Information Bureau, 575 Lexington Ave., New York, N.Y. 10017, gives data on the amount that firms spend on advertising in the major consumer magazines. But in most cases, mail-order firms spend most or all of their advertising appropriations in direct-mail or unlisted display media. *Direct-Mail List Rates and Data* gives the size of the customer lists for many firms.

There is no special reason for the order of the listings in this appendix: I have tried to keep similar lines somewhere near each other. But you may find the same line or product popping up in several different places.

In this appendix there are a number of descriptions of businesses that have been quoted and paraphrased from *Direct Marketing's* series of "Ideas in Sound" interviews.

The full interviews are available on tape from Direct Marketing, 224 7th St., Garden City, New York. The code numbers for ordering are given at the end of each description. Most of the tapes cost $8 at 1980 prices.

[I am grateful to *Direct Marketing* and to Henry R. ("Pete") Hoke for permission to use this material.]

AGENT-SOLD PRODUCTS

Look through any of the salesmen's opportunity magazines to see perhaps 500 different lines in a single issue. I shall mention some of them when I list particular classes of products.

FOOD AND DRINK

Most of the food and drink that is sold by mail is gourmet stuff—special delicacies that are not easily obtainable in nearby stores, or very high-quality foods that gourmets are willing to pay a premium for.

There have been exceptions, but generally it is not possible to sell ordinary-quality foods by mail, even if you offer special price inducements. The cost of shipping is too high relative to the weight of the food to make it possible to offer real bargains.

Liquors, on the other hand, can be offered on a price basis under special circumstances, as we shall see.

There are many mail-order food ads in *Gourmet, Signature,* and similar magazines, especially before Christmas.

Meat

Fancy steaks are shipped frozen, by the dozen, at fancy prices. Several firms in the Midwest ship all over the country.

Smoked Ham, Smoked Turkey

Fish

For many years the famous Frank Davis Company in Gloucester, Massachusetts, advertised its mackerel and other fish by direct mail and in magazines. What happened to the firm? I don't know. Maybe there is room for someone, or maybe the market is gone.

Lobsters and Seafood

A professor who got tired of teaching and who wanted to live on Cape Cod sells lobsters by mail order, far and wide.

Cheese

Cheese is a favorite mail-order food item. Distinctive cheeses are a specialty, and they travel well over long distances. Also, the price/weight ratio is good.

There are several firms in the business, selling through different techniques. Some sell direct to the consumer all year long. Others do most of their business in Christmas gifts. Still others sell their cheeses as *business* gifts. And then there is at least one cheese-of-the-month club plan. One firm distributes over 10 million catalogs a year.

Fruit

I am continuously surprised that fruit can be sold successfully by mail order. And yet, it can.

One fruit firm is responsible for a famous headline in a big ad in *Fortune*. It went something like "Imagine Harry and me advertising our pears in *Fortune!*"

Mail-order fruit is usually remarkably large and juicy and commands a stiff price. One firm sells apples by mail that are good, but I can't tell them from the extra-special apples I can buy in season right here in town (for less than half the price).

One of the most famous and successful advertising men of all time started up a mail-order fruit business, with plain and gift wrappings, after he retired from his old job.

Preserves

There's a little old lady in a dingy little store on a side street in New York who makes her own preserves by hand and sells them by mail. She has been written up in several major magazines and gets orders from all over the world.

Fruitcakes

Mary and Sam Lauderdale sell pecan fruitcakes. Sold 500 pounds first year, grossing $800, netting $400. Mary of Puddin Hill business started virtually on kitchen table at Puddin Hill, family homeplace of Mary Lauderdale whose ancestors received property as land grant in 1836 during the Texas war with Mexico. Cakes made in October for Christmas season. Couple had to store cakes in apartment during early days. Afterwards moved to 1,200 square foot plant; added 3,600 square feet and warehouse facilities including refrigeration. ("Ideas in Sound," #730222JH8)

Candy

Sold to organizations for resale to their members and others, as a fund-raising campaign.

Pastry

Available are fancy pastries and those made from special foreign recipes.

Pretzels

Pretzels are now sold in gift packages.

Doughnuts

Doughnuts can be ordered by dialing a computerized supermarket.

Pecans

Sold direct to consumers, and also to organizations for fund raising.

Coffee and Tea

My first mail-order venture was selling fancy coffee by mail. It was an enjoyable business. But it could never be very big, so I turned it over to someone else, who let it run down and die.

There are still some companies in New York City advertising coffees. Herb teas and other special teas also are advertised.

Health Foods

Look at Organic Farming, Let's Live, and Prevention magazines to see the large numbers of firms, large and small, in this line.

Health Foods

Catalog/mail order business. . . . with chain of 170 retail outlets. . . . General Nutrition Corp. . . . opened first store in depths of depression, 1935. Rang up $35 in sales first day, $25M first year. By 1960's grossed $5 million per year. Mail order accounted for 95%. Last three years, concentrated on opening stores. . . . Discovered that stores help mail order. Mail order helps stores. Mails tabloid 5 times year to promote store traffic. Store people register all new customers, send names to Pittsburgh for central data processing (some 350,000 so far this year). Mail order customers receive 80-page catalog containing 3,000 items. Now shipping 35,000 orders a week ("Ideas in Sound," 72 GNPH 12 C1)

Gourmet Foods, Full Line

There are several firms, including one on the West Coast that has a fabulous millionaire customer list, that sell a full line of fancy foods. This is probably not an easy business to enter.

Gourmet Food Business

Paprikas Weiss (1548 Second Ave., NY 10027) . . . started . . . 50 years ago. Original catalog sent out in Hungarian, German and English languages. Now catalog is English only as ethnic groups have moved and integrated into American melting pot. Recently published Hungarian Cookbook carries best selling items from catalog in back pages, plus order forms for food, spices and other gourmet treats not normally obtainable in retail stores. Advertises book on wraparound catalog cover and as stuffer with own merchandise. Also uses space in such magazines as *New Yorker*. Space ads do not offer catalog, usually hardware only. The recipient receives catalog with package. ("Ideas in Sound," 72 EWJH 8 C1)

Gourmet Merchandise

Lady entrepreneur, probably largest in MO field, now mailing over 6MM catalogs/year, has 50M active customers from '72-'73 with average sale of $18. Lillian Katz, owner of Lillian Vernon's, and division. The Country Gourmet, start of business 22 years ago. Uses space extensively mostly in shelter magazines for individual items, but advertises only gourmet merchandise for The Country Gourmet, other merchandise for Lillian Vernon's. Results: gets two markets with one basic catalog. Space not only gets new customer, but keeps name in front of public, so when catalog arrives, recipient not unfamiliar with company name. Currently mails 5 catalogs/year starting heavy in August–September. Smallest mailing goes out from Easter to June to cream of list. Mostly personalized items such as door mat with name of family. Heavy in personalization for all merchandise "wherever we can get a name or initial." About half of merchandise offered at "$1.98 . . . 2 for $3.50" or similar. "People love a bargain." Uses service bureau with success for list maintenance. Computer Directions manages. ("Ideas in Sound," 73 0 363 JH 8.)

Wine and Liquor

In big cities there are very successful dealers who solicit orders by news-papers and direct-mail advertising. A natural for anyone in the liquor business who wants to branch out into mail order.

California Wine

Tiburon Vintners selling premium California wine by mail since '64. . . . Originally sold products only in California to distributors, but at same time offered wine by mail through rented lists in "two step" selling. Mail piece told story of Tiburon wines, offered to send additional information if recipient desired. Biggest selling point was offering printed, personalized labels to buyer for self, friends or as business gifts. Label reads "Selected Expressly for the Dining Pleasure of. . . ." Now, . . . company in process of expanding into national distribution. Law forbids winery selling direct to consumer outside California, so . . . setting up label program through wholesalers who buy in case lots, send names for personalization back to Tiburon, which prints, sends labels back to wholesaler who distributes them to retailer for affixing to bottles. . . . only property was retail roadside stand, no vineyards. Sales $15M. For past fiscal year ending July, sales $5.766MM. ("Ideas in Sound," 72-PFJH 8 C1)

Duty-Free Liquor

These firms solicit tourists before they go abroad. The liquor is delivered in the United States. (Shops are located in air terminals.)

SMOKING MATERIALS

Cigarettes

Several years ago several companies in New Jersey did a thriving business selling cartons of cigarettes by mail to people in states that had higher taxes on cigarettes. But after a long fight, the U.S. Supreme Court interfered with the practice. Now firms in North Carolina have found some new more-or-less legal way to sell cigarettes by mail. Be careful.

Cigarette-Rolling Equipment

This ad has appeared for years in the classified sections of various men's magazines, sure evidence of a profitable business: "Cigarettes—Make 20 plain or filter-tip for 9¢. Facts free. . . ."

Cigarettes, Imprinted

A New York firm runs a regular 1-inch ad in *The New York Times* and other media offering cigarettes specially imprinted with "Happy Birthday," "Good Luck Joe," or whatever else you want. This is a good example of offering *personalized* goods as mail-order items.

Cigars

Many of the firms that sold cigarettes by mail turned to selling cigars by mail, and several of them are now thriving. They offer bargain offers and free trials in cigar-length one-column ads in various Sunday newspapers and mail-order sections of magazines. Their profit comes in the repeat business over a long period of time. Cigar smokers like to try various types of cigars from time to time, and the firms make their offers to their lists by direct mail.

A customer list of 25,000 to 75,000 should support a very nice business. Connections with manufacturers of cigars are very helpful in entering this business.

Fancy Smoking Articles

At least two old and famous firms in Boston, and one in New York, issue mail-order catalogs of every conceivable article and tobacco a smoker could want.

Pipes

Look for the ad that says, "Don't give up smoking until you try my pipe." It's a great ad and shows what can be done in this line by mail order.

Tobacco

There are several farm-magazine classified advertisers who sell tobacco by the pound, by mail.

Lighters

HEALTH AND MEDICAL PRODUCTS

Health and medical products, and information on these subjects, are great mail-order items. But be careful! Make sure that what you sell has real and scientifically proved value.

An advantage of this field is that most health preparations are easy to man- ufacture or to buy from a manufacturing chemist. But this advantage is also a disadvantage. Just as it is easy for you to break in, so it is easy for the competition to break in too, once it is apparent that you have a profitable line on the market.

Vitamins

Vitamins are a classic mail-order item. Fortunes have been made in this field. Large companies and tiny ones, too, have been successful. Again, how- ever, be very careful about making claims for the effect of vitamins which you can't substantiate. (As a matter of fact, I doubt that any claim of benefits for vitamins to any potential customers is scientifically reasonable. I think it is all quackery except for obvious diseases, and they require medical treatment.)

Nevertheless, people want vitamins and will continue to purchase them by mail—and in large dollar amounts every year.

Vitamins can be purchased wholesale from a variety of places, in bulk or made up into packages. A little shopping will locate suppliers for you.

The usual marketing technique is to offer a bargain rate for a short-term supply—or even free samples.

You will have plenty of competition, for there are probably hundreds of firms selling vitamins by mail. But of course that also proves what a good potential business vitamins are.

Disease Cures

Several "clinics" of various healing persuasions offer their wares by mail. I suspect that some or all of these are quackery as its worst, but of course I can't say for sure (at least, not here).

Salve

There is a firm that sells a plain petroleum jelly salve. It advertises in comic books for small-boy agents. The owner nets $100,000 yearly and plays golf most of the day, according to the account given in a recent government investigation, I'm told.

Acne and Pimple Preparations

Blackhead Removers

Prescription Drugs

Several firms are already in the business of selling prescription drugs by mail at discount prices. I would guess that this will be a big, important and respectable mail-order line in the future.

Hearing Aids

Several companies sell their hearing aids by mail, usually with the help of agents in the field.

Eyeglasses, Prescription

Look for the occasional—but successful—ad of a company in this field. It sells at prices far below neighborhood opticians. I bet there is room for many more such companies than there are now.

Good advertising media are those that go to areas in which many elderly folk live.

Eyeglasses, Magnifying

Simple and cheap magnifying spectacles. A best-seller for years. One firm sells a type that clips onto other eyeglasses for further magnification. Lighted magnifiers for special needs are another possible item.

False Teeth and Dentures

Dental-Plate Repair or Reliner Kits

Foot-Care Materials

A New York firm sells an entire line of devices for bunions, hammertoes, etc. Looks like a good field, to me.

Nose-Hair Scissors

Sold directly from ads as well as through other firms' novelty catalogs.

Reducing Preparations

If you can help people to reduce, you have a mail-order product. Dozens of different kinds of preparations have been sold. Most of them are clearly phony, and the government cracks down. Some of them have limited use, and are more or less within the law. My advice is that you don't go near this business with a 10-foot pole.

Reducing Books

Some reducing programs have real value and can be sold honestly. Others cater to the dreams of those who want a miracle way to lose weight fast. The history of mail order is replete with excursions into this field. All I can say is: Be careful; don't get sucked in by the lure of a quick buck.

Diets

There is always a market for appetizing but nonfattening meal plans.

Reducing, Exercise Equipment

Mechanical reducing ads range from $1.98 rubber-stretch gadgets to expensive exercycles. Don't try to sell massage equipment as an aid to reducing, because it just doesn't work.

Antismoking Aids

A rash of these items is hitting the market now, in the wake of recent scientific discoveries of tobacco dangers. Just what any drugs can or cannot do to stop or reduce smoking is questionable. You'll have to do a lot of research for yourself on this.

Antismoking Psychological "Programs"

One book on how to stop smoking sold over 300,000 copies. There are several "programs" selling for up to $50.

Thermal Pads

Warren F. Clark, 87, has been in direct mail for over 60 years, and is still going strong with newest enterprise, 5-year old Clark Solaray Corp . . . Company manufactures thermal pad for use under bed pad to keep sleeper warm, work out aches and pains and to improve circulation. Holder of over 50 patents, Clark rarely sells except through direct mail. Honesty in copy and good solid product best guiding principles. Comments that he hasn't seen much change in DM over the years. Biggest change . . . is in improvements in graphics and production. Over the years he has sold only one-shot items. Will not use catalog or multi-mailer techniques. Gets 1-2% return on mailings of 50-100M per year. ("Ideas in Sound," 72 SCJH 8 C1)

Sleep

One firm does well with a line of gadgets that help you sleep comfortably, read in bed, keep sound and light out, etc.

Birth-Prevention Devices

Until recently, it was not clear what the law was on selling information or devices to prevent pregnancy. But then a courageous and socially motivated mail-order firm challenged the Postal Service on this and won. Now you can freely mail contraceptive devices.

A book on the rhythm system has done well, too. Lately, at least one reputable firm has brought out a mail-order book on birth prevention and artificial contraception.

Trusses for Rupture

A classic mail-order item. One firm was already well-established in 1913, and still does well. Its ads have changed little in that time.

Posture Braces, Slimming Garments and Girdles

Several firms make and/or sell various body braces. One firm sells an entire line, and will sell you its catalog and drop-ship for you, if you have a customer list that you can use it for. They also run their own display ads.

Lately the gift catalogs are showing these devices.

Bedwetting-Prevention Systems for Children

Medical Equipment

Stethoscopes and similar small pieces of equipment are sold to the public through display advertising. Often billed as "surplus."

Noise Preventers

COSMETICS AND BEAUTY AIDS

You might guess that cosmetics would be an ideal mail-order line. They are high-markup, repeatedly bought products, easily shipped by mail. But despite these advantages, full-line cosmetics have shown little promise for mail order—probably because they require demonstration before women will buy them.

However, specialty cosmetics have succeeded in mail order, as have firms that sell through agents. In fact, two firms that sell cosmetics through agents are among the most flourishing mail-order firms.

Hair Removers (Depilatories and Devices)

Various methods of removing women's unwanted hair have done well in mail order. One firm that sells an electrolytic device has run practically the same ad for years and years in women's magazines, a sure sign of success. Another firm began in mail order and sold that way for years before converting its operation mostly to selling through drugstores.

Special Antiperspirant Products

Fingernail Preservatives

Age-Spot Removers

Perfume

Sometimes sold in a basket of many small bottles of various scents. Suffers as a mail-order item because women want to try the scent before they buy.

Wigs

Women's wigs sold successfully by mail long before the recent craze hit the nation.

Toupees for Men

A specialized, high-priced, successful mail-order item.

Men's Hair-Coloring Preparations

Cosmetics for Blacks

Special preparations, especially for the hair, sell well by mail to blacks. There is at least one large company, and many small ones, that specialize in this line. Look for their ads in magazines catering to blacks.

In-Shoe Height Raisers

Shoe Air Conditioners for Sportsmen

Electric Shavers

Must be at bargain prices.

CLOTHING

Clothing always has been, and always will be, one of the great mail-order lines. But the mail-order offer must be different from clothes offered in local stores, either in type of clothing or in price.

Women's Dresses

Johnny Appleseed . . . has "backbone" business of moderately priced women's ready-to-wear, plus Christmas catalog of gift items. Ready-to-wear catalogs sent January, March, July to total of 3MM. Christmas catalog mailed Sept. to 1M. . . . all catalogs full color, featuring artwork rather than photography. Because of style changes, new fabrics. . . . Changes 90% of items in each new catalog. His average sale of $35/order, up $5/order over past 2–3 years. Attributes increase to upgrading of quality of merchandise rather than inflation. Company provides 24 hour/day phone ordering service through local answering service. After four years, finds credit cards accounting for 15% of business, improving size, number of orders. Reorders, many from same catalog, also hold up sales volume now at $3MM/year from MO only. ("Ideas in Sound," 72 SBJH 8 C1)

A famous Pennsylvania firm offers unbelievable bargains in inexpensive women's dresses by direct mail.

Another huge firm sells frocks through agents that it recruits by a vast campaign of mail-order advertising in magazines and through direct mail.

Several exclusive dress shops sell some of their simpler styles through *The New York Times Magazine* and other media.

Bridal and Wedding Needs

[Joan Cook, Inc.] starting in '55 on Long Island, mailed Joan Cook's Bluebook for Brides, sending to newly engaged girls. At same time, published same basic catalog for bridal party shops, caterers, with individual imprint of various shops to stimulate wholesale business. Features wedding accessories, matches, gifts, decorations. Still mail half million throughout year on retail basis; have 1000 active wholesale accounts, but wedding business now only 20% of total. Seven years ago . . . began housewares, gift catalog. Most recent effort 96 pages, 32 in color in 5" × 8" format listing 500 items. Most consistent sellers: silver, silver plate serving pieces, with or without monograms. Mailed 1.5MM catalogs this year, up 300M over '71. Prospects through list rentals but each test has to return at least 35¢/catalog for continuation of list use. Average sale $25. Rents or trades own list. ("Ideas in Sound," 72 CAJH 8 C1)

Special-Size Women's Clothing

These lines are good examples of how and why mail order works. Many women throughout the country do not fit into the standard sizes of clothing offered at local stores. But the demand is not sufficient in most places for the stores to offer the additional sizes. A mail-order firm, however, can cater to the demand of these women all over the country, without having to fight local competition. In addition to dresses, coats and other clothing are sold.

Half sizes.

Extra-large sizes. One major firm also has department stores in the largest cities.

Small sizes.

Maternity sizes.

Still another firm sells used dresses—twenty dresses for $3.50—and other used clothing.

Uniforms

Many types of uniforms are sold by mail—to nurses, waitresses, etc. Men's uniforms are also a good mail-order line.

Special Brassieres and Lingerie

One firm sells a fantastic assortment of padded, stuffed, and tapered women's underwear that appear to be marvels of engineering genius. The display pictures make your eyes pop out. Some people buy their 25-cent catalog for entertainment.

Other firms sell only special brassieres, not designed to be spectacular.

A girdle firm has a mailing list of over 150,000 mail-order girdle buyers.

Stockings

Two huge firms sell women's hosiery through agents. They claim special long-wearing properties for their products, and they use imaginative and varied merchandising devices.

Women's Shoes, Wide Sizes

Furs, New and Used

Fur-Coat Remodeling

Miscellaneous Women's Clothing

Various firms sell various lines of bathrobes, bathing suits and other occasional clothing. The trick, of course, is to build a list of women who like the styles you sell.

Men's Suits

Several firms take orders for suits custom-made in Hong Kong.

Other firms have sold custom-made men's suits through agents for years and years.

And there are many exclusive (or expensive) men's shops that circularize the people who have formerly bought from them. They send out two or more brochures or catalogs each year, illustrating the styles they carry.

Men's Suit Remodeling

A specialty of at least two firms is cutting down old double-breasted suits into the up-to-date style. If you want to go into this business, you might work up an arrangement with a good tailor who wants to expand his business.

Men's Clothes, Large and Tall Sizes

Small sizes probably would not work as a specialty because of male vanity.

Men's Slacks

A famous New Jersey firm sold ties by mail for many years. Now, as far as I can tell, they are concentrating their energies on selling men's slacks. They send swatches of material in the direct-mail pieces, and offer pants made of DuPont material at bargain prices. It was probably their success that convinced Spiegel to jump into this line, in competition.

Men's Ties

One of America's great advertising men had a hand in building a mail-order firm that sold ties made by hand by New Mexico Indians.

Men's Fancy Shirts

Bathing Suits

Men's Shirts, Custom-Made

Men's Shoes

Several big companies sell men's shoes through agents. They use direct mail, match books, space ads, and all other media to recruit salesmen. This is big business.

Men's Shoes, Large and Wide Sizes

Men's Shoes, Imported

Shoes by Mail from Hong Kong

Lee Lee, owner of Lee Kee, well-thought-of shoemaker and retailer in Kowloon. 60% of business mail order, but not aggressively promoted. K.K. visitors have outline of foot and several measurements taken so that custom made shoes can be ordered by mail by simply tearing out any fashion ad in a magazine, sending it to Lee Kee to be copied for $14-$20, and mailed to U.S. Some 150–200 orders arrive each day in Hong Kong though Lee does little advertising. Depends on word of mouth and constant influx of new visitors. ("Ideas in Sound," 72 LKPH 6 C1)

A New Jersey fellow sells shoes imported from England. He advertises in classified and small display in *Saturday Review, The New York Times Magazine,* "shelter" magazines, etc.

He also runs a retail store. I've been in there, and it is a nice little business. He sends out a beautiful printed catalog.

Men's Huaraches, Imported

Moccasins

Riding Boots

Men's Uniforms

Some firms sell through agents.

Robes and Gowns

For ceremonial occasions, graduations and ministers.

Men's Outdoor Clothing and Equipment

There are at least two fine old firms that sell men everything they need to be dry, warm and good-looking in the outdoors. They also sell related equipment along with the clothing.

Stadium Blankets

Rain Suits

Western Clothing, Men's

Men's Work Clothes, Used

Small ads in lower-class men's magazines sell reconditioned work clothing for an Ohio firm.

Belts

Fabrics

Several firms sell fabrics by the yard to women who sew at home. You probably need to be near a garment center to be in this business, in order to be close to your supplies.

Fabric Remnants

Back in the 1920s, several firms did well selling remnants in large quantities at low prices. I would think there is still a good market for this proposition.

Wool

A nice little business in Connecticut sells wool to women (and men) who weave at home.

Sewing Accessories

There are a good many firms that sell women everything they need to sew at home. One firm specializes in dress dummies. Others sell a full line of notions. Look in *Workbasket* to see their offers.

JEWELRY

Diamonds

One firm sells by mail and emphasizes the investment aspect of buying diamonds. It advertises in *The Wall Street Journal*, among other media.

Pearls

Diamond Rings

Several outfits specialize in selling to military personnel. Look in *Army Times* to see their ads.

Synthetic Gems

Simulated Diamonds

Simulated diamonds with constantly changing product line "bread and butter" of OGI International. . . . Uses newest "corundum" stone under trade name "Diamint" in promotions. Stone has 9 hardness on MOH jewelers scale, compared to 10 hardness for real diamond. Early stones only registered at 5–6, were easily scratched, chipped, broken. Later development of "yags" were harder, but intense competition dropped price/karat from $50 to about $4, he says. Shaw sells corundum stones at $22/karat including mounting, sizing.

Diamints also sold successfully through credit card promotions. . . . Also tested DM using rented lists. Results "very disappointing." Then tried space in many national magazines where two-step selling technique used, i.e., prospect wrote in "for more information." Shaw says he "just traded dollars and probably lost a few." Now "asks for the order" in full-color, full-page ads. ("Ideas in Sound," 73 0304 JH 8)

This is a flourishing mail-order business. Just make sure your advertisements tell exactly what you are selling.

Watches

Richard Sears of Sears, Roebuck got his start selling watches by mail, and it's still a good mail-order business. You must offer a bargain, though.

Jewelry-Making Hobby Supplies

AUTOS, BOATS AND ACCESSORIES

Autos

The automobile manufacturers speculate that in the future they may sell a lot of automobiles from catalogs and mail order. But that's not the business for you!

Car-Purchase Criteria and Information by Computer Service

Midget Cars

Miniature Models of Cars

Miniature Cars, New and Old

After several years of scraping by with little or no financing, David Sinclair, . . . Auto Miniatures, . . . today finds more money available than he needs, now that his company is well on the road to success. Prices of the miniatures range from $2.50 all the way up to $4250. Some are kits, most are not. Sinclair finds his repeat business is very good and many collectors look upon their expenditures as an investment. Advertising in "class" magazines, he qualifies prospects by selling his 72 page catalog for $1.00. Staying with high quality merchandise, Sinclair will expand into railroads, ships, cannons and antique machinery. Last year volume topped $200,000, and he expects $1 million in five years. He uses credit cards very effectively and does not use rented lists for prospecting. . . . Four employees do the complete job for Sinclair. ("Ideas in Sound," 72 DSJH 8 C1)

Trailers and Parts

Motorcycles and Parts, Tool Bags, Models

Hot-Rod and Custom Car Parts

Auto Parts and Supplies

Several firms issue huge catalogs of accessories for ordinary stock autos.

Other firms sell parts for foreign cars, or to the hot-rod set.

There is also at least one tiny mail-order business that sells parts for the Ford Model T.

Car Caddy

Tires

For trucks, cars, sports cars—all at prices said to be below wholesale.

Reconditioned Spark Plugs

Also sold through agents.

Wheel Balancers

Auto Seat Covers

One firm solicits new-car buyers by direct mail from rental lists of new-car registrations.

Sun Glasses, Auto

Guaranteed to prevent glare. Sold by direct mail.

Auto Polishing and Washing Cloths

Car-Washing Cloths

KozaK Auto Drywash, Inc. . . . started in 1926 when cloth for dry washing demonstrator cars of dealers was needed to circumvent expensive wet wash every night. Product line now up to 16 items for household use. Include: special sponges, chamois like cloths. Price range $2 to $18. Sales were first made through distributors, wholesalers and retailers. Turned to direct mail in 1950. Company does multiple mailings each year to segmented list of 1 million. Also buys $100M in space advertising. ("Ideas in Sound," 72 KAJH 8 C1)

A small-town firm sells nothing but this item, with remarkable success. They advertise by direct mail, and in display ads in such places as the Sunday garden page of *The New York Times*.

This is an example of what can be done in the mail-order business with a good basic item, or line of items, plus a great deal of mail-order imagination.

Windshield Fog-Cleaner Cloth

This is one of the leading items in the line of a firm that sells various auto and home goods through agents.

Boats and Motors

See the outdoor magazines for the full variety of firms in this market.

Boat Equipment

Detectors for noxious gases in boats, campers, etc.

Canoes

Boat Designs (How-to-Do-It)

Airplane Designs (How-to-Do-It)

Engines and Motors for Lawn Mowers

MAGAZINE SUBSCRIPTIONS

Magazines

Proverbial kitchen table and $1500 capital starting place 34 years ago for John and Jane Shuttleworth, publishers of bimonthly *The Mother Earth News,* other publications, which stress "consume less, enjoy it more" theme by getting back to land, basic living. Company now approaching $2MM level, but, says Shuttleworth, . . . "We're still working 12-14 hours a day, seven days a week." . . . Does big business in back issues. Ten months ago launched *Lifestyle!* "the magazine of alternatives." More oriented to urban groups. Published bimonthly to fill in odd months when "Mother" not published . . . At same time, Shuttleworth says, "We get paid to promote ourselves" via syndicated column 3 × /week in 62 newspapers; radio broadcasts on ecology, related subjects, on 90 radio stations which Shuttleworth records himself in own "down home in Indiana" style. . . . In MO business with Mother's Truck Store Catalog, "tools for living the satisfying life." Sells everything from old fashioned wood burning stoves, to candle making kits. ("Ideas in Sound," 73 0349 JH 8)

Almost every magazine publisher, from *Time* to *American Bee Journal,* is in the mail-order business of selling subscriptions. And these magazines are the biggest single users of third-class mail in the country. There are literally thousands of magazines in the mail-order business in the United States.

Magazines sell subscriptions to their own magazines. But there are also various types of mail-order firms that sell subscriptions essentially as agents for the magazines.

One firm offers fifty different magazines at cut prices direct to consumers. It sells by direct mail and mails millions of pieces per year. It is a huge operation, run by the former circulation director of a major magazine. Reportedly, this operation required a large sum of money to organize, and did not become profitable for quite a while. It makes its profits, like the magazines themselves, on reorders rather than on the initial subscriptions.

Other firms make deals with department stores to enclose stuffers advertising the magazines, along with monthly bills, or to print ads on the backs of return envelopes. These firms have apparently found that they do best when they offer only a few magazines at a time.

Still other firms sell through agents that they recruit by classified or display advertising.

All these operations are drop-ship operations. They handle no merchandise. All they do is solicit orders, collect money and take out their commission before forwarding the money to the magazines. Naturally they must sell at bargain prices (though never less than half the listed rate, or the magazine does not get credit for the subscription). And they must get bedrock deals from the magazines. Since magazines themselves often expect to spend every cent they get in subscription revenues in soliciting subscriptions, it is likely that these firms are sometimes able to arrange to keep all the subscription revenue they take in.

Magazines and Newspapers, Back Date

Racing Forms, Back Date

Binders for Magazines

Some firms sell the binders. Others bind the magazines for the customer.

BOOKS

Book Clubs

From $5.5 million in '69 to $12 million in '71 is the record posted by publisher Fuller and Dees. . . . Two book clubs account for the greater portion of the mail order business and 74 million pieces of mail out of a total of 12 million were sent in 1971 soliciting memberships in the clubs. Other products include customized cookbooks, a set of books for in-home sex education of children and a treasury of Bible stories. ("Ideas in Sound," 72 JPJH 8 C1)

There is considerable overlap between this section and the sections on Correspondence Courses and Information. Whether a piece of written material is a course or a book depends mostly on the price and the way it is presented. Most correspondence-course material is also sold as books.

Some books that are good mail-order items are also mentioned in our sections on Health, Sports and other topics.

Selling books and pamphlets by mail order has many advantages and some disadvantages. Chief among the advantages is that once you know you have a salable product, you can either write the material or have it written for you. This gives you perfect control over your material and perfect independence from the vagaries of suppliers.

If you own the rights to the material, you are in a position to reap the second great advantage, that of selling books at low cost, as low as 2 cents on the sales dollar.

Books and pamphlets go through the mail very cheaply, partly because of their low weight-to-cost ratio, partly because of the preferential postal rates Congress has seen fit to legislate for books. This is one of the reasons that books and courses are the greatest of the classic mail-order items.

The greatest advantage to selling books and information is also its greatest disadvantage: the ease of entering the field. Just as it is very cheap for you to test out a printed product and then go at it full blast, so it also is very easy for competitors to get in and reap part of the profit as soon as it becomes obvious to them (by repetition of your ads) that you have a profitable item. This means that in the field of selling books and information more than in any other field, the profits will go to the most efficient operator and the best advertiser.

The best source of ideas for salable books is the mail-order ads, of course. The next best source is the catalog of the Little Blue Book Company (including the Big Blue Book catalog) of Girard, Kansas. The founder of "Little Blue Books," Emmanuel Haldeman-Julius, was one of the great mail-order men of all time, and each book in his huge series was selected with an eye to its mail-order sales appeal. The list covers practically every subject that will have mail-order appeal to a mass public. It is a gold mine of ideas, and it is also a source of books to sell while you are still testing and not ready to print your own.

Other sources of cheap books for the mail-order market include the Wholesale Book Corp., 902 Broadway, New York, N.Y. 10010; Associated Booksellers, 147 McKinley Ave., Bridgeport, Conn. 06606; Book Sales Inc., 110 Enterprise Ave., Secaucus, N.J. 07094.

Incidentally, Haldeman-Julius wrote a superb book that is a tremendous store of knowledge for all mail-order sellers. It is called *The First Hundred Million*. Unfortunately, the book is out of print.

Another source of ideas for books to sell by mail is the catalog of Lee Mountain, Pisgah, Alabama. Most of the books listed in his catalog, as well as the courses, have been successful mail-order items at one time or another. I'll mention some of the specific titles. These titles should give you a good idea of which types of books will and which won't make good mail-order items.

Sometimes you can find a good mail-order seller that is not outdated but that has fallen out of copyright. The book is then in the public domain, and you are perfectly free to duplicate it and sell it yourself without anyone's permission.

Sex Books

This class includes books of sexual knowledge, not pornography or fiction. It is a tremendous mail-order field.

One firm that sells a "marriage book" (perfectly respectable, of course) offered to rent its list of 140,000 buyers in 1962, 170,000 buyers in 1961, and 100,000 buyers in 1960. You can figure for yourself how much they grossed at $2.95 per copy. And that's only one of several items they sell. Their basic medium is display ads in men's magazines.

Other firms buy books from publishers and offer several books in their ads. Or they arrange with the publishers to drop-ship for them. All you have to do is persuade the publisher that you are a bookseller—several orders will prove that—and he will drop-ship the merchandise to your customers.

How-to-Do-It Books

Even how-to-do-it encyclopedias have sold well by mail.

Travel Books

Books on how to travel cheaply (by freighter, etc.), and how to retire cheaply in little-known places, are particularly good mail-order offers. One firm offers a line of these books.

Health Books

How to Live Long
How to Stop Smoking
How to Reduce
"Science of Keeping Young"
Home Remedies
Home Medical Encyclopedias
"How to Live 365 Days a Year"
"How to Stop Killing Yourself"
Birth Prevention

Inspirational Books

Books, Ethnic and Religious

Business and Money-Making Books

Business Books

Starting with $30,000 capital in 1971, Donald Dible, founder, Entrepreneur Press, Inc. . . . and author of "Up Your Organization—How to Start and Finance a New Business" tells . . . that sales for last year were $250,000, and he expects to do $500,000 in 1974. Book now in 5th printing after 26,000 copies sold at $14.95. Original price $24.95, but mail tests indicated greater profitability at reduced rate. Originally marketed book in space ads, but expanded to other media like co-ops, press reviews, mail, retail. Inquiries now costing about $2/piece. Converts about 30% to sales, depending on source. One-half of '73 books sold in retail trade. ("Ideas in Sound," 14-0015 JM)

You'll find a raft of these books advertised in classified space in the mechanical and outdoor magazines.

"Get Rich in Spite of Yourself" is a typical, successful title. This one sells at $1 from newspaper reading notices.
Handwriting Analysis (Graphology)
Cartooning
Show-Card Writing
Sign Painting
Restaurant Management
Shoe Repairing
"Cash from Sawdust, Coat Hangers, etc."
"990 Bizarre Businesses"
"609 Unusual, Successful Businesses"

Stock-and-Bond Record Books

Baby Books, Wedding Books, Bar Mitzvah Books, Confirmation and Graduation Books

Miscellaneous

One fellow made a nice little business out of just one book—an adult stunt book of 101 best stunts.

Auto-Repair Books

Atlases

Maps

Great Museums, Great Monuments, Milestones of History

Almanacs

Bibles

A great sold-by-agents business. Some Bibles also are sold directly by mail.

Self-Help Books

Bashfulness
Sleep Learning
Self-Hypnosis
Voice and Speaking Improvement
Dancing
Penmanship. (This was a better seller before typewriters became so common.
  But one old firm still sells its instructions.)
English
Etiquette
How to Get to Sleep
Mathematics Made Easy
Public Speaking
Conversation Improvement
Horse-Race Betting
Shorthand Systems
Fortune-Telling
How to Stop Smoking
Foreign Languages (also sold as records)
Beauty for Women
Body Building for Men (including isometrics)
Fighting Methods (karate, boxing, wrestling, judo, etc.)
Memory Improvement
Musical Instruments (especially guitar)
Personal Magnetism
Personal Efficiency
"Seven Keys to Popularity"
"Self-Mastery"
"The Knack of Remembering Names and Faces"

"Conquest of Fear"
Correct Breathing
Secrets of Strength
Psychology
Yoga
Hypnotism. (At least fifteen firms sell books and hypnotic aids.)
Methods of Success
"How to Put the Subconscious Mind to Work"
Personal Finances
Tax Saving
Social Security Benefits
Salesmanship
Handwriting Analysis
"70 Bible Lessons 25¢. Bulletin, Box 87. . . ." (A long-running classified ad.)
How to Buy Surplus from the Government. (Several firms sell these guides.)

Most self-help books are sold one at a time. However, there are several publishers who sell their whole line of books via consolidated ads in magazines. Some of them sell pamphlets at 50 cents (three for $1); others sell books at $2.

Textbooks, New and Used

When you think about mail order and books, you should remember that many, if not most, publishers of hard-cover books are in the mail-order business. This is especially true of university presses.

Coin Catalogs and Albums

Photo Albums and Photo-Mounting Supplies

Stamp Albums

Book Clubs

The Book-of-the-Month Club started a business that has burgeoned. Now there is a book club, it seems, to suit every interest: intellectuals, mystery lovers, bargain lovers, etc.

The book-club business is specialized, however, and as a beginner you won't be attempting it.

Discount Books

On one of the back pages of the book-review section of *The New York Times* on Sunday, in the *Chicago Tribune* and in other media, you will see the ads for several firms who advertise books at 25 to 30 percent off the list price. These outfits take your order, deduct the difference between your price and the publisher's wholesale price, and send money and your address to the publisher. That's all. No merchandise to carry. No investment. A nice repeat business.

I'm sure these businesses aren't getting rich. And they must be efficient to make money on their small margin.

Book Finders

The only ways to buy a book that is out of print is to get it from a secondhand bookstore or have a book finder get it for you. The book finders use several trade publications to locate the books. I don't know how they work, but I do know that at least ten of them advertise regularly in classified columns of book reviews and magazines.

Bookbinding

CORRESPONDENCE SCHOOLS

Correspondence schools are another great mail-order product. Tens of millions of Americans have taken courses in the past, and many of them have been helped to live better lives. (Look at the International Correspondence Schools testimonials in their ads!) And millions of Americans are studying hundreds of different subjects at home right now.

Correspondence schools have the major advantage that the course work travels lightly and cheaply by mail. They sell products which often cannot be studied elsewhere, or cannot be studied locally in most areas. They offer real benefits to the student—either a better job, more money or a richer life.

In addition to the correspondence schools, there are many resident schools that sell their services by mail. The auctioneering schools, for example, require that the student travel to the school, but all the selling is done by mail.

The listing of types of correspondence courses is nowhere near complete. Lee Mountain's catalog (Pisgah, Alabama) contains the fullest listing of past and present courses that I know of. The classified and display sections of *Popular Science*, *Workbasket* and the various specialized magazines will give you the complete picture of what's on the market now.

Correspondence courses go on and on, year after year. The owner of a correspondence school is not constantly hunting up new items to put into his catalog or sweating out the latest fad. He will be continuously experimenting with his advertising, year after year, but he can count on a reasonably stable income from sales of his course.

High School Home Study

A big field, and probably getting bigger even though more and more people graduate from high school.

The schools use many and various methods of promotion, including car cards and match books.

Full-Line Correspondence Schools

Most correspondence schools offer one or a few courses. Several offer five or ten related courses, such as the foreign-language schools. International Correspondence Schools and LaSalle are unique in offering many, many courses—over 250 by ICS.

"Do you make these mistakes in English?" is one of the most famous, and most effective, headlines ever written. The Sherwin Cody School has tried many other headlines and many other ads over a period of several decades. They always go back to using their original ad.

Self-Improvement

Handwriting Analysis
Child Rearing for Parents
Art. The art correspondence schools teach many different facets of art: commercial, cartooning, painting, advertising, etc.
Music. One of the schools ran the most famous headline in advertising forty years ago: "They Laughed when I Sat Down at the Piano—But when I Began to Play. . . ."

You can learn any instrument at one or more of the schools. Other outfits offer just a single course. Guitar instruction is a best-seller.

English Improvement
Conversation Improvement
Memory Improvement
Voice and Speech Training
Body Building and Muscle Building for Men
Beauty for Women

Ventriloquism
Penmanship
Home Instruction for Children

Science of Personal Success (tape cassettes)

Technical Courses

There is a wide variety of technical courses sold by mail order, ranging from navigation to welding, but we shall not discuss them here. International Correspondence Schools offers many of them, and you can check their catalog. Advertisements in technical magazines will show you others.

Business, Job and Money-Making Courses

Bookkeeping. Instructions to set up your own local business. Government manuals, which are in the public domain, probably supply the backbone of at least one of these inexpensive courses.
Accounting
Accident Investigation
Auctioneering
Watchmaking
Gunsmithing
Detective Training. Detection equipment is also sold by the outfits that sell the courses.
Piano Tuning
Practical Nursing
Restaurant Management
Swedish Massage
Invisible Mending
Millinery Design
Locksmithing
Woodworking
Typewriter Repair
Television and Radio Servicing
Photograph Coloring
Interior Decoration
Baking
Landscaping
Forestry and Conservation
Doll Making and Repair
Dressmaking
Floristry
Orchid Raising

Accident Claim Investigation
Hotel Management
Watch Repair
Meat Cutting
Taxidermy. One school has been in business over 50 years with little change in its advertising.
Exterminating. This is a course that I have never seen available, but I think it would be a good bet.
Candy Making
Photography
Child Photography
Writing
Civil Service Examination Studies
Commercial Art
Commercial Writing
Law
Metal Plating
Mirror Silvering
Baby-Shoe Metallizing
Travel Agency. I'd guess this course would be a specially good bet today, when so many people are traveling.
Cleaning and Pressing
Printing
Real Estate
Insurance

Education by Mail

Education By Mail burgeoning business of Insurors Press. . . . Three-year-old company grossed $200M in '69-70; $458M in '71; expects to go over $1 million mark this year, with more than $2 million projected for '73. Publishing firm specializes in educational materials for insurance industry, but expanding rapidly into other fields such as industrial security, occupational health and safety, humor books for doctors, dentists . . . Follows up mailing with salesmen on WATS lines. If specific name known in company, salesperson will sell 6 of 10; if name not known, sales drop to 3 of 10. ("Ideas in Sound," 72 IPJH 8 C1)

Salesmanship (sometimes with records)
Electric Appliance Repairing
Upholstering
Credit and Collection
Sign Painting
Silk-Screen Process
Flocking
General Business Training for Executives

INFORMATION SERVICES

Information services differ from books and courses in that the information must be *current and timely*, and therefore must constantly be new and up to date. Because of the high cost of gathering information, it is usually sold at a high price to a few subscribers. Information services sell their product for as high as $30,000 per year to a single firm. But most of the information services that we shall mention sell for from $2 to $100 yearly to individual or business subscribers.

Naturally enough, your information must not be easily available elsewhere, or no one will buy your service.

Information services have many similarities to magazines, and in fact, many magazines have started this way.

Stock Market Advisory Services

Look at their ads in *The New York Times* Business Section. Some are very big, some very small. Taken as a whole, this is big business.

Make sure you really are in a position to provide true information. And get clear on the laws that regulate this business.

Business Newsletters

There are several "inside dope" newsletters that provide general tips. At least one of these is a huge business.

Most major industries also have weekly newsletters that collect industry gossip, promotions, hirings, firings, alarms and anything else of interest to company executives. These letters are generally started by people who have a wide acquaintance in the industry. They have sources of information and know what executives want to know about.

Economic Information

One firm supplies leads for salespeople on all new businesses opening all over the country. Another tabulates references to economic forecasts made in all the trade magazines. A third, a huge company, provides information on new building permits.

Information Brokers

Some firms have developed an interesting trade in bringing together people who need tips on new business, mergers, etc., and people who can supply such information.

Social Security Information

Most of the information sold is extracted directly from uncopyrighted government publications in the public domain.

Retirement Information

Where to live cheaply.

Sermons for Ministers

Dress Patterns

Architects' Plans for Houses

Boat and Airplane Construction Plans

Look for the ads in the mechanics magazines.

Plans for Home-Workshop Projects

Employment and Job Information

Directories

Several firms publish directories of various types of business information: names of firms in an industry, names of buyers, names of trade associations, etc.

PHONOGRAPH RECORDS

Records have much in common with books as mail-order products. Both are readily mailable, can be offered as bargains, and often have specialized audiences.

Record Clubs

Most of the clubs are run or controlled by manufacturers, and they have a cost advantage not available to outsiders.

Language Records

Stereo Components

Children's Records

Teaching Records for Children

Popular Hit Records, Stereo Tapes and Cassettes

Combinations of the latest hits, on one record, have sold well from radio advertising. The commercial ties in with the program.

A similar scheme has worked for classical themes on television.

Religious Records

Poetry Recordings

PHOTOGRAPHY

Moving Pictures and Slides

Respectable home movies are sold via catalogs. Also 35-millimeter slides.

Religious Movies and Filmstrip

Photos of Movie Stars

Wallet-Sized Photos

Some firms make copies of photographs. At least one firm has a recent list of 95,000 buyers.

Cameras and Equipment

Cameras and Equipment, Secondhand

Correspondence Photography Courses

Photograph-Club Plans

One firm worked up a dandy business selling gift subscriptions for children's pictures taken every year on the child's birthday, from age 1 to age 6. Then they franchised the plan to local studios.

Local Studio Photography

Photographers can increase their local businesses greatly with mail-order techniques.

Baby Pictures

Film Developing

Mail-Order Film Processing

Beacon Photo Service . . . mails about 2,500 orders/day. In '71 grossed $10 million, accounting for about 3% of total mail photo processing done in U.S. yearly. ("Ideas in Sound," 72 RBJH 8 C1)

There is a large number of firms that do this work at cut-rate prices by mail. Their gimmick is that they cut out the intermediary drugstores and other pickup places from the economic chain. They advertise everywhere, in heavy volume, in many media.

GARDEN SUPPLIES, PLANTS, SEEDS, SPECIAL TOOLS FOR TERRARIUMS

Gardeners are good mail-order buyers. See garden magazines and garden sections of Sunday newspapers. Many large and small firms flourish in this field. One firm has a mailing list of 6 *million* customers. Another large firm sells through agents.

Garden-Supply–Club Plans

A different plant or seed is sent at regular intervals.

Bird Feeders and Houses

Decorative Water Fountains

Fountains by Mail

Roman Fountains, Inc. . . . turns to wholesale for bulk of yearly sales of $500M. Fountains bought principally by landscape architects and contractors, registered architects. Now testing real estate developers. . . . Most fountains sold by mail for hotels, office buildings, professional buildings, art and civic centers, shopping center malls. Smaller fountains sell for as little as $80; major jobs run as high as $50/M. Prints 80-page catalog listing 150 fountains. . . . ("Ideas in Sound," 72 JEJH 8 C1)

HOBBIES

Every year Americans have more free time and more money to spend on their hobbies. The growth of mail-order businesses in this area proves it.

Hobby Correspondence Courses

Taxidermy, Music, Horse Training and many others.

Hobby Supplies and Tools

Tools

Since 1967 when the company first went into catalog mailing, the Brookstone Company . . . has more than doubled its business each year. The product line is devoted almost exclusively to tools for the sophisticated hobbyist, miniature builders, engineer, outdoorsman. In 1971, the company realized over $1 million in sales with an average sale of $18. ("Ideas in Sound," 72 RCJH 8 C1)

Guns

Air Rifles

Antique Guns

Gun Accessories and Supplies

Gunsmith Supplies
Hunting Calls

Blank Pistols for Training Dogs

Archery Equipment

Slingshots

Animal Traps

Fishing Tackle

Rods, reels, lures, tackle of all descriptions. Some firms sell direct from ads, some from catalogs.

Fish Lures and Scents

Trophies

Dogs

Dog Equipment

Collars, kennels, shipping crates, "doors" into the house, dog "toys," etc.

Model Trains

Model Planes

Model Boats

Model-Building Supplies

Tents

Sleeping Bags

Backpacking Equipment

Portable Flush Toilets

For camping and other outdoor activities.

Golf Equipment, Club Plans

Golf Books

Personalized Golf Balls

Golf Shoes

Golf Supplies

Ball warmers, hand dryers, club covers, etc.

Pneumatic Swimming Support

A German patent, brought here. Manufacturer sells to other mail-order companies, catalogs, etc.

Diving and Scuba Equipment

Ski Supplies, Books and Clothing

Body Warmers (for skiers, backpackers or winter campers)

Barbells

Contour Joggers (for jogging at home)

Body-Building Books and Courses

Electronic Equipment, High Fidelity

Tape Recorder Tape and Supplies

Photography

Photo Travel Slides

Telescopes

Chronographs

Binoculars and Optical Equipment

Optical Equipment

The Bushnel Optical Corp. . . . deals in sports optics, spectator viewing equipment, shooting and hunting scopes. The optical equipment is made in Japan mostly under the design and supervision of Bushnell technicians. The cost vs. U.S. made products is one half or less. ("Ideas in Sound," 72 BOJH 8 C1)

Domestic and Imported

Range Finders

Scientific Hobby Equipment

Edmund started his own business by selling damaged, chipped-edge lenses for $1 through $9 classified ad. Now has 5 million per year business, mainly mail order, specializing in photographic and scientific equipment and novelties. Average sale: $3. 55,000 people per month request 4,000 item free annual catalog. ("Ideas in Sound," 72 HMNE 8 C1)

Kites for Adults and Children

Leatherwork Supplies

Musical Instruments

See the music magazines for a full display. Accordions, guitars and chord organs are sold through mass consumer media.

Recorders

One firm does well selling just this one instrument.

Astrological Horoscopes

ART

Correspondence Art Courses

Probably the most successful mail-order business in the art field.

Art Supplies

Necessary to have a retail store also, to maintain the necessary stock. Cut-rate special supplies are sold successfully.

Pottery Wheels and Kilns

Custom Paintings from Photos

Prints, Reproductions and Posters

Over the past few years these lines finally seem to have had some success.

Paintings, Imported

The firms mail out selections on approval, like stamps.

Sculpture

Statue Reproductions

Wood Carvings

Posters

Antiques

Antique Reproductions

Picture Moldings

Commemorative or Art Medals and Commemorative Plates

Origami Paper

Stamps

This is one of the great mail-order fields. There are far more than 100 firms in the field, many consisting of just one man working part time. A recent issue of *Popular Science* carried ads for seventy outfits. But you'd better know the stamp game before you try this field.

The larger stamp firms use many media, including match books.

Coins

A booming field in recent years, and will probably continue to boom.

Some firms make a dandy profit on their catalogs alone, but this may not be ethical.

Indian Relics

This is just one tiny example of hundreds or thousands of types of little-known and specialized lines that mail-order firms sell at a neat profit. They advertise in out-of-the-way places, and you must really research the field to come up with those that will be good fields for you.

Ship Models

Woodworking Supplies

Jewelry-Making Supplies

Needlework Designs and Supplies

Braided-Rug Supplies

Costume-Jewelry Supplies

Sculptured and Fancy Candles

TOYS

Toys are not a great mail-order item. Yet, under some conditions they do well. For example, the famous F.A.O. Schwartz Co. uses display advertising to solicit inquiries for its catalog before Christmas, and Penney's, among others, sends out a big catalog, too.

Electronic Computer Toys

Science Kits for Children

Dolls, 100 for $1

Huge Balloons

Balloons, 200 for $1

Magic Tricks and Novelties

PRINTING

This is a field of mail order which already thrives mightily, and which will grow even more in the future, I think, for this reason: If you went into a local printer and ordered 500 address labels, he or she would probably have to charge you $20. The shop would have to buy special paper, set up a press specially for the job, get the labels padded, etc. But a firm that makes a business of address labels can make a profit on them at 50 cents or $1. Why? Because they mass-produce them at a fantastic volume. It's the old American story, as simple as that.

The same idea holds for personal stationery, memo pads, calendars, office forms, envelopes and a hundred other types of printing.

So, if you find a printed product that people want, and if you can operate efficiently and cut costs, this can be a mighty profitable field of endeavor.

Address Labels

These are often sold as a "leader" to introduce people to a line of gifts or novelties.

Other firms sell them through agents, and through stores and women's clubs as money-raising goods.

Fancy address labels with photographs of hobbies.

Personal Stationery

Two firms sell 100 letters and 50 envelopes, good quality, at the fabulously low price of $1.50 and apparently make a nice profit. One of them was reported to gross $750,000 several years ago.

Greeting Cards

Though cards are sold all year round, the major business is for Christmas. This is a big, solid business, done mostly through agents.

Greeting-Card Kits (for making own greeting cards)

Wedding Announcements

Birth Announcements

Greeting Cards for Business

Office and commercial greeting cards for Christmas are a big business. One firm has a list of 110,000 commercial customers, very nice indeed.

Name Stamps, Rubber

Name stamps are sold for pocket use, with the personal signature engraved on them, and also just plain rubber stamps. One firm has a recent customer list of 104,000.

Book Plates

Embossing Machines

Personalized Welcome Mats

Sold direct and through agents.

Personal Signs

Metal and plastic signs are sold for all kinds of purposes: mailboxes, desks, gardens, everything. People like to see their own names in print, and that's why this is such a flourishing mail-order business.

Business Cards

Sold by mail at about $7 per thousand.

Letterheads

One firm offers to design them and print them, too.

Office Forms

Standard sales forms, invoices, etc. More complicated forms will probably continue to require a salesman. The economies of the mail-order offer are in *standardized* forms.

Legal Forms

Arizona lawyer giving up practice after 21 years to pursue new career in mail order. James E. Grant, . . . in MO part time for several years selling legal, semi-legal printed forms to other lawyers, office suppliers. Grant . . . says gross in past 12 months about $50M, but by going full time after July

1, he expects to double gross in year. So far, 75% of business in Arizona only. Difficult to sell same forms in other states because of complexities, variations in same basic laws. Now expanding into forms utilized in Federal laws such as bankruptcy sets, Federal court forms, odometer forms certifying mileage on used cars. ("Ideas in Sound," 73 0335 JH 8)

Postal Scales (pocket-size)

Job Printing

One New York firm cuts its own low prices in its direct-by-mail, cash-with-offer deal.

Mimeographing

A Chicago firm even does mimeographing for large firms whose business it solicited by mail, though I think its work is not outstanding nor its prices particularly low.

Envelopes

Mail-order envelope firms offer real economies to large users of envelopes all over the country.

Collection Aids

An entire big business has been built on collection aids and stickers for insurance offices and similar customers.

Memorandum Devices

These are big sellers to business people. *Signature,* the Diners Club magazine, is chock-full of large ads for various varieties—especially at the end of the year, of course.

Schedules and Calendars

Advertising Novelties

Many advertising novelties have the advertiser's name imprinted on the novelty.

Tarot Cards (fortune-telling)

An example of a small printed novelty that has sold for years. It has probably been too small a line for anyone to challenge, so one firm seems to have the whole market.

Book Matches, Imprinted

Usually sold through agents

Prepared Circulars and Stuffers

Various firms prepare advertising materials for cleaners, florists and other businesses, and sell them to one exclusive customer in each area.

Printing Devices

A Connecticut firm has used the identical ad to sell its low-priced printing presses for 80 years. Another firm sells presses and accessories to commercial users. Another sells mimeograph machines through agents. Still a fourth sells a postcard mimeograph machine. And there are lots more.

MONEY

Money has an advantage for mail order: it is light in weight and easily mailable. It also has a disadvantage: the person with whom you are dealing is not close at hand.

Small Loans

For a while small companies had this field to themselves. Recently a mail-order giant tested the field, and jumped in with both feet.

Business Loans

A large commercial lender mails incessantly to supermarkets and other businesses to find prospects who want to borrow money for new equipment and fixtures. They close the sales in person, however.

Coins and Bullion

Real Estate

Life Insurance

Getting bigger every day.

Health and Casualty Insurance

Growing by leaps and bounds.

Burial Insurance

Auto Insurance

I am intrigued by the "special offers" to anyone who says he doesn't drink.

Savings and Loan Associations

Dozens of them advertise for you to save with them. Two firms make a business of acting as mail-order broker for many savings and loan accounts. Stock-market firms also get into the act. One reported $60,000 in accounts for a $100 ad.

Stocks and Bonds

Regular accounts as well as voluntary investment plans for small investors.

Investment Advice and Market Letters

Betting

Betting by Mail

Betting in English football pools grossing $3MM/week for Vernons Football Pool, subsidiary of Vernons Organisation. . . . Vernons, one of five privately owned pools in England, ranks #2, gets 30% of total bets. Average bet, about one U.S. dollar. Twenty percent of customers covered by mail every three weeks with envelope containing three coupons for betting following three weeks. Bettor sends in one coupon/week. Formerly mailed 1 coupon/week but as postal rates increased, frequency moved to every two weeks; now three. Each mail drop is 1.5MM pieces; returns 600M bets/week. Remaining 80% of bettors solicited weekly by "agents" in factories or door-to-door agents. . . . Football Pool marketing director, John Kennerly, says . . . that every street and address in England on computer. ("Ideas in Sound," 73 0338 JH 8)

Collection of Debts

One firm obtains collection clients through the agents it recruits by mail.

Credit Cards

Diners Club has done a remarkable mail-order job in obtaining subscribers. It has utilized car cards and take-one advertising of all kinds, among its media.

HOME-BUSINESS EQUIPMENT AND SUPPLIES

Bees and Beekeeping Materials

Squabs

A gentleman named Elmer Rice made a remarkable mail-order success by putting people into the business of raising squabs. He was also the pet account of one of the three largest advertising agencies in the country.

Chicks and Chicken-Farming Equipment and Supplies

Years ago everyone thought it was impossible to sell chicks by mail order. Now the mails are full of them!

Fish, Partridges, Rabbits

Vending Machines

Baby-Shoe-Bronzing Equipment

Electroplating Kits

Rubber Stamp Machines

Tennis-Racket-Restringing Equipment

Printing Presses and Printing Supplies

Welding Equipment

Saw-Sharpening Machines

Plastic Molding

Synthetic Gem Making

Doughnut Machines

Rug-Cleaning Equipment

Typically, one firm sells a franchise and marketing program along with the equipment.

Furniture-Cleaning Equipment

Wall-Cleaning Equipment

Sign-Making Machines

SERVICES

When you think about what to sell by mail order, don't concentrate so much on products that you forget about services. There are many things that you can do *for* people and firms, and that can be arranged by mail—far more than you think. So search your own experience to see if you have a special knowledge that you can sell to people for profit, or if you can develop such a skill or knowledge.

Book Binding

Mentioned earlier under "Books."

Vanity Publishing

Blanket Weaving

"Send us wool for blankets. Write. . . ." reads the ad.

Comforter Recovering

Commercial Photography

Advertisement Writing and Consultation

Several hot direct-mail letter writers make a nice living this way, I'm told.

Commercial Artwork

One fellow caters to mail-order firms and does small ad layouts for them. He has done it for years.

Collection Agencies

Most of them do their collection entirely by mail. And some solicit all their clients by mail.

List Owners and List Brokers

One of them advertises in foreign newspapers and does a direct-mail business with its catalog.

Patent Search

You must be in Washington to render this service, I would guess.

Invention Marketing

Glove and Leather Goods Repairs

LOCAL SERVICES

Don't get the idea that a mail-order business must be national in scope. Many local businesses are run on mail-order principles, except that the customer calls or comes in person, or that delivery is limited to a small area. For example, a business that advertises firewood could never be national. But it might operate entirely by advertising and telephone orders, and have all the hallmarks of a mail-order business.

Local services are usually part mail-order-type, part straight retail. The two hands wash each other!

I will list only a few examples of the multitude of services that you can run this way.

Window Washing

Auto Mechanics

Rug, Furniture and Wall Cleaning

Floor Sanding

A dandy little business for some couples. He goes out and does the jobs while she minds the phone to answer the inquiries they get from newspaper classified advertising.

Duplicating and Photostat Work

Travel Agency

Some travel agents do considerable business by mail outside the local area, too.

Flower Delivery

In one major city two fellows started a successful weekly club plan. And I experimented with the idea in New York under the name "Flowers Every Friday." I gave it up in favor of another scheme at the time, though afterward I saw that it had excellent prospects. The plan was later developed for weekly delivery to banks.

Lawn and Tree Care and Treatment

BUSINESS TO BUSINESSES

For some reason, beginners in mail order always focus on products and services for consumers, ignoring the huge field of mail-order sales to commercial and industrial firms. It will be very educational to have a friend in a small office collect and show you the mail the office receives over a short time. You'll be amazed at its volume.

As an example, I will list just a few of the major types of mail-order offers that come into an ordinary insurance agency.

Office Equipment

Kole Enterprises, Inc., . . . sells corrugated merchandise, mostly for industrial use. Line includes bins for parts storage, pull drawer and office files, corrugated boxes, cabinets, related items. ("Ideas in Sound," 72 GBJH 8 C1)

Office Supplies

Everything from pencils to filing cabinets. One firm mails to a list of 3 million, among whom are a whopping 800,000 buyers.

Rubber Bands by the Pound

Specialized Books

Sales-Training Bulletins, Programs and Records

Letterheads

Stationery

Printing

Janitor Supplies

Ice-melting products, just for one example.

Building Maintenance

Wholesale Maintenance Products

Revere Chemical Corp. ... built profitable business selling assortment of building maintenance products solely by mail. ... Company distributes catalog to 100,000 customers. Careful attention to detail plus wide attention to telephone contacts, which account for 10% of sales a must. ("Ideas in Sound," 73 0352 PH 8)

Brushes, Industrial

Some sell through agents

Envelopes

Collection Aids

Specialized Magazines

Typewriters, New and Used

Adding Machines and Calculators

Imported, usually.

Electronics

Wall Charts and Display Boards

Advertising Novelties

Furniture for Institutions (Churches, Schools, etc.)

Machinery and Construction Equipment

Of every size, shape and description from chain hoists to printing presses.

Junkyard Equipment

Selling junk car crushers, heavy equipment, down to small office supplies by mail to junk yard owners turns $300M/year into $5MM/year business in three years. . . . TeleCom Industries . . . three years ago sent small flyer to 40 junk yards in NY State offering piano wire to cut out windshields, other small items. Response good, so Diefendorf got lists from associations, other sources; expanded mailings into Northeast sector of country, then Eastern seaboard. Now mails nationally to 15M/month. In view of success, company plans on expanding market into Europe with Denmark office soon. Later, will expand market to include sales of heavy construction equipment by mail. ("Ideas in Sound," 73 0158 JH 8)

HOME FURNISHINGS AND HOMES

Farms

Home Plots in Retirement Areas

Precut (prefabricated) Houses

Roofing (especially of aluminum)

House Plans (Architectural)

Lumber

For do-it-yourself builders, especially.

Fuel Oil

A local business.

Awnings

Hammocks

Wallpaper

Drapery

Burlap for Home Decoration

Custom-Made Drapes

Bedspread Caddies

Burglar Alarms

Also sold through agents.

Fire Alarms

Pumps for Miscellaneous Uses

Hardward Novelties

Door knockers, switch plates, etc.

Door Checks

Home-Workshop Equipment

Tools

Welding Equipment (Do-It-Yourself)

Rugs

Furniture

Chairs, tables, cabinets, garden furniture, all kinds of furniture.

Elevating Recliner (for handicapped or disabled)

Furniture Do-It-Yourself Kits

Chair-Caning Supplies

Bars

Bar Supplies

Novelty glasses, mixers, bars, etc.

Cabinets and Drawers

One firm that specializes in Old American style reputedly does a large business, all drop-shipped.

Bed Massage Equipment

Long-Life Light Bulbs

Sold through agents.

Wireless Light Fixtures for Closets

Miniature Chandeliers

Fire Extinguishers

Cookware

A terrific amount of cookware is sold by agents through home "parties." Other stuff is sold directly through "unbelievable bargain" ads, some of which are phony "surplus" or "liquidation."

Gadgets

Part-time, in-home catalog mail firm, Hendry House . . . still going strong after 17 years, says Mrs. Gay Hendry, owner. . . . Says she averages three-hour-day, grosses "under" $100M/year. . . . Ninety percent of 150 items shown in 32-page, 2-color, 5½" × 8" catalog drop shipped. Remainder of fulfillment done by family of five Hendry children, friends, who pitch in when busy. Mails about 100M catalogs/year spread over average three mailings. . . . Uses *The New York Times, Parade,* others for sale of single items. . . . Always on lookout for "gadgety things;" new, unusual, exclusive items. Looks for items not found in other MO catalogs. ("Ideas in Sound," 73 0088 JH $8)

China

Silverware

Basketware

Lamp Specialties

Telephones and Telephone Equipment

Plastic Freezer Containers

One firm has a list of 50,000 customers whose average purchase is $15.

Cutlery

Typewriters

Calculators

First direct marketing venture brought in over $20 million in sales for Hewlett-Packard's HP-35 pocket calculator which sold for $395 each.... Hewlett-Packard traditionally sold its line of 3000 products through own sales force. For products selling from $1000 to $100,000, $50 to $200 cost per sales call could be justified. Lesser priced calculator prohibited individual sales calls except on volume basis. Company turned to.... a direct-mail program. Result: mailing package costing 20¢ each. Mailing pieces went to cold prospects, rented list of engineers. Success of campaign induced Hewlett-Packard to use dm for all lower cost products. ("Ideas in Sound," 14-0046 KC)

Power Mowers

Lawn Markers

Lawn Furniture

Candles, Decorative

Dry Window Cleaner

Through agents.

Fabric-Mending Glue

Through agents. Also needle threader, eyeglass cleaner, etc.

Glue

Through agents.

GENERAL MERCHANDISE

Most firms in the mail-order business specialize in one or a few lines of merchandise. And I strongly advise everyone who is interested in mail order to start off with a specialty line, at least at the beginning.

However, there are also a good number of firms that sell a variety of merchandise. These general merchandisers fall into a few major classes that we shall now describe.

Department-Store Type of Firm

Everyone is familiar with the Sears, Roebuck type of operation. 'Nuff said, except to mention that at least two major firms, J. C. Penney and Singer, have entered the field more recently, testimony to the vitality of mail-order selling today.

General Agents' Merchandise

There are several prosperous firms that sell a wide variety of merchandise through mail-order-recruited agents.

Novelty and Gift Merchandise

Since World War II there has been a fabulous growth in the firms that offer novelties priced from 88 cents to $10 through catalogs. They sell knickknacks that retail stores don't carry, new and gimmicky things that are fun for customers to buy and give away. Some of these firms have been terrific success stories. One of them has a customer list of 2.6 million, and in a short 16 years has grown from nothing to an annual volume of $7 million.

This is not a field for a beginner starting on a shoestring unless you possess considerable merchandising skill and experience. Capital, too.

These firms solicit new customers in one of two ways: (1) By offering a specially attractive bargain leader in space ads. They lose money on the initial order, but make it up in later purchases. (2) By sending their catalogs to lists rented from, or traded with, competitors in the same general field.

Assorted "Bargains" and "Surplus" Specialties

Klein's Directory lists about 3,000 firms, most of which are in this category. Many of those firms make little or nothing, however, and many are in the business for only a short time.

These firms work in a variety of ways. One method is to develop a customer clientele for real or apparent bargains of all types. The firm ordinarily advertises one or more of these bargains in space advertising, then follows it up with package stuffers and direct-mail flyers of from one to eight pages of similar merchandise.

Some of the merchandise is truly bargain, imported or domestic—the result of good merchandising ability on the part of the firm. Other merchandise is government surplus. Still other firms sell phony bargains and "liquidated" merchandise that can be bought just as cheaply at retail stores.

Some firms really are able to make money with a succession of one-shot items sold directly from space advertising. But such firms are few and far between. Mostly they must depend on repeat sales for profitable volume.

MISCELLANEOUS LINES

Religious Materials

Dog Repellent

Insects

INSECTS

Terry Taylor, an entomologist and owner sells Lepidiota Bimaculata from Thailand by mail to biologists, teachers, collectors, researchers, ad agencies, artists and museums. Inventory of 3MM specimens and thousands of species in home-based laboratory. Taylor and wife operate business. ("Ideas in Sound," 73 0482 JH)

Plastic Custom Molds

Chemicals

Grave Monuments, $14.95 (in truth, that was 15 years ago)

These tombstones are made of concrete.

Bed and Sleep Furnishings

Tear-Gas Guns

Bookplates

Coin-Bank Calendars

Novelty Pets

Includes monkeys, horses, turtles.

Chalk-Talk Cartooning

Old Gold Bought

Fortune-Telling

I do not recommend this field.

Flagpoles

Coats of Arms with Family Name

In pewter or wood shield, $7 or $14.50.

Marriage Brokers

Employment Agencies

Teacher's employment agencies seem to do well by mail.

Transistor Radios

Charm-and-Treasure Jewelry

Slide Rules

Plaques and Tablets

Church Furniture

Children's Things

See mothers' magazines.

Ball-Point Pens and Refills

Pest-Control Supplies

Decorated T-Shirts

Decorative Maps

Trading Cards

There is something to be learned about the mail-order business from this example. You would never guess, from the advertising, that one firm, let alone several firms, does a very substantial volume in trading cards (baseball and other sports pictures) sold to children and collectors.

Only a few tiny ads appear each year in a couple of specialized media, accounting for only a tiny advertising budget. And yet I learned about one of these firms—a retired couple, whose large apartment was filled from wall to wall with trays of cards. The business, started as a hobby, was easily worth $25,000 when I saw it in the mid-1960s, despite the fact that many items were sold for a few cents each.

Precision Timers

The Meylan Stopwatch Corp . . . started selling regular watches by mail in 1921. However, keen competition led to stopwatch field. . . . First customers were largely sports enthusiasts or government personnel. In thirties they turned to industry where stop watches were used for time study use and industrial engineering. Most recent catalog . . . includes sophisticated timers, counter, watches and time-study boards. ("Ideas in Sound," 72 MSJH 8 C1)

Canoe Trips

Computers

Computer Service

Selling $440/year computer information service subscription by phone, only successful method found after much testing. Subscription consists of three basic volumes totalling 1804 pages, monthly update of 120 pages, unlimited phone consultation. "Most authoritative reference work in the industry," says Kalbach. Gives complete information on all types of hardware, software, new developments. Market is any company owning, leasing computers, peripheral equipment. Kalbach started in '70 when sales $250M; now $2MM and growing. Renewals "better than 80%" sell at $330/year. ("Ideas in Sound," 73 0305 JH8)

Brand-Name Items on Credit

Co-op Catalogs

Phone Catalog Grocery Sales

Grocery delivery direct from warehouse to home via phone ordering service off and running in pilot operation. Galaxy Foods, Inc., Brooklyn, NY . . . has no walk-in business, delivers only within three-mile radius of warehouse, does not sell produce, all meats flash frozen. Minimum order $7 paid for at door. Customer orders day in advance, can specify delivery time in any two hour period from 8 a.m. to 10 p.m. . . . No membership fee, no freezer to buy, no contract, money back guarantee. First order taken on spot from loose leaf catalog of 3,500 items. When merchandise delivered, new catalog goes with order and customer number given. ("Ideas in Sound," 73 0223 JH 8)

References

CHAPTER 1

1. *Establishing and Operating a Mail-Order Business*, U.S. Department of Commerce, Industrial Small Business Series, no. 46, p. 12.

2. Robert A. Baker, *Help Yourself to Better Mail Order*, Printers' Ink Publishing Co., Inc., New York, 1953, p. 4.

3. Arthur E. Swett, *Principles of the Mail Order Business*, 4th ed., Swett Publishers, 1900, p. 1.

4. "Using Labor Raises Response for Gifts-by-Mail Company," *Direct Marketing*, February 1974, pp. 55 ff.

5. "Texas Pair Saddles Career Selling Fruit Cakes by Mail," *Direct Marketing*, December 1973, pp. 24 ff.

6. "Successful Jewelry Sales by Non-Legendary Camelot," *Direct Marketing*, July 1974, pp. 55 ff.

7. Advertisement in *Advertising Age*, Oct. 22, 1973, p. 137.

8. "Thousand Dollar Investment Brings Millions in Ten Years," *Direct Marketing*, October 1973, pp. 29 ff.

9. *Direct Mail Lists, Rates and Data* (DMLRD), July 2, 1973.

10. *Direct Marketing*, October 1973.

CHAPTER 2

1. *The New York Times*, July 8, 1974.

2. *The New York Times*, Apr. 5, 1976.

3. "The World of Advertising," *Advertising Age*, special issue, Jan. 15, 1963, p. 137.

4. Joseph H. Rhoads, *Selling by Mail with Limited Capital*, U.S. Small Business Administration, Small Business Bulletin, December 1958, p. 1.

CHAPTER 3

1. Paul Bringe, *Briefs from Bringe*, August 1962.

2. *Direct Marketing*, June 1977.

3. Gerardo Joffe, *How You Too Can Make at Least $1 Million in the Mail-Order Business*, Adriano, San Francisco, 1978.

4. *Advertising Age*, May 13, 1973, p. 48.

5. Frank Vos, "How to Choose or Reject New Mail-Order Ventures," *Direct Marketing*, vol. 39, January 1977, pp. 22–26.

6. Story from *Direct Marketing*, May 1978.

7. Ibid., p. 48.

8. *The Wall Street Journal*, Sept. 21, 1978, pp. 1, 21.

9. Emanual Haldeman-Julius, *The First Hundred Million*, Simon & Schuster, New York, 1928.

CHAPTER 4

1. "Combine a Love of the Sea with True Mail Order Success," *Direct Marketing*," April 1976, p. 44 ff.

2. "How to Succeed in Business Doing Something You Enjoy," *Direct Marketing*, March 1977, p. 36 ff.

3. "Ideas in Sound," catalog no. 72, LHJK 8C1, Direct Marketing, Garden City, N.Y.

4. Maurice Segall, "Mailers and Retailers Revving Up for Marketing Revolution," *Direct Marketing*, July 1973, p. 26.

5. *Direct Marketing*, June 1974, p. 56.

6. *Advertising Age*, Feb. 4, 1974, p. 14.

7. *Direct Marketing*.

8. Murray Raphel in *Direct Marketing*, July 1965, p. 66.

9. *Direct Marketing*, "Selling Golf Clubs by Mail Brings Discounts for Duffers," March 1977, p. 46 ff.

10. "Manufacturer Sells Business to Go Into Mail-Order Sales," *Direct Marketing*, May 1977, p. 32 ff.

11. Frank Vos, "How to Choose or Reject New Mail Order Ventures," *Direct Marketing*, vol. 39, January 1977, pp. 22–26.

CHAPTER 5

1. *Advertising Age*, Feb. 3, 1964, p. 38.

2. John Moran, *The Mail Order Business*, MBA Business Associates, Syracuse, N.Y., 1949.

3. Reporter of *Direct Mail Advertising*, December 1961, pp. 22–27.

CHAPTER 6

1. *Newsweek*, Feb. 19, 1979, p. 36.

2. Morton J. Simon, *The Law for Advertising and Marketing*, Norton, New York, 1956.

3. George Rosden and Peter Rosden, *The Law of Advertising*, Matthew Bender, New York, 1974.

4. Verneur E. Pratt, *Selling by Mail*, 1st ed., McGraw-Hill, New York, 1924, pp. 50–51.

5. Samuel Sawyer, *Secrets of the Mail Order Trade*, 1900, p. 23.

6. U.S. Postal Service, General Release 25, Mar. 26, 1974.

7. *Direct Marketing*, 1979(?), p. 6.

8. U.S. Chief Postal Inspector, *Mail Fraud*, Government Printing Office, Washington, 1967.

9. Sawyer, op. cit.

10. Paul Bringe, *Direct Mail Briefs by Bringe*, March 1963.

11. Morton J. Simon, *Advertising Truth Book*, Advertising Federation of America, Washington, D.C.

CHAPTER 7

1. Paul Grant, L. W. Mail Order Survey, no date.

CHAPTER 8

1. Business Information, Inc.

2. Robert F. Stone, *Successful Direct Marketing Methods*, Crain Publishing Co., Chicago, 1975, p. 156.

CHAPTER 9

1. *The New York Times*, April 5, 1976.

2. Direct Marketing, August 1972, p. 25.

CHAPTER 10

1. Klaus Reuge, "There's More to Selling by Mail than Counting Coupons," *Direct Marketing*, January 1973, pp. 32–36.

CHAPTER 13

1. G. Lynn Sumner, *How I Learned the Secrets of Success in Advertising*, Prentice-Hall, Englewood Cliffs, N.J., 1952, p. 86.

2. Robert A. Baker, *Help Yourself to Better Mail Order*, Printers' Ink Publishing Co., New York, 1953, p. 73.

3. Paul Grant, L. W. Mail Order Survey, page not known.

4. S. D. Cates, quoted in John Moran, op. cit., p. 137.

5. Robert F. Stone, *Successful Direct Marketing Methods*, Crain Publishing Co., Chicago, 1975, p. 94.

6. Irvin Graham, *How to Sell Through Mail Order*, McGraw-Hill, New York, 1949, pp. 335-337.

7. H. K. Simon, *Mail Order Profits and Pitfalls*, H. K. Simon Co., 1961.

8. Ken Alexander (pseudonym for Alexander Segal), *How to Start Your Own Mail Order Business*, Stravon Publishers, New York, 1950.

9. J. L. Simon, Urbana, Ill., private data.

10. Robert D. Kestnbaum, ibid.

11. Robert Stone, *Successful Direct Mail Advertising and Selling*, Prentice-Hall, Englewood Cliffs, N.J., 1955, p. 50.

12. John Moran, *The Mail Order Business*, MBA Associates, Syracuse, N.Y., 1949, p. 493.

13. Robert Stone, "Where to Start, How to Test, in Direct Response Magazine Ads," *Advertising Age,* Oct. 22, 1973, p. 119.

14. Robert F. Stone, *Successful Direct Marketing Methods,* Crain Books, Chicago, 1975, p. 93.

15. Victor O. Schwab, "Successful Mail-Order Advertising," in Roger Barton (ed.), *Advertising Handbook,* Prentice-Hall, Englewood Cliffs, N.J., 1950, p. 612.

16. Moran, op. cit., p. 150.

17. Elon Borton, "Tested Facts Produce One Million Sales for La Salle in 37 Years," *Printers' Ink,* Aug. 10, 1945, pp. 19–20.

CHAPTER 14

1. Victor O. Schwab, "What 92 Split-Run Ads Tell Us," Part II, *Advertising & Selling,* May 1948, p. 38.

2. Harold P. Preston, *Successful Mail Selling,* Ronald, New York, 1941, p. 44.

3. Ibid., p. 48.

4. Victor O. Schwab, "What 92 Split-Run Ads Tell Us," Part I, *Advertising & Selling,* April 1948, p. 33.

5. John Caples, "Headlines: Your First Try Should Not Be the Only One," *Direct Marketing.*

6. Schwab, "92 Split-Run Ads," Part I, p. 60, and Part II, p. 38.

7. John Moran, *The Mail Order Business,* MBA Business Association, Syracuse, N.Y., 1949, p. 63.

8. Henry E. Musselman, *Mail Order Dollars,* Publicity Publications, Kalamazoo, Mich., 1954, p. 174.

9. David Ogilvy, *Confessions of an Advertising Man,* Atheneum, New York, 1963.

10. Schwab, "92 Split-Run Ads," Part I, p. 62.

11. Robert A. Baker, *Help Yourself to Better Mail Order,* Printers' Ink Publishing Co., Inc., New York, 1953, p. 42.

12. Stanley Rapp, "Mail-Order Inserts Increase Sales Four Times," *Media/Scope,* September 1961, pp. 79–83.

13. Schwab, "92 Split-Run Ads," Part I, p. 60.

14. William A. Shryer, *Analytical Advertising,* Business Service Corp., Detroit, 1912, p. 171.

15. Baker, op. cit., p. 49.

16. John Caples, *Making Ads Pay*, Doon Publishing Co., 1966, paperback, pages not known.

17. Baker, op. cit., p. 48.

18. D.B. Lucas and S.H. Britt, *Advertising Psychology and Research*, McGraw-Hill, New York, 1950, p. 248.

CHAPTER 16

1. Paul Bringe, *Direct-Mail Briefs from Bringe*, August 1973.

2. Stone, *Successful Direct-Mail Advertising and Selling*, p. 71.

3. Ibid., p. 70.

4. John Moran, *The Mail-Order Business*, MBA Business Associates, Syracuse, N.Y., 1949, p. 418.

5. Stone, *Successful Direct-Mail Advertising and Selling*, p. 72.

6. Ibid., p. 71.

7. Ibid., p. 70.

8. B. M. Mellinger, Mail-Order Course, published by its author, Los Angeles.

9. Verneur E. Pratt, *Selling by Mail*, 1st ed., McGraw-Hill, New York, 1924, p. 143.

10. Stone, *Successful Direct-Mail Advertising and Selling*, p. 71.

11. Paul Bringe, *Direct Mail Briefs from Bringe*, November 1978.

12. Robert A. Baker, *Help Yourself to Better Mail Order*, Printers' Ink Publishing Co., Inc., New York, 1953, p. 164.

13. Henry E. Musselman, *Mail-Order Dollars*, Publicity Publications, Kalamazoo, Mich., 1954, p. 173.

14. Paul Bringe, *Briefs from Bringe*, June 1962, quoting from Lewis Kleid, Inc., Research Report No. 48.

15. Paul Grant, L. W. Mail-Order Survey, page not known.

CHAPTER 17

1. Paul Bringe, *Briefs from Bringe*, April 1963.

2. Business Information, Inc.

3. Robert Stone, *Successful Direct-Mail Advertising and Selling*, Prentice-Hall, Englewood Cliffs, N.J., 1955, p. 26.

4. Ibid.

5. Robert F. Stone, *Successful Direct-Marketing Methods*, Crain Books, Chicago, 1975, p. 49.

6. John Moran, *The Mail-Order Business*, MBA Business Associates, Syracuse, N.Y., 1949, p. 63.

7. Paul Bringe, *Direct-Mail Briefs from Bringe*, August 1973.

8. Advertisement in *Direct Marketing*.

CHAPTER 18

1. Source not known.

2. Victor O. Schwab, "What 92 Split-Run Ads Tell Us," Part I, *Advertising & Selling*, April 1948, p. 33.

3. William A. Doppler, "A Mail-Order Test to End All Tests . . . ," *Direct Mail*, September 1957, p. 40.

4. Donald Seibert, "Exciting Concepts Are Tested in Competition for Consumers," *Direct Marketing*, June 1974, p. 58.

5. "Spot TV Sales Promotion Draws High Viewer Response," *Direct Marketing*, December 1973, p. 47.

6. Lewis Kleid, Inc., Bulletin, undated.

7. Orlan Gaeddert, in private communication to author.

APPENDIX A

1. William Berkwitz, *Encyclopedia of the Mail-Order Business*, 1906.

Index

About the Author

Currently teaching at the University of Maryland, **Julian L. Simon** started, successfully operated, and profitably sold his own mail-order firm. He has been a consultant on mail order and other aspects of business and economics to some of the largest firms in the U.S., as well as many small firms just getting started. He has also advised the Federal Trade Commission and foreign government agencies. Dr. Simon is the author of scores of articles and many books on business and economics, several of which have been used as texts at almost every major U.S. university, and his writings have been translated into 15 languages. He has also lectured widely here and abroad and appeared on national television.